Writing as Enlightenment

SUNY series in Buddhism and American Culture
———————
John Whalen-Bridge and Gary Storhoff, editors

Writing as Enlightenment

Buddhist American Literature into the Twenty-first Century

Edited by

John Whalen-Bridge and Gary Storhoff

Foreword by Jan Willis

Cover photo credit: © Photographer: Stephen Coburn / Dreamstime.com

Published by State University of New York Press, Albany

For information, contact State University of New York Press, Albany, NY
www.sunypress.edu

Production by Diane Ganeles
Marketing by Anne M. Valentine

Library of Congress Cataloging-in-Publication Data

Writing as enlightenment : Buddhist American literature into the twenty-first century /
    edited by John Whalen-Bridge and Gary Storhoff.
        p. cm. — (SUNY series in Buddhism and American culture)
    Includes bibliographical references and index.
    ISBN 978-1-4384-3920-4 (pbk. : alk. paper)
    ISBN 978-1-4384-3919-8 (hardcover : alk. paper)
    1. American literature—Buddhist authors—History and criticism. 2. American
literature—Buddhist influences.   3. Buddhism and literature—United States.
4. Buddhism in literature.   I. Whalen-Bridge, John, 1961–   II. Storhoff, Gary,
1947–   III. Title: Buddhist American literature into the twenty-first century.

PS153.B83W75 2011
810.9'382943—dc22   2011005365

10 9 8 7 6 5 4 3 2 1

John Whalen-Bridge would like to dedicate his work on
Writing as Enlightenment:
Buddhist American Literature into the Twenty-first Century
to Professors John L. Abbott and Milton R. Stern.

Gary Storhoff would like to dedicate his work on this volume
to Professor Yakira Frank.

Writing is the final enlightenment.

—*Don DeLillo*

Contents

Acknowledgments

Reprinted with permission from the University of Massachusetts Press: pp. 107–26 from the introduction to Chapter 3, "The Emergence of Black Dharma and *Oxherding Tale*, in *Charles Johnson in Context* by Linda Fergerson Selzer. Copyright 2009 by University of Massachusetts Press and published by the University of Massachusetts Press.

For Jackson Mac Low's poetry, permission granted by Anne Tardos and the Jackson Mac Low Papers in the Mandeville Special Collections Library at the University of California, San Diego.

We wish to thank our families especially, and writers who have made so much time for this project: Keith Abbott, Reed Bye, Charles Johnson, Maxine Hong Kingston, Joanne Kyger, Elizabeth Robinson, Andrew Schelling, Gary Snyder, and Jan Willis. We wish to thank our authors for perfect patience—this has been a slow train comin'. Several research assistants kept the slow train a-movin': Angela Faye Oon, Nirmala Iswari, Loh Waiyee, Heidi Virshup, and Jane Wong.

We have had the pleasure of working with Nancy Ellegate, Diane Ganeles, Janice Vunk, and Diana Altobello. It is always a great pleasure to work with Team SUNY.

John Whalen-Bridge would also like to thank National University of Singapore for sabbatical release in 2009 and Lenz Foundation & Naropa University for the opportunity to hunker down in the Allen Ginsberg Library for four months.

Foreword

Jan Willis

In the eighth century AD, an Indian Buddhist poet and philosopher named Shantideva penned, in verse, a treatise on compassion that immediately became—and has remained—a classic work of Buddhist literature. Entitled *The Way of the Bodhisattva*, the poem eloquently describes how the thought of enlightenment (*bodhicitta*)—that spark of compassionate caring for others that ignites in the hearts and minds (for *citta* in Sanskrit means both "heart" and "mind") of those entering on the Mahayana path—arises, is maintained, increased, and strengthened. No small feat for a poem of just slightly more than nine-hundred verses and for a poet-philosopher who was known in his day as a lazy, good-for-nothing monk!

Thankfully, writing has continued to help enlighten us. Even in this so-called postmodern age, literature and art can still be employed in the service of human beings. How this is done, in manifold and distinctive ways, is the subject of this volume, *Writing as Enlightenment*, the third in the series on American culture and Buddhism, co-edited by Gary Storhoff and John Whalen-Bridge.

Buddhism has been evident on American shores and in the minds of some Americans since the mid-nineteenth century. To the West Coast it came along with the earliest Chinese laborers who toiled anonymously in the gold mines and on the railroads. On the East Coast a small band of well-known dissidents, the Transcendentalists, saw in the ancient teachings of "the Orient" a new and useable system of thought and spirituality. Then, in 1893, the great Parliament of World Religions was held in Chicago, the nation's heartland, and Buddhism officially arrived.

Today, more than a century removed from that Parliament, we live in a world that is, in many ways, smaller and closer than ever before. Scientific and technological advances have brought us together in ways that would have been unthinkable for inhabitants of centuries past. Today, for having said that "East is

east and west is west and never the 'twain shall meet," poor Mr. Kipling would
have to eat the proverbial crow. One consequence of this global postmodernity
is that Buddhism is no longer novel on American shores. Rather, it has become
familiar. Whether through the giant jumbotron depicting the Dalai Lama and
telling us to "Think different" that for months dwarfed all other advertisements
in New York's Times Square, or the Tibetan monks in burgundy robes on TV
commercials jostling playfully with their fellows for access to mobile cell phones in
various regions of Nepal, Americans have come to regard Buddhism as a familiar
feature of their world. Even so, there can be little denying that Buddhism has
had far more a *cultural* impact here than a religious one. The latest demographic
figures say that less than .7 of 1 percent of the U.S. population claims any official
religious affiliation with Buddhism, and the great majority of these Buddhists are
first- and second-generation ethnically Asian Buddhists.

What, then, accounts for such easy familiarity and for such disproportionate
cultural impact? The simplest answer might be, art; a more specific one perhaps
might be, literature (and, more recently, film and the visual technologies). It
clearly seems that, from the Transcendentalist writers of the mid-nineteenth
century to the Beat poets and novelists of the 1950s and 1960s, Americans
have been receptive to a sort of literary, although not necessarily or primarily
religious, transmission of Buddhism.

In this wonderfully rich collection of offerings, the authors represented here
speak to us about Buddhism's place in America's postmodern culture. When
Julia Martin and Allan Johnston take yet another look at the prodigious work
of Buddhist writer and environmentalist Gary Snyder, they do so with a focus
on his work since the mid-1970s and with special attention focused on his 1996
Mountains and Rivers Without End. They address Snyder's process as well as what
he has termed "the real work," done without a view to rewards, completion,
or even possibility. Jane Falk illumines for us the this-worldly savvy of the two
renowned Zen representatives at the Parliament of Religions, Shaku Soen and
Okakura Kakuzo, and suggests that these two men consciously determined how
best to present Zen to the West by emphasizing its secular and cultural features
rather than any that might be characterized as religious. The pieces here by
Jonathan Stalling, John Whalen-Bridge, and Linda Furgerson Selzer introduce the
reader directly to the practices of artists and writers who are guided by Buddhist
principles. Stalling's evocation of the work and the artistic process of Jackson
Mac Low is enthralling. Whalen-Bridge's interview with Charles Johnson and
Maxine Hong Kingston is captivating—from Johnson's evocation of the Buddhist
notion of selflessness as the collapsing of dualisms, to Kingston's magical and
fleeting image of the firefly as a representation of a moment of enlightenment.
And Selzer's discussion of the history of "Black American Buddhism" brings
us again full circle to our racialized history as a nation, whether our focus is
on ethnically Asian Americans or other people of color on these shores, who

find real value, and the possibility of *liberation*, in the teachings of Buddhism. Were this not the case, as Shantideva once pointedly remarked, we might as well give up the practice and resort to gambling and alcohol.

In the end, no matter how brilliant, translucent, or beguiling the words, writing can only point the way; it cannot of itself enlighten us. Only our own actions can do that. As Shantideva deftly observed more than thirteen centuries ago,

> *But all this must be acted out in truth.*
> *For what is to be gained by mouthing syllables?*
> *What invalid was ever helped*
> *By merely reading in the doctor's treatises?*

Introduction

John Whalen-Bridge and Gary Storhoff

Is it not singular that, while the religious world is gradually picking to pieces its old testaments, here are some coming slowly after, on the sea-shore, picking up the durable relics of perhaps older books and putting them together again?

—Henry David Thoreau, Letter to Ralph Waldo Emerson, 1844

Now that Buddhism has taken root in America—a process characterized by Zen pioneer Sokei-an as "holding the lotus to the rock"—those who have managed to survive their first enthusiasm are busy tending the new growth. The ground has been broken and we are now in a period of cultivation and settlement.

—Rick Fields, How the Swans Came to the Lake

In his recently published *North American Buddhists in Social Context* (2008), Paul David Numrich wonders if scholarly research on American Buddhism really constitutes a "field of study." Although the interest in Buddhism in North America is, as Thomas A. Tweed asserts, much greater currently than in the past (2000, xv),[1] Numrich feels that it is too early to tell whether Buddhist Studies in the United States represents a true field of study. In fact, Numrich equivocates in his judgment, concluding that in the first decade of the twenty-first century, Buddhist study in North America has attained only the status of a "protofield," not having "progressed beyond the earliest stages of development" (8). In order to evaluate the strength of Buddhist Studies in North America, Numrich devises three criteria:

1. specialization, which includes scholarly training, research questions, and professional commitment;

2. organization, which includes meetings and conferences, academic programs, university departments, and so on; and—perhaps most important

3. publications such as books, refereed articles, and journals (1–13).

Even though Numrich acknowledges that the impressive number of publications in North American Buddhist Studies constitutes the best case for a field-of-study status, he also is concerned that there is yet to be a "high level of cross-disciplinary productivity, sophistication, and integration" on the topic of Buddhists in America. He concludes, "scholars have yet to achieve significant interdisciplinarity" (9).

Our series from the State University of New York Press, *Buddhism and American Culture*, is an important interdisciplinary milestone, for it is the first edited collection on the comprehensive topic of Buddhism in the expressive arts and living styles in the United States. In short, the series answers Numrich's urgent, timely call for a cross-cultural discussion of Buddhism in the United States. This series attempts to increase understanding of how Buddhism has become an important cultural dimension of America, and it is necessary to look at the contexts of literature, film, visual art, and social thought—to name just four domains—to do this work. The first volume of this series, *The Emergence of Buddhist American Literature*, demonstrates the profound influence of Buddhism on American literature since the beginning of the twentieth century; the eleven essays included in that volume constitute an astute examination of literary work within the context of a decidedly immigrant faith. Indeed, *Emergence* represents the most complete treatment to date of Buddhism in literature, including discussions of seminal writers of High Modernism such as Ernest Fenollosa and Ezra Pound; innovative treatment of the Beats, such as Allen Ginsberg and Jack Kerouac; and—perhaps groundbreaking for contemporary studies of American Buddhism—analyses of Buddhist principles in literary works by contemporary writers of color, such as Maxine Hong Kingston, Lan Cao, and Charles Johnson.

Our second volume in this series, *American Buddhism as a Way of Life*, explores in wide-ranging essays how Buddhism has been transmitted to America spiritually and materially in the late twentieth and early twenty-first centuries. Rather than focus solely on a cultural practice such as literature, however, this volume considers particular social problems as a way to understand the social context of American Buddhism. We have become used to a discourse in which "Buddhism is a philosophy rather than a religion," but to the degree that this is so, Buddhism is also at variance with traditional approaches to philosophy. We can think of it as philosophy as a "way of life"—to paraphrase Pierre Hadot, from whose book *Philosophy as a Way of Life* we took our title. American Buddhism is "a way of life, both in its exercise and effort to achieve wisdom, and in its goal, wisdom itself. For real wisdom does not merely cause us to know: it makes us 'be' in a different way" (Hadot 265). In eleven far-ranging chapters in this volume, authors consider the developing social needs of Americans as they face the new millennium. Contributors explore the ethical challenges posed by contemporary medicine; the special needs of gay persons as they search for refuge in Buddhism; feminism and a Buddhist response to the abortion debate; and the Japanese-Americans as they found solace in Buddhism while experiencing discrimination after Pearl Harbor.

Writing as Enlightenment: Buddhist American Literature into the Twenty-first Century, the third volume in this series, is meant to re-engage literary scholars. The literary richness characteristic of early Buddhist texts has now become an important part of American literary history in the late twentieth and early twenty-first centuries, and literary scholars schooled in Buddhist thought know that to dispense with literary features identifiably Buddhist is to engage in one more futile dualism of ancient, doctrinal texts versus contemporary expressions of the dharma. In the discipline of anthropology, "indigenization" refers to transformations that occur within an imported cultural system, changes that enable it to better fit local customs. And a certain degree of indigenization is only to be expected when Buddhism migrates to America. Buddhism underwent indigenization when it moved from India to Tibet, and when it crossed from India to China and then to Japan. Certainly, Buddhism is undergoing this process as it moves from Asia to the United States. But when any cultural system undergoes indigenization, some people will discover creativity and innovation—as Buddhism finds contemporary expression in literature, film, and life writing—whereas others will bemoan the loss of authenticity as ancient texts, doctrines, and principles are adapted and transformed to an American culture. The study of indigenization as Buddhism engages with America is the project of this series on *Buddhism and American Culture*.

There is much to explain and interpret, despite the resistance to interpretation that some strands of American Buddhist discourse have occasionally foregrounded. This resistance to an analysis of a text is common to Buddhist critical discourse broadly understood—to interpretations, explanations, and ratiocinations generally. The Buddhist reader will remember that near the end of Buddha's life, he took his disciples to a pond for instruction, and instead of a usual philosophical discussion, Buddha simply reached into the pond, picked a lotus flower, then twirled it in his hand. Although many of his disciples attempted to analyze the gesture, explain the symbolism, and interpret the scene, Buddha approached his follower Mahākāśyapa, who simply smiled in understanding.

Buddha replied to the followers, "What can be said, I have given to you; and what cannot be said, I have given to Mahākāśyapa"—and it was Mahākāśyapa, not the interpreters, who became Buddha's successor.

In yet another wonderful story, the interpretive endeavor itself is mocked. A visiting monk admits to defeat in a dharma contest by a one-eyed monk. The visiting monk relates the nature of his defeat:

> First I held up one finger, representing Buddha, the enlightened one. So he held up two fingers, signifying a Buddha and his teaching. I held up three fingers representing Buddha, his teaching, and his followers, living the harmonious life. Then he shook his clenched fist at my face, indicating that all three come from one realization. Thus, he won.

His interpretive discourse, however, collapses under the testimony of the one-eyed monk, who has an entirely different interpretation of this dharma contest:

> The minute he saw me he held up one finger, insulting me by insinuating that I have one eye. Since he was a stranger, I thought I would be polite to him, so I held up two fingers, congratulating him that he has two eyes. Then the impolite wretch held up three fingers, suggesting that between us we have only three eyes. So I got mad and started to punch him, but he ran out and that ended it.

If, as Dōgen tells us, enlightenment cannot be achieved unless the practitioner "ceases to cherish opinions," literary critics are apparently quite far away from satori; we are much more like the visiting monk or Buddha's followers at the pond. We *need* to explain.

This volume is composed of chapters written by those who indeed have opinions, but do not "cherish" them, as Dōgen warns us against. Instead, the authors in this volume wrestle with the question of Buddhism's place in America's postmodern culture. The volume's first section, "Widening the Stream: Literature as Transmission," begins with a study of how America came to Buddhism originally, and how that origination persists into twenty-first century American culture. How is it that America, known for its pragmatism and muscular Christianity, would embrace a religion that seemingly is its opposite, especially given the orientalist stereotypes current at the turn of the century? These early, negative stereotypes of Buddhism are discussed in Jane Falk's "The Transmission of Zen as Dual Discourse: Shaku Soen and Okakura Kakuzo," which discovers a major source of postmodern America's fascination with Zen Buddhism in its transmission by two Japanese, Soen and Kakuzo, whose contributions to the origination of Buddhism in America have heretofore been underestimated. Falk argues that they presented Zen to America as a "dual discourse," its duality residing in Zen's emphasis on both a spiritual and an aesthetic dimension. In Buddhism's introduction in America (generally considered to be the World's Parliament of Religions in 1893), the Japanese cultural emphasis on the arts predominated in early twentieth-century America, and this aesthetic aspect of Zen strongly influences American culture even today.

As Falk shows, both Shaku Soen and Okakura Kakuzo were seminal in the creation of this dual discourse. Soen was a Rinzai Zen priest, and Kakuzo was an art historian. Falk's chapter shows how these two teachers confronted a suspicious American audience, saturated with anti-orientalist religious propaganda that emphasized the inferiority of Zen as compared with Christianity: Zen, as detractors claimed, is passive and contradictory, whereas Christianity represents an engaged spirituality coupled with a confident sense of a secure, absolute Truth. However, both Shaku and Okakura countered this published Western bias by emphatically emphasizing Zen's aestheticism, both at the Parliament and throughout their careers. In so doing, Falk writes, they performed a kind of jui jitsu, a "reverse orientalism" where the seeming deficits of Zen were—within the time's cultural contexts—seen as its actual strengths. For example, Zen's nontheism, Shaku emphasized, was much more consistent than Christianity's monodeism with Western modernity, industrialism, and scientific ideas of the early twentieth century.

But it was on the aesthetic plane, Falk explains, that Shaku and Okakura were the most effective as apologists for Zen, even contributing to the "Japan Craze," an American fad of collecting Japanese artifacts at the turn of the century. Although a Zen priest, Shaku emphasized his avocation as poet and calligrapher—almost eclipsing a spiritual discourse of Zen in favor of an aesthetic discourse. Most notably, Shaku presents meditation primarily as a relief or refuge from the Western rat race and commercialism—in terms a twenty-first century American would readily recognize. Okakura was likewise emphatic in focusing on the pragmatic and aesthetic as opposed to the religious planes of Buddhist experience. For instance, Okakura wrote an illustrated catalogue for the Exposition, intensifying American collector's interest not only in traditional Japanese art in Meji Japan but also in how Zen Buddhism influenced Japanese culture. Okakura's most famous book, *The Book of Tea* (still read today) recommends the advantages of Eastern thought and life practices in contrast to Western materialism and anxiety-ridden modernity. As Falk demonstrates, the tea ceremony becomes a refuge set against the perceived restlessness and disharmony of the West. For Falk, recognizing the "dual discourse" that informs the early transmission explains "the privileging of the aesthetic [as] a factor in the continuing Americanization of Zen in the 21st century."

Not all commentators would agree, of course, that Buddhism in America uniformly privileges Buddhism's aesthetic dimension. The second chapter on transmission, Linda Furgerson Selzer's "Black American Buddhism: History and Representation," focuses on perhaps the most recent development in the transmission of Buddhism to America: the "Black Dharma"—African Americans who have converted to Buddhism or who are fellow travelers. For African Americans, Selzer argues, Buddhism provides a spiritual but also a political refuge from discrimination and the contemporary subtleties of institutionalized racism. Selzer shows how African Americans were most likely exposed to Buddhism in the mid-nineteenth century through their association with Chinese immigrants who worked on the railroad; however, the most important moment in the transmission process occurred during the World's Parliament of Religions in 1893. In her analysis of the pamphlets and news reports written during that seminal event, Selzer shows that despite the racism and Euro-American ethnocentrism in the discourse, African Americans played an important shaping role in the Parliament in conjunction with Asian Buddhists, advocating for their civil rights within a religious context.

A generating question in Selzer's chapter is why so many African Americans turn to Buddhism rather than conventional Christianity. African Americans must still contend with racial stereotypes in their embrace of Buddhism, but a constant challenge is race-inflected. Is the "Black Dharma" *black* enough? In response to this problem, Selzer demonstrates the importance of Buddhism to African Americans by exploring the depth and breadth of Buddhist commitment among African-American writers such as Charles Johnson, bell hooks, Jan Willis, and others. Selzer shows that their motivations result from the social pressures emerging from racism, but also from their recognition of the wider sense of spiritual resources that became available during and after the Civil Rights Movement. The First Noble Truth—All life is suffering—is especially relevant to African Americans who have faced discrimination; as Selzer writes, "Buddhism resonates deeply with their situated experience as black Americans." Buddhism also provides many of these writers, Selzer shows, with a spiritual but also practical method of dealing with this suffering. Especially important to African Americans is Thich Nhat Hahn's "Engaged Buddhism" movement, which employs Buddhism as means of attaining social and political reform, and Nhat Hahn enhanced Buddhism as a this-worldly tool for attaining human rights, in the United States and the world itself. Nhat Hahn's personal association with Martin Luther King Jr., solidified the importance of Buddhism in the minds of many African Americans.

The second part of this volume, "The New Lamp: Buddhism and Contemporary Writers," examines Buddhism's aesthetic principles in recent American literature. One exemplary Buddhist writer is Gary Snyder, and Allan Johnston's far-ranging essay "Some of the Dharma: The Human, the Heavenly, and the 'Real Work' in the Writings of Gary Snyder" (Chapter 3) explores Buddhist doctrines in Snyder's entire career. What, asks Johnston, is the generating principle in Snyder's oeuvre? This Johnston discovers in Snyder's conception of the "real work"—a term that Snyder has consistently used in his poetry and in interviews. Although Snyder's "real work" has been considered by other critics primarily in terms of its political and artistic dimensions, Johnston's argument is that the term *real work* is more comprehensive and stratified than has been previously considered, as it refers to Snyder's attempt to intensify human awareness of reality on *all* levels—certainly the political and aesthetic planes, but also the mundane and quotidian, as well as the spiritual and religious. In this way, Johnston argues, Snyder engages his reader at all dimensions of life, and Johnston's chapter is a study of the various forms "real work" assume in Snyder's career. Johnston argues that it is critical for a Snyder reader to distinguish the heavenly from human action in nature and culture. This distinction has been a theme, according to Johnston, throughout Snyder's career. Meditation is used by Snyder to pass into a sense of "overwhelming nature" that transcends human reason.

A conception of the *dharma* is central to Johnston's argument. He carefully considers the variety of definitions of the *dharma*, then demonstrates how throughout Snyder's career, Snyder has made "real work" correspond to the *dharma*. Johnston isolates a passage from Chuang-Tzu's Autumn Flood's section, which Snyder taught in his "Wilderness and Literature" class at UC Davis in 1986:

> Jo of the North Sea said, "Horses and oxen have four feet—this is what I mean by the Heavenly. Putting a halter on the horse's head, piercing the ox's nose—this is what I mean by the human."

In this depiction of the nature–culture division, culture cannot rule out nature; to approach an issue through the heavenly as opposed to the human bespeaks a different *aim*, not a different *object*. In this way, Johnston tactfully works through Snyder's career in ways that invite an interrelation among political, poetic, and spiritual levels. To achieve this ambitious goal, Johnston also must situate Snyder's religious vision within American culture; and adjunctive to this abstract enterprise is Johnston's explanation of how Snyder resists the dualistic self–object split, an understanding of the world that underlies American individualism. Snyder instead adopts the Buddhist doctrine of no-self (*anātman*). For Snyder, the self–object split divides the human being not only from nature but also from heaven. For Johnston, the challenge of Snyder's poetry resides in exposing the reader to "heavenly nature" through poetic discourse, and meditation, as an analogue for "real work," assists the reader in achieving spiritual as well as political liberation.

In distinguishing his chapter from earlier Snyder criticism, Johnston supports his argument with imaginative, technical readings from selected works, largely atypical heretofore in Snyder's criticism. He demonstrates that Snyder's poetry—whose previous critics treat almost exclusively for its themes—evinces an aesthetic self-consciousness and a deliberate attention to poetic detail: a marshalling of imagery, syntax, tone, diction, meter, and rhyme to shape the reader's response. Johnston's analyses of such poems as "Mid August at Sourdough Mountain Lookout," "Piute Creek," "Fire in the Hole," "Milton by Firelight," and "Toward Climax" increase our respect for Snyder's careful construction of poetic elements and the beauty of his work.

Johnston's chapter reveals, then, not only Snyder's profound political principles—a consensus of Snyder criticism is his politically radical stance—but also his careful attention to poetics. Yet in Chapter 4, Jonathan Stalling shows that few poets even come close to the radicalism of Jackson Mac Low. Stalling's chapter, "Listen and Relate: Buddhism, Daoism, and Chance in the Poetry and Poetics of Jackson Mac Low," demonstrates conclusively that well before post-modernist theory had taken hold in America, Mac Low was at the vanguard of experimental poets by employing Asian philosophy in his avant-garde work, especially in his undermining of a Western substantialist self. Stalling explains how in Mac Low's early career, Mac Low was influenced primarily by the Daoist conception of *wuwei*—meaning human *non*intervention in allowing a being to become itself, including a poet's refusal to interfere in allowing a poem take its own poetic form. As Stalling writes, "he was the first American poet to explore the dynamic possibilities of chance operations in the composition of poetry." Stalling explains how Daoism leads Mac Low to "stand out of the way" of the performer/reader, or of the role of chance in his poetry.

As Mac Low studied Buddhist principles under D. T. Suzuki, the direction of his work shifted from "getting out of the way" of his poetry—and permitting chance to beome a sole poetic principle—toward a more inclusive investigation of *anātman*, the Buddhist belief in the illusory nature of the ego. Nevertheless, the concept *wuwei* did not entirely disappear in his work either, since he attempted in a nondualist way to bring together *wuwei* and *anātman* in his admonition to his audience to "listen and relate: 'Listen' to bring non-judgmental attention to phenomena, and 'relate' without interfering with the *zirzan* [the mysterious unfolding of the other]." Stalling analyzes in detail Mac Low's "Mani Mani Gatha" to demonstrate how Mac Low's work nondualistically unifies Daoist and Buddhist principles. Because the performance of "Mani Mani Gatha" at least partly is shaped by the performers in their unpredictable choices of movements and intonations, the work is to a large extent aleatoric; because the performers' choices are to pay close attention to what happens around them, the performance could never be self-determined, leading to a sense of the evacuation of the self—a "non-egoic," or non-ego reinforcing composition. Like the performer of Mac Low's poetry, the audience is urged to "listen and relate," and Mac Low hoped, work "through what each of us thinks of as 'my self.'"

Archie J. Bahm argued many years ago for a "Buddhist aesthetics," and the next chapter expands and clarifies what a Buddhist aesthetic might look like. To what extent does a Buddhist aesthetic help illuminate the texts of postmodernist writers who do not necessarily self-identify as Buddhists? Gary Storhoff begins this discussion with his chapter, " 'A Deeper Kind of Truth': Buddhist Themes in Don DeLillo's *Libra*," (Chapter 5), in which he considers DeLillo's characters in relation to Buddhist ideas about selfhood. DeLillo does not overtly acknowledge his affinity for Buddhist thought, and has in humility acknowledged that the Buddhist inflections in his work do not imply his profound understanding of that religion. Yet there is a persistent pattern of references to Buddhism (and other spiritual disciplines and religions) in his novels—this pattern created by an author who avows that he is a "spiritual person." Are these merely parodic allusions to Orientalist culture, or does DeLillo disclose a deeper affinity to Buddhism? In previous scholarship on DeLillo, a perpetual debate is the extent and depth of the spiritual dimension in his work, and Storhoff's discussion of Buddhist ideas that emerge in *Libra* contributes to that debate, especially because many of DeLillo's aesthetic obsessions—the materialist craving of contemporary America, the emotional sterility of Americans after Kennedy's assassination, the potentially nihilistic vision of postmodern media, and the deconstruction of a Western ideal of individualism and self-identity—offer a spiritual resolution for the reader. For Storhoff, DeLillo's purpose in *Libra* is therapeutic in nature, leading his reader toward an understanding of self and its interrelationship with all things. As Storhoff writes, "If we see DeLillo's fiction within a Buddhist framework, we add another dimension to the view that literature expresses fundamental truths about how we live."

Storhoff shows that DeLillo's novel is about the various forms of craving in the novel, the most important being the obsession over a substantialist self. Like David Loy, whose writing recommends *anātman* as a relief for the radical anxiety about self in western civilization, DeLillo offers no sense of an anchor in a solid identity. Indeed, *Libra*, in Storhoff's words, "enacts key Buddhist themes that clarify the nonexistence of the self." As Storhoff demonstrates, throughout the novel DeLillo "employs the *memento mori* theme common to both Christianity and Buddhism so as to reveal where reality may be truly found." Yet the novel offers a refuge from death and the radical loss of self. In a way that passes the understanding of many of these characters, to be "a zero in the system" is in actuality the therapy that DeLillo (and Buddhism) recommends as relief from suffering. This therapy, ironically, is dramatized not by any of the male characters—in this very masculine book—but by the female characters, who seem through their actions to intuit a more profound conception of the self. Storhoff's chapter, then, suggests a way of looking at DeLillo that rescues him from the category of postmodernist, nihilist writers.

This volume ends with the section "Speaking as Enlightenment: Interviews with Buddhist Writers." Buddhism in America is more than occasionally seen as enigmatic, even disturbing, to Asians who grew up in established Buddhist traditions. One Asian-American student who took my (Storhoff's) course in Buddhism and American literature at the University of Connecticut cautioned me to be sure to have at least one Asian Buddhist in my class to assure other students that Buddhism is "real" for practitioners, although she took considerable pride that an entire semester was devoted to an acceptance of her faith in a secular, public university. This section demonstrates conclusively that Buddhism is indeed a heart-felt religion among contemporary writers, although there is little doubt that America presents a new model of Buddhist practice to meet the demands of American postmodern culture.

The section begins with Chapter 6 by Julia Martin, "The Present Moment Happening: A Conversation with Gary Snyder." Snyder's most influential books of poetry often are paired with a collection of prose—for example, *Mountains and Rivers without End* (1996) with *Practice of the Wild* (1990). Martin catches Snyder between his poetic collection *Danger on the Peaks* (2004) and its prose partner *Back on the Fire* (2007) to interview him about developments in his views on the interrelationships between poetry and environmentalism. As a serious devotee of Buddhism since the "Buddha Boom" of the 1950s and an originary figure of Buddhist American literature, Snyder has persevered in his vow, made when he was only fifteen years old, to offer therapy to the planet that has become increasingly threatened by ecological destruction, despite the end of the Cold War and nuclear brinksmanship. Returning from his first ascent of Mt. St. Helens in 1945, Snyder read newspaper accounts of Hiroshima and Nagasaki, and then he vowed to fight against the destructive powers of the world. How, asks Martin, does Snyder now reconcile himself to an apparently even more precarious world, where nature itself is endangered by, in Snyder's words, "the half-million-year long slow explosion of human impact"?

In response, Snyder discusses the relationship between human value and nature in terms framed by Robinson Jeffers, and Jeffers' distinction between "Inhumanism" and anti-humanism. No "anti-humanist," Snyder stresses that the personal and the human have their place in the world and in an artist's representations of the world, but as an Inhumanist, Snyder avoids the egotistical inflation of the human element on the planet. The profundity of Snyder's commitment is obvious in the interview; but so too is his good cheer and humor—this interview is not a testimony of gloom from one of America's foremost poets, and his laughter throughout the interview leavens his description of his "despair at how the human world goes down." More than sixty years after his vow, Snyder is still speaking out against the forces of commercialism and overdevelopment, but he also understands the "limits of who we are, and the limits of what our world is. . . . I had to learn what is actually possible in the world." Perhaps his most moving statement in this interview is his admonition to "honor the dust," a statement that registers his courageous resignation combined with his devotion to the seemingly mundane and nonhuman features of earth.

Buddhism in American literature has evolved considerably since Kerouac's 1958 *Dharma Bums*, and Whalen-Bridge's interview in Chapter 7 with Charles Johnson and Maxine Hong Kingston, "Embodied Mindfulness: A Discussion with Charles Johnson and Maxine Hong Kingston," reveals this artistic development. Both National Book Award winners, Johnson and Kingston have commented in their literary work on Buddhist American writing after the Beat period. Johnson is perhaps the most explicit writer who distances himself from the Beats, as evidenced in the chandoo episode in *Oxherding Tale*, and in Chaym Smith's representation of the black dharma bum in *Dreamer*. For Johnson, the bohemian path forged by the Beats toward freedom is a first step but never a resting place. In comparison, Kingston's characters, such as Wittman Ah Sing in *Tripmaster Monkey: His Fake Book*, often look back not necessarily in anger but in disappointment at the orientalism and misunderstanding of such predecessors as Jack Kerouac.

Whalen-Bridge's interview is useful to scholars of contemporary literature because Johnson and Kingston cover so much ground—*anātman* (the no-self doctrine), Christianity, phenomenology, karma, and reincarnation. Johnson acknowledges his emotional commitment to Christianity—the religion that was firmly grounded in his own family-of-origin, and is now practiced by his wife and children. But Johnson elaborates on his Christian background by discussing the importance of Thich Nhat Hahn's Order of Interbeing in his work. Nhat Hahn's statement that "a good Buddhist is a good Christian, and a good Christian is a good Buddhist" seems central to Johnson's worldview; Johnson is consequently not disturbed by Buddhist ideas that to the casual observer seem antithetical to orthodox Christian theology, the most important of these ideas, perhaps, being *anātman*. For Johnson, seeing an opposition between Christianity and Buddhism is only one more perceptual dualism that must be overcome. Johnson's commentary is important to an understanding of all his fiction, and Whalen-Bridge probes him on his dramatization of enlightenment in such works as his *Oxherding Tale* and his short story "Dr. King's Refrigerator." For Johnson, enlightenment almost solely resides in emotional and intellectual acceptance of *anātman*: from that acceptance flows an understanding of the interrelatedness of all things (Nhat Hahn's concept of interbeing). Yet perhaps because of American culture's tradition of individualism, Johnson recognizes that this acceptance is difficult—hence, the resistance of even renowned philosophers like Paul Tillich to *anātman*.

Maxine Hong Kingston also comments on her treatment of enlightenment in her work, but her representation of Buddhism is considerably more circumspect and tentative than is the somewhat "muscular" passages of the Beats that pronounce on enlightenment. In contrast to writers such as Kerouac, the dramatic representation of enlightenment for Kingston is the epitome of her art, yet she will only venture to depict enlightenment imagistically, not with Kerouac's blustering confidence, didacticism, or overheated philosophy. The image of a firefly, for Kingston, summarizes the precarious and evanescent moment of enlightenment: flickering, beautiful, but gone in an instant. Although enlightenment is central to her art, she will only present enlightenment briefly and with utmost subtlety, in keeping with her understanding of that experience. In her interview with Whalen-Bridge published in *The Emergence of Buddhist American Literature*, "Buddhism and the Ceremony of Writing," Kingston goes into further detail about her relationship to Buddhism, where she also discusses her less well-known works such as *Tripmaster Monkey: His Fake-Book* and *The Fifth Book of Peace*. The interview with Kingston in this section and in *Emergence* together should be of considerable help to any scholar interested in her Buddhist references, and how Buddhism partly shapes her aesthetic and spiritual aims.

Whalen-Bridge's (Chapter 8) interviews with writers affiliated with Naropa University, "Poetry and Practice at Naropa University," concludes this volume. The institutional center for American literary Buddhism—although the name of the writing program at once asserts and dismisses the importance of institutional embodiment—has been Naropa University's Jack Kerouac School of Disembodied Poetics. The program was created in 1974 when Trungpa asked Allen Ginsberg, Anne Waldman, Diane di Prima, and musician John Cage to develop a writing program, to which the quasi-Beat assemblage gave a fruitfully ironic and iconoclastic name. Despite its considerable accomplishments, Naropa is more often remembered in the context of Tom Clark's *Great Naropa Poetry Wars* (1980), an account of events that occurred at a Halloween party in 1975. During one of Trungpa's three-month Buddhist seminars, poet W. S. Merwin and his girlfriend Dana Naone refused to attend this party and behaved in other ways that offended Trungpa, who ordered his "Vajra guards" to force them to participate. This involved stripping them naked against their will. Trungpa's defenders argued that the guru was attempting, out of compassion and a radical teaching mode called "crazy wisdom," to peel away the delusions of ego. Kenneth Rexroth felt otherwise, comparing Trungpa to Buddhism's Judas-figure, Devadatta: "Many believe Chögyam Trungpa has unquestionably done more harm to Buddhism in the United States than any man living."[2]

It may seem as if the Poetry Wars crystalize the clash between Asian traditions (of asceticism, collectivism, and respect for teachers) and an American emphasis on sexual expression, democracy, and egalitarianism. The interviews in this chapter expose the apparent clash between Asian traditions and American values, and this collision is not going to be avoided by simply ignoring the many cultural traditions inherited from Asia. But it is far from clear what conclusions should be drawn.

John Stevens argues in *Lust for Enlightenment: Buddhism and Sex* that there has never been one simple message of sexual repression within Buddhist discourse, and psychologist Mark Epstein provocatively presents Buddhist as a path toward greater intimacy in *Open to Desire: the Truth about What the Buddha Taught*. Is this pro-sex Buddhism an American projection? Is Tantric transgression an alibi for countercultural, antinomian lack of discipline? Marcus Boon's essay "John Giorno: Buddhism, Poetry, and Transgression," in *Emergence of Buddhist American Literature*, juxtaposes transgressive elements that are from the Tibet of one-thousand years ago with transgressive sex of post-Stonewall America—images of the Tibetan saint Padmasambhava are juxtaposed shockingly with the poetic lines "when you shoot your load/ up/ my ass" (*Emergence* 65). Boon glosses philosophical emptiness with scholarly references to canonical texts of Tibetan Buddhism, but readers might object that there is no "queer dharma" in medieval Tibet. The tradition of veiled, highly metaphorical "twilight language" allows for the expression of actions that would have been flatly transgressive if understood plainly, and we look forward to the possibility that scholars in decades to come will better be able to work with the stormy ground of "Comparative Transgressive Studies." This is a complicated issue that warrants its own separate volume of essays, and it must be remarked that what follows in this volume is, hopefully, a set of initial forays into what will develop into a rich vein of writing. We are in the middle of this story.

Whalen-Bridge's interviews with Joanne Kyger, Reed Bye, Keith Abbott, Andrew Schelling, and Elizabeth Robinson concern such topics as the evolution of contemplative poetics at Naropa, attempts to develop a pedagogy that balanced the Beat and Buddhist inspirations behind the program, and the grueling difficulties faced by devout practitioners as they attempt to accommodate their faith with their committed American values such as freedom of expression, democracy, and self-reliance.

Probing, tentative, and provisional—these chapters look for ways to open up new approaches to the complex interaction between Asian Buddhism, that of second-generation American teachers, and American writers from the mid-1970s through the new millennium. It is in this spirit that each of the contributors to this volume—Falk, Selzer, Johnston, Stalling, Storhoff, Martin, and Whalen-Bridge—studies the dynamic and hybrid philosophical traditions of Buddhism and how Buddhism partly shapes the forms and meanings of American literature. This volume is yet another episode in the evolution of a genuinely global mixture of discourses and practices, an exchange that is transforming life on both sides of the Pacific.

One more Zen story—and the cultural echo-locution around such telling and retellings humbles anyone who would say it is an "Asian" or an "American" story too quickly. It is said that Tokusan, one of the great interpreters of the Diamond Sutra, met an old woman, who asked about a huge bundle he carried on his back, and he answered that it was his interpretative writings on the Diamond Sutra, compiled after many laborious years of study. The old woman then reminded him of a passage in the Sutra: "The past mind cannot be held, the present mind cannot be held, and the future mind cannot be held." Astounded at the old woman's astuteness, Tokusan returned to his study under a Zen master, and it is said that he later burned his commentaries.[3]

We hope the reader will enjoy these chapters. If they must be burned, may they give you light!

Notes

1. Tweed has stipulated in a different essay that Buddhism is a "new subfield of Asian religions in America" (1997, 190), enfolded in the domain of American religious history. Charles S. Prebish also points out that there are more academic hirings of professors specializing in Buddhist Studies than in the past (74–78).

2. Rexroth's words appear on the back cover of Clark's book as an endorsement.

3. The Zen stories are paraphrased from *Zen Flesh, Zen Bones*.

Works Cited

Boon, Marcus. "John Giorno: Buddhism, Poetry, and Transgression." John Whalen-Bridge and Gary Storhoff, eds. 63–81.

Clark, Tom. *The Great Naropa Poetry Wars*. Santa Barbara, CA: Cadmus Editions, 1980.

Epstein, Mark. *Open to Desire: The Truth about What the Buddha Taught*. New York: Gotham Books, 2006.

Hadot, Pierre. *Philosophy as a Way of Life: Spiritual Exercises from Socrates to Foucault*. Ed. Arnold I. Davidson. Trans. Michael Chase. Oxford: Blackwell, 1995.

Numrich, Paul David. "North American Buddhists: A Field of Study?" *North American Buddhists in Social Context*. Ed. Paul David Numrich. Brill: Boston, 2008. 1–17.

Prebish, Charles S. "Studying the Spread and Histories of Buddhism in the West: The Emergence of Western Buddhism as a New Subdiscipline within Buddhist Studies." *Westward Dharma: Buddhism beyond Asia*. Eds. Charles S. and Martin Baumann. Berkeley: University of California Press, 2002. 66–81.

Stevens, John. *Lust for Enlightenment: Buddhism and Sex*. Boston: Shambhala, 1990.

Storhoff, Gary and John Whalen-Bridge, eds. *American Buddhism as a Way of Life*. Albany: State University of New York Press, 2010.

Tweed, Thomas A. *The American Encounter with Buddhism, 1844–1912: Victorian Culture and the Limits of Dissent*. Chapel Hill: University of North Carolina Press, 2000.

———. "Asian Religions in the United States: Reflections on an Emerging Subfield." *Religious Diversity and American Religious History: Studies in Traditions and Cultures*. Eds. Walter H. Conser Jr., and Sumner B. Twiss. Athens: University of Georgia Press, 1997. 189–217.

Whalen-Bridge, John and Gary Storhoff, eds. *The Emergence of Buddhist American Literature*. Albany: State University of New York Press, 2009.

Zen Flesh, Zen Bones: A Collection of Zen & Pre-Zen Wrings. Ed. Paul Reps. Rutland, VT: Charles E. Tuttle Co., 1957, 1998.

PART I

WIDENING THE STREAM

Literature as Transmission

Chapter 1

The Transmission of Zen as Dual Discourse

Shaku Soen and Okakura Kakuzo

Jane Falk

The seemingly widespread awareness of Zen Buddhism in American culture today is evident from the use of Zen as a catchword in everything from beauty advertisements to self-help manuals. A recent edition of *Books in Print* lists approximately 450 titles under the subject of Zen, although many of these books deal with the arts and self-help rather than with religion. *Zen and the Art of Modern Eastern Cooking* and *Zen Key to Your Undiscovered Happiness* are prime examples of this phenomenon. Whether writers or readers of such texts have a firm grasp of Zen as spiritual practice is questionable. To gain a better understanding of how Zen is understood, the *Oxford Dictionary of World Religions* provides a general definition, beginning with a summary of Zen tenets in the four lines attributed to Bodhidharma, Zen's first patriarch: "A special transmission outside the scriptures / Not founded on words and letters / By pointing directly to mind / It allows one to penetrate the nature of things to attain the Buddha nature." It concludes by emphasizing "the immense cultural consequences of Zen" (Bowker 1066). Although one might find variations on this definition in other Western reference books, Zen usually is understood as having both a spiritual and a cultural dimension. Transmission of Zen to the United States in the 1950s, for example, relied heavily on a Zen of dual dimension, with an emphasis on Zen and the arts. It is the transmission of what I have termed this *dual discourse* of Zen to America and the privileging of the aesthetic that is the particular subject of this chapter. Such an understanding of Zen has its originary moment in the Columbian Exposition of 1893 and its World's Parliament of Religions with two Japanese figures, Rinzai Zen priest Shaku Soen and art historian Okakura Kakuzo, instrumental in this process.

Shaku Soen is best known as the first Zen teacher to visit the United States as delegate to the Parliament, whereas Okakura Kakuzo most often is associated with his 1906 work, *The Book of Tea*, a key text for the understanding of an aestheticized Zen. This work strongly influenced American perceptions of Zen and Japanese culture in the early twentieth century, is still in print, and is widely read today.

Zen in America Before the Columbian Exposition

To better understand why Zen was introduced and presented as dual discourse by the Japanese, it is necessary to go back to the 1880s. As might be expected, early interest in Zen at this time came from the religious community of ministers and educators brought in by the Meiji government to help modernize Japan. They most often saw Zen as a curious and problematic spiritual practice especially in regard to Christianity.[1] Their commentary ranges from the objective, interested, and informational to the more subjective and judgmental, the latter view of Zen predominating. Zen's practices are often disparaged and seen as contradictory and flawed in comparison with Christianity, especially in relation to Zen's claim for transmission without words or the aid of scriptures. Additionally, some commentators use the somewhat esoteric Zen as a form of cultural capital and a way to prove their ability to speak about and for Japanese culture and religion. Hence, their information about Zen is often presented without acknowledging Japanese informants by name.

Typical of a somewhat negative presentation of Zen is M. L. Gordon's article of 1886 published in the *The Andover Review*, a periodical with a strong theological purpose. Although Gordon's treatment appears to be straightforward, he has a hidden agenda directed toward missionary types who need information about Buddhism in order to gain an advantage in proselytizing. As he puts it, a better understanding of Japanese Buddhism will give us less of a "disadvantage" (310). Gordon emphasizes the authenticity of his information while downplaying his source and his own interest in Buddhism, characterizing his nameless informant as a "disciple of the sect employed recently to teach the essentials of their belief" to "an unpromising pupil," implying Gordon himself. Zen is described as the "Dhyana" or a contemplative school introduced into China from India by Bodhidharma, characterized by its claims to be "sutra-less." Gordon contrasts this with Zen's inconsistencies in its use of certain sutras as aids to "contemplation." He also points out incongruities in Zen's use of images in its temples for which his informant has only a "shrug of the shoulders in reply," thereby indicating Gordon's skepticism (305). However, Gordon is not much more understanding toward other sects he describes, his point being to demonstrate the varieties of Japanese Buddhism as contradictory, with implicit comparison to a supposedly noncontradictory Christianity.

Around the time of the 1893 World's Parliament of Religions, the number of articles on Japanese Buddhism and Zen increased, as might be expected.[2] One of these, "Developments of Japanese Buddhism" by Rev. A. Lloyd, provides more factual details about Zen while continuing to allude negatively to its contemplative practice. Like Gordon, Lloyd describes Zen's practice of "abstract contemplation," transmitted heart to heart without words, and includes the story of wall-gazing Bodhidharma as bringing this "silent understanding" to China. Although Lloyd's treatment of Zen sometimes seems appreciative, he ends by branding it as an "utterly impractical method of arriving at Truth," and characterizes Zen's meditating practitioner negatively: "to think unthinking, i.e., he is to sit in a kind of mesmeric condition, with an entire absence of all formulated thought" (430, 437).

Zen as Dual Discourse and the Columbian Exposition of 1893

In contrast to such written descriptions, Zen became a physical presence in the United States for the first time at the Columbian Exposition of 1893, the World's Fair to commemorate the quadricentennial of Columbus' discovery of America.[4] Zen's religious aspect was personified by Shaku Soen, a Zen priest of the Rinzai sect who came as one of the members of the Japanese Buddhist delegation to the World's Parliament of Religions, one of the congresses held in conjunction with the Exposition. Unconventionally prepared by his teacher, Kosen, with a university education and travels abroad to India and Sri Lanka, Shaku Soen looked to establish Zen in the West. However, as has been demonstrated, Zen's appearance in the person of a Zen master was less an originary moment than a shift in a conversation that had already begun in the decade before the Parliament, the consequences of which will inform Shaku Soen's presentation of Zen.[5] The aesthetic aspect of Zen was represented by Japan's exhibition at the Exposition, the Ho-o-den, a replica of a Buddhist temple whose decoration and catalogue were masterminded by Okakura Kakuzo, a Japanese art historian, director of the Tokyo Art Academy, curator of the Imperial Museum, and former pupil, translator, and assistant to American Japanophile, Ernest Fenollossa.[6] As of 1884, he had become an authority in his own right and espoused the cause of traditional art in Meiji Japan. In comparison with Zen's presentation from the American clerical point of view that saw Zen as puzzling, contradictory, and lacking in comparison to Christianity, both men present Zen to the American public at the Exposition in a positive light, by associating it with modern ideas and nonreligious aspects of Western philosophy and culture.

Shaku Soen and other Japanese delegates made a positive impression on their American audience.[7] Shaku is presented as an important religious figure in the published proceedings of the Parliament. His bibliographical note at the end of the second volume report of the Parliament proceedings identifies him as "Shaku Most Reverend Soyen . . . head of the Engakuji division of the Rinzai Zen sect; a scholar in the sacred books and doctrines of Buddhist sects . . ." (Barrows 1589). Here his title, given in Eastern and Western terms, designates his elevated religious position, while enabling his reception as a type of religious figure familiar to Americans with an air of the exotic.

Using interpreters, he spoke twice at the Parliament, once on the eighth day and once on the sixteenth. The theme of the eighth day was ecumenicism and the need for religious sympathy and the unity of all religions to counteract the rise of science and skepticism. However, although Shaku Soen personified Zen for his Western audience, his message in this first speech did not specifically describe or allude to Zen tenets.[8] Entitled "The Law of Cause and Effect as Taught by Buddhism," it presents Buddhism in a way that shows it to be both in keeping with Western morality and a religion (unlike Christianity) well able to encompass new developments in Western science such as Darwin's theory of evolution. Shaku begins by describing the natural world and asks why the universe is "in a constant flux," responding with Buddhism's "one explanation, namely, the law of cause and effect," a natural law by which our deeds of the past create our present existence today. His speech develops these ideas effectively while simultaneously inserting comments that subtly question and challenge Christian tenets: "God did not provide you with a hell, but you yourself," for example (829, 830–31).

His rhetorical strategy here is a reverse orientalism, using Western stereotypes of Buddhism to his advantage. In this way, he turns a popular Western critique of Buddhism, lack of a personal God, to his advantage by demonstrating how Buddhist philosophy can respond to the pressures of both Western scientific ideas and modern life.[9] This pattern will be evident in Shaku Soen's subsequent presentations of Zen to a Western audience, as he speaks and writes about Mahayana Buddhism in general, emphasizing its compatibility with Western modernity in comparison to Christianity. His strategy thus uses the pragmatic Buddhist concept of *upaya* or skillful means, the idea that bodhisattvas or Buddhist teachers may use all means at their disposal to guide beings to enlightenment.

Although the Parliament and Shaku Soen represented the religious aspect of Zen, the Exposition itself made connections between Zen and Japanese material culture. American world's fairs were important venues for the introduction of Japanese and other foreign cultures into the United States in the nineteenth century, and the Columbian Exposition was no exception. One aspect of these fairs was that Japanese culture was presented as collectible commodity to the American public. This emphasis on Japan and the aesthetic also dovetails with the American collecting mania for Japanese art objects and enthusiasm toward Japan in the nineteenth century, a fad known as the Japan Craze.[10] An aspect of this craze was that Japan epitomized the aesthetic for Americans who also saw in Japanese culture a panacea for modernity. Collecting and appreciating Japanese art was a way for American Japanophiles to renew and recover a connection with the handmade and artisanal. Art historian William Hosley describes American interests in Japanese culture as both a "diagnosis and a cure for the Victorian's growing cultural malaise" in which the "throbbing pulse of industrialization had taken its toll" (29).[11]

Japan's exhibition, the Ho-o-den or Phoenix Palace, a replica of the Buddhist Phoenix Temple of Uji, was given one of the choice locations of the fair, the Wooded Isle. Joe Earle in his study of Meiji Era art suggests a reason for this almost favored status in that Japan's monetary contribution for the centennial or the amount that its government committed to spend was the largest of any other participant (32).[12] The building was constructed on site by workers sent from Japan and contained displays of Japanese material culture. In a statement for the *North American Review* on Japan's participation in the Exposition, Japanese Minister Gozo Tateno describes this building as an example of historical Japanese architecture, "unique in design and construction," illustrating three different epochs of Japanese cultural history with the left wing in the style of the Ashikaga Period, the right wing in the style of Fujiwara, and the main hall in the style of Tokugawa (39). Its interior was decorated by members of the Tokyo Art Academy under the direction of Okakura Kakuzo.[13]

Okakura also wrote the illustrated catalogue for the Ho-o-den, which presents not only Japanese culture to an American audience, but a culture influenced by Zen Buddhism. Describing the Ho-o-den as a replica of the Phoenix Hall adapted for "secular use," he cites Buddhism as influential in bringing Chinese art to Japan, the Ashikaga period representing a style that "began a new art-life under the influence of Zen Buddhism" (an " 'orthodox' sect of the Northern, Mahayana, School of Buddhists") and the teachings of Chinese philosophers of the Sung dynasty. The Ho-o-den also featured a tea room, described by Okakura as an aspect of Ashikaga culture in which all "appliances" are "noted for simplicity of taste" (13, 20, 23).[14] He described the wing's study as a place its master used to practice Buddhism.

Okakura's catalogue was not the only publication where average fairgoers could read about Zen influences on Japanese art and material culture, however. *History of The World's Fair*, a souvenir book, devotes a chapter to the Wooded Isle, in which the "Hoodo" or "Japanese building" is named as one of the "gems" of the fair with its three pavilions each representing three epochs in Japanese art history. Describing the Ashikaga period as one when Japan, "emerging from the war of the two dynasties, started into a new art-life under the influence of Zen-Buddhism and Lung [Sung] philosophy" with "purity and simplicity" as the motto, the author seems to paraphrase Okakura's catalogue without acknowledgment (Truman 431). Both documents are significant in demonstrating that Zen associations with the artistic culture of Japan were presented to the American public at this time in a popular context, complementing the spiritual presentation of Zen embodied in Shaku Soen's appearance at the Parliament.

The continuing American fascination with Japanese culture and the increasing presence of Japan on the world stage as the Asian power to be reckoned with due to Japan's military victories at the turn of the century kept both men before the public eye. They would feed interest in Japanese religion and culture with articles and books for an English-speaking audience from the 1890s into the twentieth century. Additionally, both men were physically present in the United States in the new century. Shaku Soen toured the United States giving lectures in 1905–1906, and Okakura Kakuzo made Boston his American base, as advisor, then curator, at the Museum of Fine Arts from 1904 until his death in 1913.

Zen Discourse after the Fair: Shaku Soen

After the Parliament, Shaku Soen's contribution to Zen transmission was not only to embody Zen as honored dignitary in the Buddhist religious hierarchy, but also to take on new roles of poet and calligrapher. In keeping with his pattern at the Parliament, Shaku Soen would continue to allude only sparingly to Zen and its unique practices and qualities, perhaps because as previously noted, Zen tenets were seen as too "curious" by Americans.[15] It is ultimately the fact of his appearance, the aura of authenticity, along with artistic, scholarly, and elitist associations that will be most significant in his transmission of Zen at the turn of the century in person and in print.[16]

Shaku's articles and talks emphasize both his persona as Zen poet and that of polemicist for Buddhism, the aesthetic discourse becoming almost as strong as the spiritual. For example, in January 1894, *The Monist* printed one of his poems, "The Universality of Truth," written in Chinese characters with literal translation as well as extensive footnotes. The editor adds the comment that "it takes a scholar to write such poetry," implying both that Shaku is a poet and scholar and that Zen priests write poetry. The four-line poem describes the world's races as one in righteousness and equality under a moon that shines down on all. His vision is of a world of racial harmony in contrast to the actual discrimination and racism of the West, especially in relation to the yellow races, his point made not through sermonizing but through poetic imagery ("Universality" 161).

Shaku is again presented as both poet and calligrapher in an article of February 1899, in *The Open Court*, in an essay entitled "Japanese Calligraphy."

Here he acknowledges Buddhism's similarities to Christianity in a positive way, describing an image of Jizo (a Bodhisattva) as "omnipresent, fatherly love" in his four-line, calligraphed poem with translation into English:

> Throughout the three worlds I am everywhere
> All creatures as my loved children I cherish.
> And though e'en time and space may perish.
> I shall ne'er cease to embrace them in prayer.

The obvious parallel here for an American audience is between Christianity's benevolent God, the father, and Jizo (120–21).[17]

The next time that Shaku comes to prominence for the American public (again as priest and poet) is during the time of the Russo-Japanese war when Japan is frequently in the headlines. Two articles, "Buddhist View of War," and "At the Battle of Nan-Shan Hill," for *The Open Court* present him as a Japanese spokesperson for the war.[18] Although it seems contradictory for a Buddhist priest to condone war, Shaku does so, in the process rationalizing Japanese imperialism for an American audience. In the latter article, he states that war is an evil, "but war against evils must be unflinchingly prosecuted till we attain the final aim," adding that Japan has sought to subjugate evils "hostile to civilisation, peace, and enlightenment" ("At the Battle of Nan Shan Hill" 708). Is he making a play on words here with enlightenment's Buddhist connotations? This article ends with a poem the priest composed on the field of battle, suggesting that he is civilized indeed if he can compose verse on the tragedy of war, while reinforcing his poetic persona for his American audience. He combines religion and art in this article to glorify and justify war as well as to reassure American readers that Japan's aggression is necessary. In relation to Japanese militarism, poetry and Zen priest form an enlightened front, while poetry and the aesthetic have the last word.[19]

Shaku's major work published at this time, *Sermons of a Buddhist Abbot*, a collection of talks given on his American lecture tour, again includes few specific details about Zen. Most of the essays deal with a generalized Mahayana Buddhism, privileging it over Christianity as a religion better suited to modern life. However, it is in this context that he does address a key aspect of Zen, its meditation practices, in an essay titled "Practice of Dhyana," *dhyana* being an alternative term for Zen in some Western texts about Buddhism in the late nineteenth century. Although Shaku does not make this term's connection with Zen clear, he does define *dhyana* as contemplation, necessary for the "realization of the Buddhist life" along with moral precepts and wisdom ("Practice" 135). He equates it with self-examination, pacification, equilibration, and tranquilization, while pointing out that it is not trance or self-hypnotism. *Dhyana* brings practitioners to a state of *samadhi*, which he defines as "perfect absorption of thought into object of contemplation" ("Practice" 138–39).[20] Instead of describing how meditation is practiced, however, Shaku presents its benefits as an antidote for the pace of the modern world and explains it using Western scientific terminology as a "sort of spiritual storage battery" ("Practice" 140). He concludes by stating that "besides its being an indispensable religious discipline for attaining enlightenment, it is one of the most efficient means of training oneself morally and physically" ("Practice" 145).[21] In this way, he indirectly refutes ideas that meditation is impractical or curious. By not discussing his doctrine too specifically, but emphasizing its physical and mental health benefits, Shaku presents Buddhism in the West's terms in this essay, recalling his presentations at the World's Parliament of Religions. For a Western audience, Buddhism becomes a practical self-help kind of religion which can better cope with modernity than can Christianity.

Zen, Aesthetics, and Tea: Okakura Kakuzo

In contrast, Okakura Kakuzo would continue to present more specific information about Zen to his Western audience, especially in relation to art and culture, bearing out the pattern he had established in his catalogue for the Exposition. In the process, Okakura would also play a prominent role in the American art world. Because of his Western connections with such influential Japanophiles as William Bigelow and John LaFarge, he was asked by the Boston Museum of Fine Arts to act as advisor to their Asian art collection in 1904 and the next year became curator, dividing his time between Boston and Japan.[22]

Thus, Okakura became known as representative of Japanese culture to a certain, albeit elitist, segment of the American public. A more general audience also came to know him through his appearance in magazines of the day, partly due to his command of English. The magazine *The Critic* and its gossip column of literary news, "The Lounger," had this to say about Okakura and his facility with English in relation to his 1904 book, *The Awakening of Japan*: "If the reader was not told so in the publisher's preface . . . he would scarcely believe that the book was written entirely in English by Mr. Okakura. It is not alone English, but good English . . ." (13–14). Numerous reviews of his books appeared in magazines such as the *Nation* and the *Dial* and chapters of his most popular work, *The Book of Tea*, were excerpted in such periodicals as *The Critic* and *The International Quarterly*.[23] For these reasons, Okakura was able to disseminate his perspective on Zen to a fairly broad segment of the American public.

Of his books published in the early twentieth century, *The Ideals of the East* and *The Book of Tea* present Zen in some detail with specifics of history and practice, especially in relation to its influence on Japanese material culture.

The information about Zen, however, often is used not only to discuss art and aesthetics, but to support his position in regard to a comparison of East and West on spiritual and philosophic grounds, also. His point is to demonstrate not only how the West and East differ, but paradoxically, how the East can be considered superior to the West. For example, the East's way of conquest is not outwardly (as England conquered India), but inwardly, through self-control, which leaves humans ultimately at one with other beings and nature. His tactics and use of Zen to prove the superiority of East to West are reminiscent of Shaku Soen's approach in "The Practice of Dhyana."

His earlier work, *The Ideals of the East*, presents Okakura's argument about Asian traditions threatened by Western imperialism. He claims that Asia is one, and the best place to study and understand its two major traditions, Indian and Chinese, is Japan, a kind of museum for the study of Asian culture. It is within this context that Okakura describes Zen's major contribution to Japanese aesthetics, giving a brief history of Zen and its introduction to China via Bodhidharma. He claims that its main impact was felt in the Ashikaga period, which had its idealistic basis in the Zen sect. Okakura especially emphasizes Zen individuality and ideals of "self-control and strength of will" in relation to the Samurai (*IE* 159). He also describes Zen's transmission without words and its dynamic iconoclasm, wherein thought was to be freed from "trammels of mistaken categories" through methods of self-control, "the essence of true freedom" (*IE* 173). Zen becomes a means of "freeing thought from the fetters in which all forms of knowledge tend to enchain it" (*IE* 172). Thus, Okakura presents Zen not only as a driving force behind Japanese aesthetics and material culture, but also as an idealistic philosophy privileging individuality and power. In giving the history of Japanese art, Okakura also presents an alternative to Western views of both the Japanese and Buddhists as passive and introspective with his polemical use of Zen as argument against Western stereotyping of the Japanese. With Zen a key support, Okakura defines the idea of individuality in a way that turns the Western orientalist notion of Japanese inferiority back on itself.

The Book of Tea, his most widely reviewed and highly recommended work at the time of publication, builds on dichotomies presented in *The Ideals of the East*. His premise here is that the West does not understand the East and judges it as inferior, when in actuality the East is superior to the West in quality of life. It is through a discussion of tea, a drink enjoyed by both East and West, and the tea ceremony that Okakura will make his point. In the process of discussing tea's impact on Japanese culture and aesthetics, he provides much information about Zen's history and tenets, its affinity with Taoism, and its special contributions to Eastern thought. He begins with the history of tea drinking and Buddhists who used the beverage to keep awake during meditation, picturing Zennists drinking tea before an image of "Bodhi-Dharma." This

Zen ritual would develop into the tea ceremony in fifteenth-century Japan.

Connections between Zen and the aesthetics of the tea ceremony include what Okakura calls the Abodes of Fancy, Vacancy, and the Unsymmetrical. He explains these respectively as relating to qualities of ephemerality; simplicity and emptiness; and imperfection and lack of completion (*BT* 74). Additionally, these all have connections with Buddhist, specifically Zen, ideals and monastic practice. For example, the simplicity of the teahouse is modeled after that of Zen monastic buildings, while its lack of symmetry relates to Zen's "dynamic nature" and its interest in process rather than perfection (*BT* 95). Significantly, he is among the first to connect Zen with Taoism, noting that both "worship" relativity, "advocate" individualism and believe that truth can be attained through the "comprehension of opposites" (*BT* 65).[24] In this context, he describes the stories told by Zen masters, providing as example a koan from the Mumonkan, number 29. For Zen, words are an encumbrance to thought, and the mundane is as important as the spiritual. The tea ceremony demonstrates these ideals and Zen's teaching that there is greatness in the smallest details of life.

As has been suggested, Okakura's underlying purpose within the context of a discussion of the tea ceremony and Zen is to contrast West and East, to the detriment of the West. At the beginning of *The Book of Tea* he notes a paradox: "You have gained expansion at the cost of restlessness; we have created a harmony which is weak against aggression. Will you believe it?—the East is better off in some respects than the West" (*BT* 5). The rest of the book is in a sense the proof of that statement moving from considerations of the physical use of space to issues of materialism and cultural values, in the process criticizing Western lifestyles. For example, Okakura contrasts Western interests in symmetry and "useless reiteration" in relation to the "simplicity of the tea-room and its freedom from vulgarity" that makes it a "sanctuary from the vexation of the outer world" (*BT* 63). Similarly to Shaku Soen, Okakura brings modernity into his argument when he ends his discussion of the tearoom with the claim that industrialism makes "true refinement difficult" and the tearoom "more of a necessity" (*BT* 41). His message is that the values of the tea ceremony prove superior to contemporary ones (synonymous with those of the West), again demonstrating his privileging of the East over the West, especially in the aesthetic and spiritual realms. However, in comparison with Shaku Soen, Okakura provides the American public with much more specific information about Zen as religious and aesthetic practice.

What They Transmitted

In describing the transmission of Zen to the West by Shaku Soen and Okakura Kakuzo as an originary moment for the understanding of Zen as dual discourse, the privileging of the aesthetic over the spiritual has become evident. The complexity of Zen's transmission and the fluidity of its signification in the late nineteenth and early twentieth centuries also have become apparent. On an obvious level, more positive attitudes are demonstrated toward Buddhism and Zen by the Japanese themselves, as might be expected. Along with this comes an emphasis on Zen aesthetics in the face of the West's denigration of Zen as curious spiritual practice. Perhaps for these reasons, Shaku Soen downplays Zen's unique contemplative practice, knowing that the West's more negative responses come from its seemingly contradictory and peculiar spirituality. Additionally, both men present Buddhism as a religion able to counter the negative effects of modernity. This especially is true of Shaku Soen's essay on *dhyana* and the way in which he emphasizes meditation as a panacea for the West and its "industrial and commercial civilization" where people have little time for "spiritual culture" ("PD" 139–40). Demonstrating Zen's modernity in the scientific and personal spheres adds to its Western appeal, while shifting the emphasis away from Zen as religion.

Furthermore, Zen's influence on Japanese aesthetics and material culture, emphasized by Okakura, permitted appropriation without conversion, and appreciation instead of practice for the American public, already used to appropriating material aspects of Japanese culture through the Japan Craze.[25] It is in the context of aesthetics that Okakura Kakuzo provides much specific information about Zen religious practices, philosophy, and tenets. That American appreciation for Japanese aesthetics also included an interest in Japanese spirituality is evidenced by Okakura's translation of Zen tenets into terms Americans could readily assimilate. Providing Zen as an idealistic and aesthetic alternative to American materialism points to underlying compensatory and appropriative needs in American culture that the understanding of Zen as dual discourse addresses. This might have been another reason why Shaku Soen presented himself as scholar, poet, and calligrapher as well as priest. These were effective roles for his transmission of Zen, demonstrating his use of the Buddhist tenet of skillful means. Both figures privilege Zen's affinity with the arts to good advantage.

Zen transmitted as dual discourse also points to an understanding of Zen as an orientalist discourse against a backdrop of American and Japanese imperialism of the late nineteenth century. The translation of Zen as an aspect of Japanese aesthetic culture to an American context is perhaps a way for Americans to see Japanese imperialism's military triumphs over China in 1895 and Russia in 1905 as less threatening. At this time, Japan continues to be seen as a producer of art rather than artillery. For the Japanese, however, the presentation of Zen in relation to Japanese culture is used to demonstrate the superiority of the East to the West in the modern age.[26] A seemingly informational discussion of Zen becomes a polemical one, and a reverse Orientalism, what James Ketelaar calls Occidentalism, occurs (37–56).

Ultimately, these Japanese commentators use Western stereotypes of Japan and Buddhism to their advantage with lasting consequences for the transmission of Zen to America.[27] Both Shaku Soen and Okakura Kakuzo define Zen in ways that emphasize its ability to show Japanese culture as modern in Western terms, while continuing to link Zen to aesthetic practices and the cult of the individual. In the process, they both capitalize on and contradict Western stereotypes of Japan. In all these ways, the discourse about Zen at this time demonstrates the possibility for mutual understanding and communication between the two nations. As well, it looks ahead to Zen's further naturalization in the United States, where Zen as aesthetic and cultural practice almost overshadows Zen as spiritual and meditative one. This especially is true of the Zen boom of the 1950s, also a period when Japanese militarism significantly impacts East–West relations. Indeed, the understanding of Zen as dual discourse with the privileging of the aesthetic is a factor in the continuing Americanization of Zen in the twenty-first century.

Notes

1. The *Oxford English Dictionary* gives the earliest citation for Zen as an article by J. M. James, entitled "Descriptive Notes on the Rosaries as Used by the Different Sects of Buddhists in Japan," published in the *Transactions of the Asiatic Society* in 1881. This article is significant not so much for detailed information on Zen, but to demonstrate the common practice of comparing Zen with Christianity at this time. Commodore Perry's opening of Japan to the West in 1853 marked the beginning of close ties between the United States and Japan and was an added reason for the Meiji government's reliance on American expertise in modernization. Many of the early educators also were missionaries or ministers because of the necessity to be literate in English in order to read the Bible. Commentaries on Japanese religion often appeared in periodicals with a theological purpose, such as *The Andover* Review. Other minister/educators wrote for the *Transactions of the Asiatic* Society, an important venue for information about Japan and Japanese culture for a more general American audience.

2. A number of articles on Buddhism were published in *The Open Court,* which showed a more positive attitude toward Zen. An article by C. Pfoundes, for example, describes the Dhyana sect's principle of " 'abstract and profound meditation' " more positively as " 'thinking out' the great problems for one's self" (4373). Note that the terms *Dhyana sect* and *Zen* were used interchangeably at this time.

3. Rev. Lloyd was a missionary who also taught in Japanese universities and schools of higher learning. Despite this negative attitude, Lloyd also summarizes the Soto system of contemplation in Dogen's *Fukanzazengi,* including instructions on how to meditate. Note that Percival Lowell's book *Occult Japan* also alludes to Zen in a discussion of meditation as trance.

4. Instigated by Protestant minister John Barrows, the Parliament was envisioned as a major religious and ecumenical event, although the closing addresses assume all

nations as one under Christ. Seager's study characterizes it as ideological landscape against which the East–West debate could be read (46). See McRae's essay for a discussion of the fair as missionary movement.

5. A number of commentators on Zen's transmission to the West begin with Shaku Soen's appearance at the Parliament, considering it key. See Tworkov and Fields, for example.

6. American Japanophiles such as Fenollosa or Morse came to Japan to teach, but unlike the missionary types, they were more philosophically and culturally oriented. Many of these Japanophiles were interested in preserving unique aspects of Japanese culture rather than in totally abandoning them in the process of Westernization. See Lears, *No Place of Grace*, for more on these men.

7.. The interest of American news media and public in the exotic appearance of the Asian delegates, including the Japanese delegation, was part of the orientalizing aspect of the Parliament. In "Strategic Occidentalism," Ketelaar notes one Japanese priest's statement that the West's interest in and obsession with the ways Japanese Buddhists dressed in silks and velvets implied the West's materialistic attitude and its dwelling on surface values (51–52). It is interesting that Okakura also capitalized on the West's fascination with traditional Japanese dress, primarily appearing that way during his stay in the United States in the next decade.

8. The speech on the eighth day was about the law of cause and effect and that on the sixteenth day was about war and the importance of arbitration to prevent war. McRae makes a similar point about Shaku's refraining from using Zen "logic-busting technique" in the United States (25). But see Ketelaar's book-length study for the point that much was lost in the translation of Shaku's speeches for the Parliament from Japanese to English (151). Shaku Soen did not speak English, hence the need for his English-speaking secretary, D. T. Suzuki, and for his speeches to be read by others at the Parliament.

9. See Paul Carus' *Buddhism and Its Christian Critics* for more on the debate between Buddhists and Christians.

10. The characterization of American interests in Japan as a craze was first made by Edward S. Morse in his 1886 study, *Japanese Homes and Their Surroundings*. He dates the beginnings of fascination with things Japanese to the Philadelphia Centennial of 1876.

11. A major discussion of the Japan Craze with epicenter in the 1880s can be found in this catalogue.

12. The sum was placed by Robert Rydell in *All the World's a Fair* at $630,000, who points out that this major contribution indicates Japan's interest in "furthering commercial ties with America" (48), proving it worthy of inclusion with western European nations. Additionally, for the first time at a world's fair, Japan had been given the privilege of displaying its art in the Palace of Fine Arts, the only non-European nation to be asked to do so. In return, Japan with its successful modernization in the Meiji Era was, according to Rydell, expected to have an "uplifting—that is, Americanizing—influence on an otherwise backward Asian continent," while American attitudes toward the Japanese were often "patronizing and demeaning" (50–51). For more on the importance of world's fairs, see Rydell who points out that these fairs were hegemonic spaces in which the ruling elite of "corporate, political and scientific leadership" were able to demonstrate proper attitudes toward "race, nationality, and progress" as well as

to emphasize Western racial superiority to the non-European cultures on display (2). See Ronald Takaki for more on American attitudes toward the Japanese at this time.

13. According to Earle, Okakura also guided the officials who were in charge of the selection of all exhibits for the 1893 Exposition.

14. Note that Okakura would again make connections between tea and Zen in his later work, *The Book of Tea*. Thanks to Prof. Thomas Kasulis for pointing out that this presentation of Zen as "orthodox" is not at all a non-Zen characterization. Okakura presents Zen as equal in stature to "orthodox" Southern Buddhism, namely Theravada, the focus of British scholarship on Buddhism in the mid-nineteenth century.

15. Relative to the American difficulty of understanding the Zen point of view, Zen master Nakagawa Soen relates an anecdote about one of Shaku Soen's lectures to an American audience in 1905 and the laughter aroused by his paradoxical statement about his forty-year study of Buddhism. He understood after all those years that, as he put it, " 'I do not understand anything' " (128).

16. Print venues would primarily be *The Open Court* and *The Monist*. Both were known to present articles on alternative spiritualities and philosophies with an underlying scientific and empirical bent. *Open Court* was a successor to *The Index*, an organ of the "Free Religious Association, a group formed by New England religious liberals, according to Tweed (32). Its banner at this time reads: "Devoted to the Work of Conciliating Religion with Science." The Open Court publishing company also put out a book of Shaku Soen's collected essays to commemorate his American tour, *Sermons of a Buddhist Abbot*.

17. The editor describes the image as "the omnipresent law of love and righteousness, as a father cherishing the animate creation like a child, in paternal affection, and bears a certain resemblance to the Roman Catholic representation of St. Joseph with the Christ child" (120).

18. These articles also suggest the interest the United States took in Japan's conflict with Russia and American sympathy with the Japanese who were seen as more Western and civilized than the Russians. Such interest is also evident in the fact that "At the Battle of Nan Shan Hill" was excerpted in a more widely disseminated periodical, *The American Monthly Review of Reviews*, entitled "A Buddhist Priest on the War." The article was accompanied by a drawing of Shaku, the caption alluding to him as a "leader of Japanese Buddhist thought" (233). Other articles on the war are featured in this issue.

19. It is interesting to note that similar connections between Buddhism and war appear in his essay "Buddhism and Oriental Culture," included in *Sermons of a Buddhist Abbot*. Here, Soen relates Buddhism and aspects of Oriental culture through practices of "patriotism, filial piety, faithfulness, and abnegation of self" (180).

20. This is an infrequent use of Buddhist terminology on Shaku's part. However, in more scholarly articles for *The Open Court*, he does use Buddhist terminology, another example of skillful means in action, and his awareness of the levels of sophistication of his American audience.

21. Here, Shaku may be capitalizing on American interests in *jiu jitsu* and Japanese practices in relation to physical health and well-being, popular at the time.

22. His importance for this group is evident in LaFarge's dedication of *An Artist's Letters From Japan* to him: "I wish to put your name before these notes . . . because for a time you were Japan to me" (ix). Not only did he epitomize Japan for these men, he

also helped establish them as Western authorities on Japanese culture. Similarly, Shaku Soen was equally important to Paul Carus, helping to authenticate Carus as Western spokesman for Zen Buddhism and in turn adding to Carus's cultural capital.

23. He also published in Boston's *Museum of Fine Arts* Bulletin. It is important to note that bulletin articles by Okakura were not the only ones that discussed Zen, which was frequently mentioned and even defined in connection with art of the Ashikaga Period in articles by other members of the curatorial staff, perhaps under his influence.

24. Connections between Zen and Taoism were emphasized in *The Dial*'s book review.

25. In fact, the association of Zen with aesthetics in the 1890s and early 1900s shows the continuing influence of that Craze. Hosley points out the irony that "Japan emerged as a symbol of Western anti-modernism at the same time that she was exchanging her traditions for modernization" (28). In fact, Japan's modernization was built with income from these supposedly handmade exports of premodern, nonmachine-made art objects, the production of which under increasing demand from the West became increasingly mechanized (41). Such modernization led to Japan's own imperializing as it defeated both China and Russia.

26. The East–West conversation centering on Japan is of great concern to Japanophiles at this time, as well as the general public. Among the key discussants is Lowell in *The Soul of the East* (1888), who considered that the East was doomed to be eclipsed by the West if it didn't change from an emphasis on the impersonal and absence of Self as put forth by Buddhism. Fenollosa wrote several articles and poems relating to the meeting of East and West, including the 1898 article "The Coming Fusion of East and West." He is more optimistic about possibilities for mutual understanding than either Lowell or Okakura. Interestingly, the obituary for Okakura in the *Museum of Fine Arts Bulletin* ends by noting his "grasp of the best intellectual products of the highest civilizations on both sides of the world, completely invalidating Kipling's famous line: 'Oh, East is East, and West is West, and never the twain shall meet.' They met in Okakura Kakuzo" (Bigelow and Lodge 74–75).

27. Associates of both Shaku and Okakura carry on their respective missions. D. T. Suzuki, Shaku's interpreter and associate of Paul Carus at Open Court, continues to present Mahayana Buddhism, rather than Zen, in his 1905 work, *Outline of Mahayana Buddhism*. Anesaki Masaharu, Japanese historian of religions lecturing at Harvard, took over Okakura's lecture series at the Boston Museum of Fine Arts after Okakura's death. He devoted a chapter of his study *Buddhist Art in Its Relation to Buddhist Ideals* (1914) to Zen influences on Japanese art, even quoting extensively from Dogen on the practice of sitting meditation. Both men continued to publish well into the twentieth century. Suzuki most notably wrote about Zen for an American audience in the 1950s.

Works Cited

Barrows, John Henry, ed. *The World's Parliament of Religions*. Vol. 2. Chicago: The Parliament Publishing Company, 1893.

Bigelow, William Sturgis and John Ellerton Lodge. "Okakura Kakuzo." *Museum of Fine Arts Bulletin* 11, no. 67 (December 1913): 72–75.

Bowker, John, ed. *The Oxford Dictionary of World Religions*. Oxford: Oxford University Press, 1997.

"A Buddhist Priest On the War." *The American Monthly Review of Reviews* 31, no. 2 (Feb. 1905): 233.

Carus, Paul. *Buddhism and Its Christian Critics*. Chicago: The Open Court Publishing Company, 1899.

Earle, Joe. *Splendors of Meiji: Masterpieces from the Khalili Collection*. St. Petersburg, FL: Broughton International Publications, 1999.

Fields, Rick. *How the Swans Came to the Lake*. Boston: Shambhala, 1992.

Gookin, Frederick W. "The Cult of the Cha-Jin." Review of *The Book of Tea* by Okakura Kakuzo. *The Dial* 41, no. 485 (September 1906): 105.

Gordon, M.L. "The Buddhisms of Japan." *The Andover Review* 5, no. 27 (1886): 301–11.

Hosley, William. *The Japan Idea: Art and Life in Victorian America*. Hartford, CT: Wadsworth Atheneum, 1990.

James, J. M. "Descriptive Notes on the Rosaries (Jiu-Dzu) as Used by the Different Sects of Buddhists in Japan." *Transactions of the Asiatic Society of Japan* 11 (1881): 173–82.

Ketelaar, James. *Of Heretics and Martyrs in Meiji Japan*. Princton, NJ: Princeton University Press, 1990.

———, "Strategic Occidentalism: Meiji Buddhists at the World's Parliament of Religions." *Buddhist-Christian Studies* 11 (1991): 37–56.

La Farge, John. *An Artist's Letters From Japan*. New York: The Century Company, 1897.

Lears, T. J. Jackson. *No Place of Grace*. Chicago: U. of Chicago Press, 1983.

Lloyd, Rev. A. "Developments of Japanese Buddhism." *Transactions of the Asiatic Society of Japan*. 22 (1894): 337–506.

"The Lounger." *The Critic* 46, no. 1 (1905): 10–14.

Lowell, Percival. *Occult Japan*. 1894. Reprint. Rochester, VT: Inner Traditions International, Ltd. 1990.

———, *The Soul of the Far East*. 1888 Reprint. New York: MacMillan, 1911.

McRae, John. "Oriental Verities on the American Frontier: The 1893 World's Parliament of Religions and the Thought of Masao Abe." *Buddhist-Christian Studies* 11 (1991): 7–36.

Morse, Edward S. *Japanese Homes and Their Surroundings*. 1886. Reprint. Rutland, VT: Charles E. Tuttle, 1972.

Okakura Kakuzo. *The Awakening of Japan*. New York: The Century Co., 1904.

———, *The Book of Tea*. New York: Duffield & Co., 1912.

———, *The Ideals of the East*. 1903. Reprint. Rutland, VT: Charles E. Tuttle Company, 1970.

———, *The Ho-o-den (Phoenix Hall) an Illustrated Description of the Buildings erected by the Japanese Government at the World's Columbian Exposition, Jackson Park, Chicago*. Tokyo: K. Ogawa Publisher, 1893.

Pfoundes, C. "Religion in Japan." *The Open Court*. 11, no. 4 (1895): 4372–4374.

Rydell, Robert W. *All the World's a Fair*. Chicago: The University of Chicago Press, 1984.

Seager, Richard Hughes. *The World's Parliament of Religions*. Bloomington: University Press, 1995.

Senzaki, Nyogen, Soen Nakagawa, and Eido Shimano. *Namu Dai Bosa*. Ed., Louis

Nordstrom. New York: Theatre Arts Books, 1976.

Shokin, Furuta. "Shaku Soen: The Footsteps of a Modern Japanese Master." *Philosophical Studies of Japan.* 8 (1967): 67–91.

Shaku, Soen. "At the Battle of Nan-Shan Hill." *The Open Court.* 18, no.12 (December 1904): 705–09.

———, "Japanese Calligraphy." *The Open Court.* 13, no. 2 (February 1899): 120–21.

———, "The Law of Cause and Effect, as Taught by Buddha." *The World's Parliament of Religions.* Edited by John Henry Barrows. Vol. 2. Chicago: The Parliament Publishing Company, 1893. 829–31.

———, *Sermons of a Buddhist Abbot.* 1906. Reprint. New York: Doubleday, 2004.

———, "The Universality of Truth." *The Monist.* 4, no. 2 (1894): 161–62.

Takaki, Ronald. *Strangers from a Distant Shore.* Boston: Little, Brown, 1989.

Tateno, Gozo. "Foreign Nations at the World's Fair: Japan." *North American Review.* 156 (January 1893): 34–43.

Truman, Ben C. *History of The World's Fair.* 1893. Reprint. New York: Arno Press, 1976.

Tweed, Thomas. *The American Encounter with Buddhism: 1844–1912.* Bloomington: Indiana University Press, 1992.

Tworkov, Helen. *Zen in America.* New York: Kodansha International, 1994.

Chapter 2

Black American Buddhism

History and Representation

Linda Furgerson Selzer

Being both Black and Buddhist in our society seems a cultural oddity. . . .
A "Black Buddhist" confounds people's expectations.

—Ramon Calhoun

In one compelling scene in the racially controversial film *Crash* (2004), a successful black television producer and his beautiful wife—Cameron and Christine
Thayer (played by Terrence Howard and Thandie Newton)—are pulled over by
a racist cop and his reluctant young partner. The scene quickly escalates from
an ostensible case of mistaken identity to one of full-blown police intimidation.
Just before pulling the couple over, Officers Ryan and Hansen (played by Matt
Dillon and Ryan Phillipe) had received a police alert describing two armed black
men in their twenties traveling in a stolen, late-model, black Navigator similar
to the one in which the couple is riding. Although both officers clearly are
aware that neither the license plate of the couple's Navigator nor its occupants
match the dispatcher's description, senior Officer Ryan, motivated by a sim-
mering racism that has recently been brought to a boil by a black insurance
agent who refused medical aid for his ailing father, decides to pull the couple
over for his own purposes. Early in what will become an increasingly abusive
encounter, Officer Ryan places his hand on his police-issued Glock and tells
Cameron to get out of the car. At that moment Christine attempts to defuse
the situation and defend her husband by pointedly telling the officers, "He's a
Buddhist, for Christ's sake!"

Within the context of director Paul Haggis's Oscar-winning film, Christine
Cameron's "Buddhist defense" of her husband lends itself to several interpretations.

Most immediately, Christine uses the observation to suggest that her husband would never drive drunk (although she herself is somewhat inebriated, the couple having come from a celebratory awards ceremony). More important, Christine seems to use her husband's Buddhism in an attempt to distinguish him from the officers' stereotypical expectations, or as a defense against racial profiling. By implication, Cameron's Buddhism suggests that he is not an "angry black man," but a peace-loving and nonthreatening citizen. As the scene develops, however, the pacifism implied by Cameron's Buddhism takes on disturbing overtones when Officer Ryan forces Christine to submit to a humiliating and sexually abusive body search while her husband stands passively by. Finally, Cameron's Buddhism is positioned by the film not simply to imply that Cameron doesn't fit the officers' stereotypical profile, but also to suggest that he is *in fact* racially and culturally inauthentic—charges the black couple aim at each other in a later scene, when Christine tells her husband, "the closest you ever got to being Black was watching the Cosby show," and Cameron replies, "at least I didn't watch it with the rest of the equestrian team." *Crash* therefore gestures toward the growing number of black Americans who are practicing Buddhism, while the film simultaneously raises questions (both intended and otherwise) about the cultural representation of Buddhists and black people, especially in relation to issues of cultural and racial authenticity.

Since the 1990s, black Buddhists themselves have been writing about their religious practice with increasing frequency, addressing in their own voices the complexities generated by their multiple cultural identities. Such writings offer an invaluable firsthand account of the challenges—and opportunities—that confront contemporary black American Buddhist practitioners. At the same time, the emergence of a black Buddhist voice in American letters prompts serious consideration of the cultural history of this group. This chapter examines what *Turning Wheel: The Journal of Engaged Buddhism* has called "Black Dharma" by analyzing black American Buddhism from its early roots in the nineteenth century to its contemporary expression in a variety of articles and books that have been recently published by black practitioners, including works by figures such as bell hooks, Charles Johnson, Angel Kyodo Williams, Jan Willis, and fellow traveler, Alice Walker.

Black Dharma in the United States: Early History

Black Americans who traveled on transnational routes as free people—or, what is more likely, as slaves—may have had the opportunity to meet practicing Buddhists on board ships or in foreign countries in the early part of the nation's history. It is likely, however, that African Americans first encountered Buddhism on American soil through unrecorded encounters with Chinese immigrants in the

1800s, when the California Gold Rush and the building of the Transcontinental Railroad drew waves of Asian immigrants to the United States.[1] As Buddhist scholar Rick Fields points out, by the 1860s Chinese immigrants comprised as much as one-tenth the population of California, and as early as 1853 the first Buddhist temple in the United States had been established in San Francisco (70–71). In the nineteenth century, literate black Americans also may have been exposed to Buddhism through the many Buddhist-inspired translations, commentaries, and literary works produced by English-speaking writers, including those by Ralph Waldo Emerson and Henry David Thoreau (in addition to the wide circulation of the extremely popular English poem "The Light of Asia," published by Sir Edwin Arnold in 1879).

An important moment in the mutual history of black people and Buddhists in the United States, however, occurred in 1893 at the World's Parliament of Religions, part of the historic World's Columbian Exposition in Chicago. African-American representatives at the parliament included Frederick Douglass, Benjamin William Arnett (bishop of the African Methodist Episcopal Church), and Fannie Barrier Williams (a Unitarian laywoman). Buddhist representatives included Anagarika Dharmapala from Ceylon (now Sri Lanka) and Japanese Buddhists Zenshiro Negachi, H. Rev. Zitsuzen, Horen Toki, and Zen Master Soyen Shaku. Although the extent of personal exchange between various delegates cannot be known, at the opening ceremonies a small number of both Buddhists and blacks joined four-thousand other attendees in the Hall of Columbus to inaugurate what Parliament historian Richard Hughes Seager calls "a first-of-its-kind event in the history of the world" (*Dawn* 8). The list of names for those sitting on the platform during the ceremonies includes Bishop D. A. Payne and Bishop B. W. Arnett from the African Methodist Episcopal Church and Buddists H. Rev. Zitsuzen, Horen Toki, and A. Dharmapala (Barrows 1: 64–65). Held on September 11, a day that more than a century later would become infamous for a tragedy that seemed to epitomize the kind of religious antagonism that the World's Parliament of Religions—taken at its best—sought to surmount, the opening ceremony began as the Columbian Liberty Bell was rung ten times and delegates from the "world's ten great religions" entered Columbus Hall arm in arm.[2]

The Parliament of Religions holds a special, if problematic, place in the history of religious pluralism. Specifically designed to commemorate the four-hundred-year anniversary of Columbus' "discovery" of the Americas, the Columbian Exposition mounted a grand display of national, cultural, and racial supremacy. In order to protest the Exposition's treatment of African Americans, Ida B. Wells published *The Reason Why the Colored American is Not in the World's Columbian Exposition* (1893), a work that documented the lack of black representation in the early planning stages of the event, the fair's denial of good-paying jobs to black workers, and the Exhibition's racist showcasing of "primitive" African peoples. Certainly, a large impetus for the Parliament of Religion was the display of national and Christian triumphalism and, as John Burris suggests in *Exhibiting Religion* (2001), the elaborate staging of colonial interests. Not surprisingly, the great majority of speeches at the Parliament of Religion were by white Christians, whereas other religious traditions and racial and ethnic groups were more meagerly represented. Native Americans were represented in part by a white woman ("Miss Alice C. Fletcher of Cambridge, Massachusetts"), African Americans by a disturbingly small delegation, and Africans and South Americans largely by scientists with an anthropological perspective (Barrows 2: 812). Additionally, many white Christians used the Parliament to speak out against religious pluralism and against the call by some speakers—notably the popular Swami Vivekananda—for the development of a universal religion. Representing Vedantic Hinduism, Vivekananda argued, "every religion is only . . . evolving a God out of the material man; and the same God is the inspirer of all of them" (2: 977). He also spoke in favor of a form of global religious unity in which religions still maintained their distinctiveness: "each must assimilate the others and yet preserve its individuality and grow according to its law of growth" (1: 170). On the other hand, Christian William K. Wilkerson argued against religious pluralism, arguing that "men need to be saved *from* false religion; they are in no way of being saved *by* false religion." He suggested further that the attitude of Christianity toward other religions must be one of "universal, absolute, eternal, unappeasable hostility" (2: 1249). Although the Parliament often is pointed to as a landmark event in the history of religious pluralism, Christian ecumenicism, and the development of comparative religious studies, its relation to all of these movements is obviously culturally and racially complex.

But it would be a mistake to read the participation of African-American and Asian delegates at the Parliament simply in terms of the racist representations by whites. Indeed, both blacks and Buddhists advocated for their own interests and criticized Western Christianity openly in their papers. For example, Fannie Barrier Williams, whose speech was received enthusiastically in the hall and reported upon favorably by the press, emphasized that white Christians brought black people to the country "for the use of Christians" (142). She also pointed out that 50 percent of fundamentalist churches were still "denying membership" to people of African descent, and that white Christian Americans were continuing to deny black men and women their full civil rights (149). Although some speakers worried about the degree to which the insights of other religions could be properly assimilated into Christianity, Williams argued that "the hope of the Negro and other dark races in America depends upon how far the white Christians can assimilate their own religion" (149). Although the extent of criticism levied against Christianity differed among various Asian delegates, some of the most popular speakers at the Parliament were Asian representatives who openly criticized Western Christianity, especially for its materialism and Christian Imperialism, while advocating for their own religious and nationalist interests.[3] In particular, Hirai Ryuge Kinzo spoke out boldly against the work of Christian missionaries in Japan, and Anagarika H. Dharmapala did the same against their practices in India and Ceylon, asserting that "the selfishness and intolerance of the missionary" ensures that "not an intelligent man will accept Christianity" (2: 1093).

However problematic a place the 1893 World's Parliament of Religions holds in the history of religious pluralism, the event's importance to the establishment of Buddhism in the West is undeniable. As Seager observes, the Parliament marks the beginning of "full-scale Asian missions to the Western nations" (*Dawn* 10). Significantly, one of the Asian delegates to the Parliament was the first Buddhist Zen master to visit the United States, Soyen Shaku, who was asked by Paul Carus, publisher of *Open Court* (and editor of *The Monist*), to stay in America in order to translate books on Asian religion.[4] Although Shaku declined, one of his students, D. T. Suzuki (1870–1966), came to the United States in 1897 to work with Carus on a translation of the *Tao Te Ching* (Verhoeven 217). Thus began the career of perhaps the twentieth-century's leading Buddhist scholar in the West. As a result of the World's Parliament, other Asian religious groups also sent representatives to begin missions in the United States—a consequence that the Parliament's planners had probably not anticipated.

Although other Asian Buddhists also were important to the dissemination of Buddhism in the West, Suzuki's influence on Western Buddhism over the course of the twentieth-century as a translator, writer, teacher, spiritual leader, and lecturer is especially significant. He was important to both the growth of Beat Buddhism in the 1950s and to the "Buddhist Boom" in the 1960s and 1970s, a period during which many of the black Buddhists practicing today were first drawn to the Dharma, including bell hooks. Well-known white literary figures such as Jack Kerouac, Allen Ginsberg, and Gary Snyder also admired Suzuki's writings, and all of them met him in person (although Suzuki criticized Beat Zen for being poorly disciplined in both its meditative practice and its ethical conduct).[5] Suzuki's work was also of interest to Bob Kaufman and to LeRoi Jones (Amiri Baraka), and may have influenced the selection of the name *Yugen* for the Beat literary magazine that Jones edited with his first wife, Hettie Cohen, a Jewish woman whom he married in a Buddhist temple in New York in 1958. In any case, Suzuki's knowledge of several languages, his extensive travels across Europe and the United States, and his influence as the leading scholar on Zen Buddhism during his lifetime were critical to the introduction of Zen Buddhism in the West.

In addition to the active missionary efforts of various Buddhist organizations, two other important factors contributed to the dissemination of Buddhism in the twentieth-century United States: the return of servicemen from overseas with wives who carried their devotional practices with them; and the liberalization of immigration laws in 1965, which led to a new influx of immigrants from Sri Lanka, China, Thailand, Cambodia, Laos, Burma, Taiwan, and Vietnam (Seager "Buddhist Worlds" 252). Today, Asian immigration to the United States is second in numbers only to Hispanic. In "The Dharma Has Come West: A Survey of Recent Studies and Sources," Martin Baumann estimated that in 1997 that there were three to four million Buddhists in the United States with fewer than 100,000 of them being convert Buddhists (198). In fact, the precise number of black people participating in Buddhism is extremely difficult to ascertain. Part of the difficulty in obtaining reliable numbers stems from the fact that the scholarly study of American Buddhism is itself a young discipline. As Charles Prebish points out, Buddhist Studies did not begin to emerge as a "significant discipline in the American university system" until the 1960s ("Academic" 186). Because the study of American Buddhism took time to establish itself as a legitimate field of study, secondary literature in the field was modest through the 1980s. Thus, information on black Buddhists in the United States was especially limited until the 1990s, when people of color themselves began writing about their Buddhist practice in greater numbers.

Moreover, up to the 1990s, American Buddhism tended to focus on issues of "ethnicity" and "race" almost exclusively in terms of the differences between the so-called "two Buddhisms"—ethnic Asian Buddhism and white American convert Buddhism. As Scottish-Japanese-American Buddhist Addie Foye points out in "Buddhists in America: A Short, Biased View," this classification tended to obscure both the differences among various Asian Buddhist traditions and the participation of non-whites in American Buddhism (57). For the survey on which he based "The New Buddhism: Some Empirical Findings" (1991), James Coleman reports that only about one in ten respondents identified themselves as black, Hispanic, or Asian ("The New Buddhism" 92). Whatever figures he might have obtained with a more explicit survey would not have been conclusive, however, because Coleman did not include the Soka Gakkai Buddhist organization in his survey, a significant omission because Soka Gakkai is not only the largest Buddhist organization in the United States but also the most racially diverse (Chappell 184). The rationale for this omission was that the practices of Soka Gakkai differed from those of other convert Buddhists to such an extent that "a separate study would be required to do them justice" (92). The omission is unfortunate, however, because the picture of "The New Buddhism" that it creates is by definition largely white. On the other hand, David Chappell's analysis of the Soka Gakkai found that blacks represent 32.8 to 34.6 percent of the organization's total membership—a figure almost three times that of the ratio of black people in the nation's total population. In 1996, estimates of the total membership figures for Soka Gakkai ran from a low figure of 100,000 to a high of 330,000. Although membership numbers are a matter of continuing debate, by using these figures one would assume a baseline range of 32,000 to 100,000 practicing black Buddhists in the United States—a figure, it must be emphasized, that does not include black people practicing in Buddhist traditions other than Soka Gakkai, such as Charles Johnson, Jan Willis, hooks, Angel Kyodo Williams, Ralph Steele, and Choyin Rangdrol, to name a few of the nation's most visible black Buddhists.

Coming Out: Recent Developments in Black Dharma

Whatever the precise number of black people practicing Buddhism today may be, their visibility increased dramatically from the 1990s to the early 2000s, when a number of Buddhists of color began to speak out more publicly about their religious affiliation in a variety of Buddhist publications, such as *Shambhala Sun*, *Tricycle: The Buddhist Review*, and *Turning Wheel: The Journal of Socially Engaged Buddhism*. Tina Turner's film *What's Love Got to Do With It* dramatized her own conversion to Buddhism on the large screen at movie theaters across the country in 1993. In a 1994 *Tricycle* issue that included a section on "Dharma, Diversity, and Race," hooks declared that the "time has come for more people of color in the United States to move out of the shadows of silence and speak about the nature of their spiritual practice" ("Waking Up" 44). By 2003, interest in black practitioners had grown to the point that *Turning Wheel* published a special issue entitled "Black Dharma," which included pieces by Alice Walker, Jan Willis, and Charles Johnson, among others. In the pages of Buddhist journals, in recent collections of articles such as *Dharma, Color, and Culture* (2004), edited by Hilda Gutierrez Baldoquin, and in books such as Johnson's *Turning the Wheel*, Willis' *Dreaming Me: An African American Woman's Spiritual Journey* (2001; reissued, *Dreaming Me: Black, Baptist, and Buddhist: One Woman's Spiritual Journey*, 2008), Angel Williams' *"Being Black": Zen and the Art of Living with Fearlessness and Grace* (2000), and Faith Adiele's *Meeting Faith: The Forest Journals of a Black Buddhist Nun* (2004), the work of black Buddhists provides new perspectives upon and contexts for understanding the character of American Buddhism. From the late 1990s on, scholarly studies of American Buddhism also have demonstrated a greater awareness of the need to account for an African-American presence in Western Buddhism, as is reflected in Christopher S. Queen's *Engaged Buddhism in the West* (2000) and Queen, Prebish, and Keown's *Action Dharma: New Studies in Engaged Buddhism* (2003), as well as in articles in scholarly journals such as the *Journal of The International Association of Buddhist Studies* and the *Journal of Buddhist Ethics*. By 2007, Rep. Hank Johnson, from Georgia, became the first black Buddhist to be sworn in to the U.S. Congress.

Recent developments demonstrate that in response to the greater visibility of Buddhists of color, some Buddhist organizations are changing in order to examine more deeply and widely the needs of African-American practitioners.

For example, since 1999, the Spirit Rock Meditation Center near San Francisco has held an annual seven-day retreat for people of color. Additionally, a 2000 African-American Retreat and Conference led to continuing meetings specifically designed for black Buddhists. At the same time, sitting (meditation) groups for people of color have been established in various cities across the United States, while "untraining" sessions that use meditation to help white people unlearn racism have been initiated. Internet resources for black Buddhists have grown rapidly in the past ten years, and now include the Spirit Rock web page (which posts some of the diversity training materials used at the African-American Retreat and interviews with various African Buddhist practitioners); an Internet listserv for black Buddhists (Blackbuddhists-subscribe@yahoogroups.com); the Rainbow Dharma Web site (www.rainbowdharma.com) established by Choyin Randgrol (an African-American lay teacher in the Tibetan Buddhist tradition and author of two booklets, *Buddhist Meditations for African Americans* and *Black Buddha: Living Without Fear*); a Web site for the racially diverse Soka Gakkai organization (www.sgi_usa.org) and one specifically for black practitioners of Nichiren Soshu Buddhism (www.proudBlackbuddhist.org), among others. More recently still, black Buddhist bloggers are debating the dharma on sites such as "Blogging While Black" and "Zen Under the Skin: Reflections of an African-American Practitioner." From cyber-sanghas to structural changes within established Buddhist organizations, to the active outreach of Soka Gakkai to people of color, to the increased public presence of black Buddhists, African-American practitioners are beginning to reshape the outlines of American Buddhism.[6]

Taking into account the experiences of black Buddhists will necessarily alter the understanding of the history and practice of Buddhism, as well as provide an important context for approaching the creative work of practitioners such as Charles Johnson, hooks, Jan Willis, and Buddhist sympathizers such as Walker and Trey Ellis. For example, it often has been pointed out that one of the characteristics of Western converts to Buddhism is that they commonly encounter Buddhism for the first time by reading a book rather than through proselytizing efforts. Many Beat Buddhists, for example, first encountered Buddhism in the library through Suzuki's writings (Coleman, *The New* 62). Indeed, the importance of books to convert Buddhism has been read as a marker of the elite, upper middle-class, white nature of American convert Buddhism. But such assumptions become complicated when the experiences of black Buddhists are taken into account. Soka Gakkai members state that they are most likely to learn of Buddhism through personal contact with another Soka Gakkai member (Chappell 193). More important, perhaps, the meaning attributed to cultural practices such as reading books can take on a new significance when the situated experience of black Americans is considered. For example, consider the experience of black Buddhist Merle Kodo Boyd, who in "A Child of the South in Long Black Robes" discusses the importance of books to her as she was growing up in a segregated Texas in the 1940s and 1950s: "In the South of my childhood, Jim Crow laws defined my world. There were many places we were forbidden to go, but once I could read, I discovered that any place I found in a book was open to me" (102). Like others in American convert Buddhism, Boyd was first introduced to Buddhist practice through books, her "first teacher" (102). But Boyd's experience speaks powerfully to a different understanding of the social significance of literacy than the one commonly attributed to it by Buddhist scholars. Willis writes of her own battles for literacy growing up near Birmingham as a "struggle to be smart, to read, against all the powers that told me not to" ("Already" 32). As these examples make clear, taking account of race complicates the standard interpretation of the significance of literacy as a marker of privilege in Western Buddhism.

Black or Buddhist?

As their participation in American Buddhism becomes more visible, black Buddhists often encounter a unique set of social pressures. In particular, they are frequently put in the position of having to defend either their Buddhism or their "blackness." Many black Buddhists write about the covert disapproval or overt antagonism they receive from both white and black people when others learn about their Buddhist observance. Thus, hooks has felt "singled out" for her interest in Buddhism when white people question her suggestively, "Why are you interested in Zen?" ("Waking Up" 42). In "Moving Toward an End to Suffering," Marlene Jones, an African-American woman who practices in the Theravada Buddhist tradition, describes being asked by white Buddhists, "What would a black person be doing at a meditation center? I thought that you liked Baptist churches and dancing" (43). As black Japanese practitioner Ramon Calhoun suggests, being both black and Buddhist "confounds people's expectations" (39). Calhoun attributes people's reactions to certain cultural preconceptions, such as the belief that Asian Buddhists are "serene, contemplative, deliberate," whereas blacks are "outspoken, expressive, emotional" (39). Such expectations can easily degenerate, as the experiences of many black Buddhists would seem to suggest, into forms of racist and Orientalist essentialism.

Black Buddhists also face criticism from African-American Christians who worry that the practice of Buddhism constitutes an abandonment of black people's traditional religious heritage in America. Concerns range from religious anxieties that individual Buddhists may be putting their immortal souls in danger to the more culturally based criticism that a conversion to Buddhism simply continues the cultural devastation of black Americans wrought by Western slavery and its aftermath. In an article in the 2000 *Cleveland Plain Dealer*, Buddhist La Vora Perry writes of being told by another African-American woman with whom she had been having a friendly chat in the waiting room of a maternity ward, "Your father didn't raise you right, that's your problem" (3E). Ironically, Perry identifies the religious training she received from her father—a Baptist minister—as important preparation for her later conversion to Buddhism. To those who suggest that she is a cultural sell out for not being a protestant Christian, Perry responds: "When I'm labeled a cultural sell-out for not being Christian, I reply that, like many Blacks, I believe that Jesus probably had African ancestry, but most folks also believe he lived in the Middle East, and that area's not known for having much American-style, 'it's-a-Black-thing' flavor" (2). hooks may name the cultural anxiety that lies at the heart of these objections when she suggests that converting to Buddhism, for some black people, is in fact "synonymous with choosing Whiteness" ("Waking Up" 42). Given the majority white membership in most convert Buddhist organizations, some black Buddhists argue that fears of cultricide are legitimate, and they point to the difficulties that blacks have experienced in incorporating black cultural practices into various Buddhist communities as evidence that American Buddhism must adapt to the needs of black Americans. It is clear to many black people that the primarily white membership of Buddhist centers actively discourages their attendance: As Rangdrol describes, "It feels as though there is no such thing as practicing Buddhism without assimilating to Asian culture. . . . To African Americans this can appear to be a destructive cultural process that goes against the grain of their historicity, their heritage, and their legacy in America as survivors of cultricide" (Rangdrol 23).

The response of black Buddhists to racial, cultural, and religious criticism of their practice is of necessity emotionally and intellectually complex. Against the accusation that they are not being "black enough" in choosing Buddhism, some black Buddhists point out that Christianity served the oppressor's interests until black people adapted it for their own spiritual, social, and political needs. Their point resonates with the analysis offered by Lawrence Levine in his classic study of slave culture, *Black Culture and Black Consciouness* (1977), in which he argues that enslaved people were not "passive receptors" of Christianity, but rather that they "selectively" chose those parts of the religion that spoke to their oppressed situation, and by doing so, turned the oppressor's religion into an "instrument of life, of sanity, of health, and of self-respect, the means of preventing legal slavery from being spiritual slavery" (70). In a 2005 article, "Buddhism and the Body Problem," African-American Buddhist scholar and sympathizer Lori Pierce points out that despite the popularity of Protestantism among African Americans, some "members of the black community have made other religious choices" during their history in America (such as the choice to become a black Muslim). These choices, she asserts, also reveal a "deliberate attempts to create a new, empowering ethnic and religious identity that validated and expanded the African American experience" (21, 22). The writings of black

Buddhists demonstrate that they understand their participation in convert Buddhism as part of a similar process of transformation and adaptation—one that may require, as Alice Walker suggests, that they give themselves "permission to posit a different way from that in which [they were] raised" ("This was not" 17). Or, as Carol Cooper succinctly suggests in an interview with hooks, black Americans "tend to transform the things we embrace" (1).

Although some black Buddhists simply claim as a basic human right the freedom to choose the religious affiliation that they find best satisfies their spiritual needs, others argue that one need not give up Christianity to become a practicing Buddhist. Jan Willis, for example, has called herself a "Baptist Buddhist" ("Dharma" 221). Because Buddhism sometimes has been classified as more of a philosophy or a mental and spiritual discipline than as a religion in the usual Western sense of the word—at the World's Parliament of Religions Anagarika Dharmapala called it a "Philosophical Religion" rather than a "theology" (Barrows 2:863)—it is probably not surprising that many practitioners do not see a conflict between their Buddhist practice and the religious beliefs they maintain from other traditions. As hooks explains in a 1995 feature in *Shambhala Sun*, "in the morning I sit zazen [Zen meditation], but then I always take time to say my Christian prayers at the same time. It's like those two traditions have walked with me through my life and I haven't been able to just choose one as the right one for me. I still feel like the sweetness of both of them enhances my life" ("bell hooks" 8). Like many other black Buddhists, hooks frequently cites the writings of Vietnamese Buddhist monk Thich Nhat Hanh (who was nominated by Dr. Martin Luther King Jr. for the 1967 Nobel Peace Prize) as further support for blending Christian and Buddhist traditions. In *Living Buddha, Living Christ* (1997), Hanh emphasizes the similarities between Buddhism and Christianity; and in *Going Home: Jesus and Buddha as Brothers* (2000), he suggests that Buddhists who have felt anxious about leaving their Christianity behind can reclaim that religion while still participating in Buddhist practice, despite the differences that admittedly remain between the two traditions. Other black practitioners argue further that Buddhist practice can enhance their Christianity: As Willis explains, "I can use *Buddhist* methods to practice *Baptist* ideals" ("Dharma" 221).

In addition to encountering accusations that they are not being black enough, African-American practitioners also find themselves charged by white Buddhists, ironically if not surprisingly, with being *too* ethnocentric. As one might suspect, this is especially the case for those who work to change the cultural climate of Buddhist organizations. Additionally, because Buddhists are trained to recognize the ways in which reified categories—what Charles Johnson calls "calcified, prefabricated thinking" in "Reading the Eightfold Path"—may limit understanding, one's national, ethnic, and racial practices can sometimes be interpreted from a Buddhist perspective as limiting forms, something to overcome rather than to celebrate (138). In "Black Buddha: Bringing the Tradition Home," however, Rangdrol argues that culture can be used for enlightenment and that blacks should insist on the legitimacy of both their cultural practice and their Buddhism: "African Americans can use their own culture, too. No one questions Tibetan, Japanese, or Chinese culture in Buddhism, but the moment African Americans say, 'this is my culture, and I am Buddhist,' people say we are being ethnocentric" (24). Rangdrol's position would seem in keeping with the Buddhist teaching of dependent co-origination, which argues that because everything arises from a complex set of causes in a particular situation, its appearance is necessarily contingent. In short, as Lewis Wood, the guest editor of the "Black Dharma" issues of *Turning Wheel* suggests, "*all* Buddhism is culturally hyphenated Buddhism" (2).

But if black Buddhists encounter negative reactions to their practice that range from the mildly inquisitive to the forcefully disrespectful, they also find that Buddhism resonates deeply with their situated experience as black Americans. In particular, practitioners of African descent write eloquently about their powerful responses to Buddhism's emphasis on suffering and liberation, about the efficacy of their Buddhist belief in providing concrete practices for realizing spiritual goals (especially for combating the debilitating psychological effects of racism), and about their attraction to Buddhism's radically egalitarian values, particularly as those values are realized in what has been termed *Engaged Buddhism*.[7]

Several black Buddhist practitioners assert that the history of black oppression in America led them to respond powerfully to the First Noble Truth expounded by Buddha, "There is suffering." As Johnson writes, "the black experience in America, like the teachings of Shakyamuni Buddha, begins with suffering" ("A Sangha" 46). Willis suggests further that black people's history of oppression may enable them to grasp the discussions of suffering in Buddhist thought more quickly than those from other backgrounds: "people of color, because of our experience of the great and wrenching historical dramas of slavery, colonization, and segregation, understand suffering in a way that our white brothers and sisters do not, and, moreover . . . this understanding is closer to what is meant by the Buddhist injunction [to understand suffering]" ("Dharma" 220). The historical oppression of black people both serves as a compelling motivation for some African Americans' initial attraction to Buddhism and provides them, as Willis asserts, with a sort of "head start" in comprehending Buddhist philosophy (217).

It is not only the historical experience of oppression that enables black practitioners to respond to the Buddhist emphasis on suffering, but, as several black Buddhists insist, the depth of black people's present psychological, spiritual, and social suffering. Black Americans, as Walker observes, are "being consumed" by suffering ("This Was Not" 15). In a 2001 interview, hooks ties her decision to become more open about her Buddhist practice specifically to a concern for such distress: "That's why I've been coming out of the closet myself about spirituality period. Because I don't think we can afford to stay in the closet, our circumstance is too dire. . . . I came out of the whole, 'my spiritual practice is private bag' because I just thought, hey, our people are suffering" (Cooper 3). Furthermore, hooks emphasizes, the extent of black people's suffering goes largely unrecognized in American society. As she indicates in *Rock My Soul* (2003), "Throughout our history in this nation, Black people as a whole have wanted to minimize the reality of trauma in Black life. It has been easier for everyone to focus on issues of material deprivation . . . than to place the issue of trauma and recovery on our agendas" (*Rock* 23). For some black people, the Buddhist emphasis on the truth of human suffering seems to validate both the historical and the contemporary experience of black Americans, providing Buddhism with the power, as Rangdrol explains, "to reverberate down to the core of the hurt so many of us carry" (23).

It is important to note that although black Buddhists may understand their suffering as a manifestation of the universal validity of the First Noble Truth, they nonetheless insist on the distinctive historical and cultural character of that suffering. As Ralph Steele explains in an interview with William Poy Lee, "Being a Black person in a particular land or culture leads to a particular kind of suffering" (2). Steele, born on Pawley's Island in a Gullah Gee Chee community, experienced racism both in the United States and in Japan, where he moved with his military family as a youth. While serving as a tail gunner in the Vietnam War, Steele reports, he developed a heroin addiction, and afterward, post-traumatic stress syndrome. He credits Buddhist practice with enabling him to overcome the traumas of racism and his war service. Subsequently, he spent a year abroad in retreat and was ordained as a monk in the Theravadan Buddhist tradition ("Teaching" 77). Other black practitioners also testify to the power of Buddhism in enabling them to overcome the traumatic effects of racism, from the more subtle forms of "mental colonization" that are one consequence of growing up in a racist society to the debilitating effects of psychic trauma caused by terroristic acts. Growing up near Birmingham, Alabama, Willis participated in the Birmingham Campaign led by Dr. King in 1963. Afterward, the Klu Klux Klan burned a cross in her family's yard in response to a newspaper account that she had won a scholarship to Cornell. Buddhism, she contends, enables her to transform her rage so that it is not self-destructive ("You're Already" 32). Black Buddhist Sala Steinbach writes of the time when she was growing up close to the naval station at which her father had been stationed near Lake Forest, Illinois, a well-to-do suburb north of Chicago. When the woods near her house caught fire and her white neighbors gathered to watch, she realized that they were cheering the blaze on in hopes that it would reach her home ("Stories" 89). Sala credits meditation with enabling her to overcome the traumatic impact of this event. For many black practitioners Buddhism seems to provide, as Johnson asserts, "the richest of refuges from a predominantly white, very Eurocentric and culturally provincial society . . . completely blind to the dignity and deeds, well-being and needs, of people of color" ("Reading" 127). Or, as Johnson summarizes—Buddhism serves as "an exquisite manual for survival" ("Reading" 128).

Westerners often tend to understand meditation and chanting as contemplative activities with few practical consequences. While insisting on the cultural specificity of their suffering, however, black Buddhists such as Steele, Willis, Steinbach, and Johnson emphasize that Buddhism provides them with a *practical* means for transforming suffering. As Merle Kodo Boyd writes, Zen practice offered her a "new way of defining suffering and a new way to end it" (102). In particular, black adherents write of the personal empowerment and increased sense of agency they discovered through Buddhist practice: Not surprisingly, they frequently refer to Buddhism as something they "do" rather than something they "believe." It is not uncommon for practitioners to compare the rigors of Buddhist training (especially as it is taught in the meditative traditions) to physical training in the martial arts. Indeed, many American Buddhists, black and white, first become interested in Eastern thought through the martial arts.[8] Steele, Angel Williams, and Johnson all practiced the martial arts before becoming Buddhists. Johnson also codirected the Twin Tigers kung-fu studio where Martin Hughes, future Abbot of the Daigoji Temple in Osaka, trained when he was living in Seattle.[9] Many black Buddhists argue that just as physical exercise is a practical way to transform the body, so mental and spiritual exercise offers an effective way to reshape one's attitudes, thinking, and habits. Willis elaborates on the practical character of meditative practice when she explains just how she uses "Buddhist methods to practice Baptist ideals." When she found herself having difficulty practicing the Christian injunction to "love your enemy," Willis practiced a series of meditations specifically designed to develop loving kindness by progressively leading from the cultivation of compassion for oneself, to the practice of compassion for loved ones and friends, to—finally—the practice of compassion toward those from whom one has experienced hostility ("Dharma" 221). Moreover, a belief in the practical benefits of meditative practice also has led some black Buddhists, like Willis and Rangdrol, to create new meditations specifically aimed at changing racist attitudes.

Significantly, in addition to attesting to Buddhism as a practical tool for personal transformation, a large number of black Buddhist practitioners advocate what Hanh labeled *Engaged Buddhism*, or the practice of Buddhism as a tool for social reform.[10] In his study of Engaged Buddhism, "Responding to the Cries of the World," Donald Rothberg points out that the phenomenon includes "a broad range of approaches, unified by the notion that Buddhist teachings and practices can be directly applied to participation in the social, political, economic, and ecological affairs of the nonmonastic world" (268).

By leaving the monastery to work among the war-stricken populace during the Vietnam War, Hanh provided an exemplary illustration of such practice: As he explains in support of engagement, "Once there is seeing, there must be acting" ("Peace" 91). Engaged Buddhists undertake various kinds of social reform, ranging from grassroots activism (such as working in local shelters and providing AIDS volunteerism), to participating in antipoverty, peace, and civil rights movements worldwide. Willis is active in prison outreach programs in the United States, a growing Buddhist service. Indeed, outreach to the imprisoned has grown to such an extent that African-American Shu Shin priest Joseph Jarmen has suggested that the "vast majority" of black Buddhist practitioners in the United States today may in fact be prison inmates (Pintak 4). At the same time, Buddhist organizations like Soka Gakkai, an official nongovernmental organization of the United Nations, are active in various international civil rights, relief, and peace movements (Hurst 94). On the other hand, Lawrence Ellis practices Engaged Buddhism through his regular employment, which he understands as an application of the Buddhist concept of "right livelihood." A graduate of the University of North Carolina and former Rhodes Scholar, Ellis serves as an organizational consultant for Amnesty International, various health organizations, and other large corporations, where he applies "values-based strategies" to make large organizations more "just" (Lee "Interview" 2). According to Ellis, Buddhism offers "concrete tools" that can be used to transform "institutions that perpetuate systematic suffering, domination, and violence" (Lee 3).

Engaging Buddhism and Engaged Buddhism

A focus on systematic as well as personal transformation is, according to white Buddhist scholar Christopher S. Queen, a defining characteristic of twentieth-century socially Engaged Buddhism.[11] In his contributions to four edited collections, *Engaged Buddhism: Buddhist Liberation Movements in Asia* (Queen and King 1996), *American Buddhism* (Williams and Queen 1999), *Engaged Buddhism in the West* (2003), and *Action Dharma* (Queen et al. 2003), Queen develops an argument that socially Engaged Buddhism emerged in the late nineteenth-century as developing forces of globalization brought together diverse religious and reform movements in novel forms of "cultural interpenetration" (*Engaged Buddhism: Buddhist* 20). Attributing a "multicultural parentage" to Engaged Buddhist practice that links the Asian religious traditions to Western religious, political, and human rights traditions, Queen interprets the emergence of engaged practice as a significant new direction in the history of Buddhism (*Action* 1). For example, Queen identifies the India movement of Dr. B. R. Ambedkar (1891–1956) as one twentieth-century model of an activist Buddhism growing out of an international exchange of ideas about social progress and human liberation.[12] An "untouchable" who studied at three different Western universities in three different nations—at Columbia (with John Dewey), at the London School of Economics, and at the University of Bonn in Germany— Ambedkar later served on Nehru's cabinet and drafted the Indian constitution. His national movement on behalf of civil rights for untouchables, or Dalits, included a rejection of Hinduism—which he believed to be inseparably implicated in the maintenance of the caste system—and led to a mass conversion of more than 500,000 Dalits to Buddhism on October 14, 1956. Although Ambedkar died only seven weeks after this ceremony, Dalits continued to convert to Buddhism by the hundreds of thousands and their conversion to Buddhism is the largest in the twentieth-century. (Another mass conversion was accomplished in 2006 for the anniversary of the 1956 event). The unique blend of anticolonialism, nationalism, civil rights reform, and Buddhism embodied in Ambedkar's movement illustrates well the characteristics of Engaged Buddhism that Queen identifies: It emerges out of a global conversation on human rights, reveals a new emphasis on the systematic dimensions of suffering and liberation, and demonstrates a willingness to use secular means in pursuit of its goals—means such as "education, mass communication, political influence and activism, jurisprudence and litigation . . . even fundraising and marketing" (*Engaged Buddhism: Buddhist* 11).

Although their published writings on their Buddhist practice suggest that a majority of African-American practitioners are drawn to some form of Engaged Buddhist practice, since the 1980s scholars of Western Buddhism have demonstrated a growing interest in evaluating the "legitimacy" of Engaged Buddhist practice in relation to traditional Buddhism. One area of concern is the degree to which a socially activist practice may conflict with fundamental Buddhist teachings on liberation, suffering, and the nature of the self. Obviously, such a conflict would be of concern to all Engaged Buddhists, but especially so to those who are members of oppressed minorities. Bardwell L. Smith identifies one potential conflict in his discussion of whether certain twentieth-century "reinterpretations" of Buddhist teachings on liberation run the risk for confusing "what is primary" in Buddhism with what is not:

> The primary goal of Buddhism is not a stable order or a just society but *the discovery of genuine freedom (or awakening) by each person.* It has never been asserted that the conditions of society are unimportant or unrelated *to this more important goal,* but *it is critical to stress the distinction between what is primary and what is not.* For Buddhists to lose this distinction is to transform their tradition into something discontinuous with its original and historic essence. (106; qtd. by Deitrick 261; italics added)

Smith identifies an important possible disagreement between contemporary practices of "engagement" and traditional understandings of the character of "enlightenment" in a Buddhist economy of liberation (or soteriology). In an article titled "Engaged Buddhist Ethics," James Deitrick warns that Engaged Buddhism can misinterpret key Buddhist teachings on suffering by confusing social and material suffering with a "more profound" spiritual suffering (265). Elsewhere, Derek S. Jeffreys also seems to undermine the grounds for an Engaged Buddhist practice by arguing that the adoption of human rights discourse by Engaged Buddhists is "philosophically problematic." Such rights are historically and logically grounded, Jeffreys argues, in a Western conception of the individual as a "stable agent who possesses certain rights"—a conception obviously in conflict with the Buddhist teaching of "no self" or the view that a belief in the existence of an unchanging, substantive self is merely an illusion (271). By raising questions about the degree to which Engaged Buddhists may be altering central Buddhist teachings about suffering and liberation and by pointing to possible philosophical inconsistencies in Engaged Buddhists' espousal of human rights, these scholars question the degree to which socially active Buddhists' practice of "engagement" coheres with traditional Buddhist teachings on "enlightenment."

Such historical, religious, and conceptual challenges to an Engaged Buddhist practice recall Max Weber's well-known critique of Buddhism (in *The Religion of India: The Sociology of Hinduism and Buddhism*, 1958) as an "anti-political status religion" (206). Rather like Jeffries, Weber argues that a social ethic based on the "value of the individual human soul" must appear under Buddhism only as a "grand and pernicious illusion" (213). Weber defines Buddhism primarily as a path for other-worldly salvation—"the most radical form of salvation-striving conceivable" (206). Weber also critiques the Buddhist understanding of compassion, which he believes reduces concern for others to a mere marker of one's own "progressive intellectual development," something to be abandoned when one achieves enlightenment for "the cool equanimity of the knowing mind" (213). To such a critique of the political potential of Buddhism, Jacqueline I. Stone's 2003 essay "Nichiren's Activist Heirs" adds the point that the Buddhist emphasis on the individual's power to overcome suffering may have a "flip side": An emphasis on individual agency may minimize the role that social forces play in creating oppression, thereby ruling out a serious consideration of "exploitation or discrimination" (76). Extending Weber's criticism of the practice of compassion in Buddhism as a mere marker for inner cultivation, Stone raises the important question of just how far a focus on inner cultivation can be taken "before it becomes an endorsement of the present system" (76).

To articulate a response to such criticisms and to explain their own practice, Engaged Buddhists draw on several textual, historical, and philosophical justifications for their practice. The description of Buddhism as a passive religion concerned only—or even primarily—with inner cultivation is countered as a mischaracterization of traditional Eastern Buddhism (one that is fueled, perhaps, by an unconscious Orientalism).[13] More precisely, to rebut the assertion that historical Buddhism advocates ascetic quietism, scholars cite textual and historical antecedents for twentieth- and twenty-first century engaged practice. Additionally, Engaged Buddhists offer careful interpretations of Buddhist teachings on "suffering," "no-self," and "dependent co-origination" in order to demonstrate that the tradition either provides room for, encourages, or in fact *requires* engaged practice.

For example, the claim that the Buddhist conception of "no self" undermines the grounds for supporting human rights is countered by arguments that suggest that the concept of no self has been mistakenly interpreted in the West in nihilistic terms, when it should be interpreted to mean something closer to the claim that there is no "permanent, essential self." Such an understanding of the self does not require that one give up an appreciation of personal dignity, defenders of Engaged Buddhism argue, but rather that one give up a Western understanding of the source from which that dignity arises. Understanding the self as necessarily impermanent, for example, can imply a respect for others that is grounded in their very capacity to change: a person cannot logically be dismissed as *being* a liar or a thief if one does not believe in a permanent self, because there always is an expectation that the person can change.[14] Similarly, Hanh finds the grounds for compassion and a respect for others in "emptiness," which he translates not in terms of nothingness but through the neologism "interbeing." Rather than an essentialized state of nothingness, he understands "emptiness" to mean *empty of* individual essences. Johnson explicitly discusses Hanh's claim that "there is no such thing as an individual" ("Reading" 132), explaining that it does not entail nihilism but rather an understanding of reality as a "*We*-relation" (132). Understanding reality as a we-relation obviously does not pose the same philosophical problems for justifying compassion for others as does an understanding of human reality as composed of atomistic individuals (although it may well raise other philosophical problems of its own, such as those involving individuation).

To justify their activist practice, socially Engaged Buddhists also point to specific textual and historical antecedents, beginning with the Buddha himself. Viveka Chen, a member of The Friends of the Western Buddhist Order (whose Web site announces the intent "to create *new* Buddhist *traditions* relevant to the 21st century)," calls Buddha "a freedom fighter who launched a spiritual movement empowering people to end mental, physical, and spiritual enslavement" (111, italics added). Although the designation "freedom fighter" is a somewhat contemporary vernacular, the Buddha did admit people of different castes, classes, nationalities, and genders into his religious community, an action considered by many scholars to be a radical one for the period.[15] Another historical precedent for engaged practice that is mentioned frequently is King Asoka of India (c273-c232 BCE), an emperor who converted to Buddhism, turned from warfare to public works, and established free public hospitals and public assistance programs, as well as instituting a number of other progressive social reforms. Support for an Engaged Buddhist practice also is offered by the scholarly analysis of mainstream Buddhist texts. Stephen Jenkins finds in traditional Indian Buddhist sources (*contra* Deitrick) a "clear concern for material forms of suffering" (44). According to Jenkins, these sources suggest that material suffering in fact has a priority over spiritual forms of suffering, because "in order to create the conditions necessary for benefiting people spiritually, one must first attend to their material needs" (46). Interestingly, Jenkins' textual research seems to provide support for Queen's claim that "a just society . . . is a *necessary* and *prior* condition for the discovery of genuine freedom (or awakening) for each person," although it simultaneously undercuts his claim that twentieth-century Buddhism comprises a radical new direction in the history of Buddhism (*Action* 20).

Many Engaged Buddhists find particularly important conceptual and historical antecedents for their practice in Mahayana Buddhism, which is believed to have emerged in the first century CE in reaction to Theravada Buddhism's emphasis on the necessity of monastic practice for achieving enlightenment. In Sanskrit, *yana* means "cart" or method of conveyance: different *yanas* thus signify different methods of conveying—practicing or disseminating—Buddhism. The Theravada method is primarily that of the ascetic, who separates from the world in order to achieve enlightenment through rigorous monastic training. The Mahayana method, by contrast, emphasizes the path of lay people who seek enlightenment while engaged *in* the world. Because it understood itself to be opening the path of enlightenment to all, Mahayana Buddhism disparaged Theravada Buddhism as "Hinayana," the "smaller" vehicle, while naming itself the "greater" ("Maha"). In addition to articulating a Buddhist economy of enlightenment in a way that emphasizes immersion in the world, Mahayana Buddhism stresses the ideal of the *bodhisattva*, a figure frequently evoked as providing a precedent for Engaged Buddhism. As Johnson discusses in "Reading the Eightfold Path," the bodhisattva is a person of great spiritual achievement who "due to his compassion, renounc[es] full immersion in nirvana in order to work indefatigably for the salvation of all sentient beings" (136).

Civil Rights Movement and Contemporary Buddhism

In addition to offering conceptual arguments and historical or textual precedents for Engaged Buddhist practice, Western Buddhists—especially but not exclusively

Buddhists of color—discuss their practice through comparisons to the U.S. Civil Rights Movement. Although such a validation may seem both historically and culturally confused, by reading Buddhism through the history of civil rights (and by reading the history of civil rights through their Buddhism), Buddhists of color enact a type of existential heuristic characteristic of the dissemination of religious thought. In describing the religious world of enslaved black people, Levine emphasizes that slaves appropriated Christianity selectively by focusing on those passages of Biblical texts that had special resonance with their own condition, such as the exodus of the Israelites out of Egypt or Daniel's escape from the lion's den. In effect, slaves brought an existential hermeneutics to sacred text, one that functioned to foreground certain meanings available in holy writ while de-emphasizing others. Black Buddhists writing in the post-civil rights decades also adopt an interpretive heuristic in their appeal to the history of the civil rights movement to illuminate their practice. By so doing, they translate ancient Buddhist teachings into a contemporary American and African-American cultural language, while selectively emphasizing certain meanings available in both the history of the Civil Rights Movement and in Buddhism. By reading Buddhism from a post-civil rights location, black Buddhists participate in the kind of global conversations that Queen finds characteristic of twentieth-century Engaged Buddhist practice as they create an innovative, hybrid form of Western Buddhism.

In particular, Western Buddhists find intellectual and historical support for their Engaged Buddhist practice in the civil rights philosophy and practices of Dr. King, whose association with Eastern religious and moral philosophy provides a limited historical warrant for such an identification. Certainly, King's relationship to Eastern thought deepened over his lifetime through an increasingly sophisticated engagement with Gandhi's writings; through his work with a number of self-avowed "Gandhians" who had adopted the Indian reformer's methods for social transformation (notably former Communist Party member Bayard Rustin and Rev. Glenn Smiley); through his contact with Gandhians from India who were sent to the United States to support civil rights workers; through his trip to India in 1959 (as a guest of the Gandhian Peace Foundation); and through his increasing familiarity with the ideas of Hanh, one of the factors that contributed to King's taking a public stance against the Vietnam War. King formally announced his opposition to the war while sitting next to Hanh at a press conference in 1967. Although historical associations such as these tie King more to Eastern thought in general (and to Hinduism) than they do to Buddhism, King's willingness to combine insights from the African-American social gospel tradition with those of Eastern religious and moral thought, and his forging out of that combination the nonviolent protest method of "direct action," provide Engaged Buddhists with a powerful example of a social reform movement regulated by a religious or moral ideal. As King described his civil rights practice, "Nonviolent resistance . . . emerged as the technique of the movement, while love stood as the regulating ideal" (qtd by hooks, "Surrendered" 52).

In April 2003, the San Francisco Zen Center offered a retreat on "The Dharma of Martin Luther King." Just how such a *dharma* (a Buddhist teaching or way) might be understood by black Buddhists is suggested in the Winter 2005 issue of *Shambhala Sun*, which features a close-up of King on its cover and includes a special section inside on "The King We Need Now More Than Ever." Both hooks and Johnson contributed articles to the issue (which also includes an interview with Maxine Hong Kingston about how her Buddhism affects her life and her work).[16] In their essays, hooks and Johnson foreground King's commitment to nonviolence, both as the basis for social action and as "a Way, a daily praxis people must strive to translate into each and every one of their deeds" ("The King" 48). The analysis by hooks centers on two important conversions that she believes King's practice demanded: a personal conversion to nonviolence and a collective conversion of values ("Surrendered" 52). Johnson also emphasizes King's moral commitment to nonviolence, which the civil rights leader illustrated in dramatic fashion on the night of January 30, 1955, when King responded to the bombing of his house in Montgomery by calming an angry crowd of black people, some of them armed, who had gathered to defend (and possibly to avenge) him and his family ("The King We Need" 48). To document the commitment to nonviolence that guided civil rights workers in Montgomery, Johnson reprints in full the "commitment blank" signed by members of the Southern Christian Leadership Conference, which begins, "I hereby pledge myself—my person and my body—to the nonviolent movement" (48). Elsewhere, in "Reading the Eight-Fold Path," Johnson specifically ties that document to Buddhist ethical principles by inviting readers to compare the "ten commandments" in the commitment blank to the "Eightfold Path," the primary dharma of the Buddha's teachings. Both hooks and Johnson find in King's example the implication that a radical revolution in values is needed to regulate social reform efforts if those efforts are to be both effective and just. In his most recent novel, *Dreamer (1998)*, Johnson, as Whalen-Bridge emphasizes, "boldly reinterpret[s] King's life in recognizably Buddhist terms" (518).[17] By representing Buddhism in dialogue with King, black Buddhists draw on King's moral authority to buttress their own practice of nonviolence, while they simultaneously cite the early successes of the Civil Rights Movement as a historical warrant for the efficacy of nonviolent reform movements.

In addition to linking King to the Buddhist ethic of nonviolence and the dharma of the "Eightfold Path," black Buddhists also evoke the Civil Rights Movement (perhaps more surprisingly) to explain specific Buddhist teachings on matters such as the character of the *sangha* (religious community), suffering, no self, and interbeing. Boyd, for example, draws on Rosa Parks and the 1955–1956 Montgomery bus boycott to explain the Buddhist distinction between "pain" and "suffering." Although Buddhism teaches that all sentient beings are subject to pain, suffering itself is understood as a particular relation to that pain, a distinction Boyd illustrates in her description of the hardships faced by the boycotters who gave up their transportation to work during the yearlong bus boycott. She writes, "People in Montgomery, walking miles back and forth to work, were probably in pain, but they were not necessarily suffering" ("Child" 105). Willis makes a similar point when she describes her experience marching in the 1963 Children's Campaign in Birmingham as a fifteen-year-old. Although she marveled to learn that "water could *burn* so," she nonetheless also discovered that "because we knew we were morally and spiritually right, we were physically energized" (*Dreaming* 60).

For many black Buddhists the civil rights movement in general—and the example of King in particular—seem to function as an intellectual catalyst for their personal decisions to convert to Buddhism. In describing the "typical" conversion pattern for white Western Buddhist converts, Jan Nattier points out that they often first read about Buddhism in a book—or learned about it through classes or from other literary sources—and then traveled to "exotic" locales to study it firsthand. This conversion pattern, as Nattier points out, requires "money and leisure time" (43). The experience of black Buddhists frequently overlaps with this model. Boyd and Willis first learned of Buddhism through books (although, as I have noted, the cultural meanings of their literacy may differ from that of white converts), and hooks did so through her relationship to literary figures like Gary Snyder. Yet important distinctions remain in the conversion patterns of black Americans and those of whites—and one of these differences lies in their cultural, emotional, and intellectual connections to the Civil Rights Movement. Indeed, the Civil Rights Movement and the Black Power movement occupy a central place in the "conversion narratives" told by many Buddhists of color. In particular, many black Buddhists discuss their conversion to Buddhism in terms of a reaction against developments in the Black Power movement that led them to turn toward Buddhism in an attempt to recapture the spiritual and moral idealism of the Civil Rights Movement.

Some black Buddhists were themselves active in the Civil Rights Movement, as in the case of early participation by Willis in the children's marches in Birmingham. In "In Search of Our Mother's Gardens," self-described fellow traveler Alice Walker describes working for voter registration with the Atlanta movement while she was a student at Spelman from 1961 to 1962 and again when she moved to Mississippi in the late 1960s and early 1970s, after being inspired by King's call during the 1963 March on Washington for people to go "Back to Mississippi" to work for civil rights (*In Search* 162). Named by *Time* magazine in 2000 as one of six "spiritual innovators of the millennium" and currently Walter A. Crowell Professor at Wesleyan University, Willis went from marching in King's Birmingham campaign in 1963 to participating in an armed student takeover of the student union at Cornell in 1969 to becoming the first African-American scholar-practitioner of Tibetan Buddhism in the United States.

Willis' journey from the periphery of the Black Power movement to the center of mainstream Western Buddhism provides a dramatic example of the type of political, intellectual, and spiritual motivations that led black converts to Buddhism in the post-civil rights era. Willis arrived at Cornell in 1965, the only woman out of eight African Americans on campus. (At the same time there were approximately 250 Africans studying at Cornell.) She was immediately drawn to a major in philosophy and took a course in Wittgenstein (eventually studying at Cornell with Norman Malcolm, a student of Wittgenstein's) and to Buddhism through her reading of D. T. Suzuki (*Dreaming* 81). In her junior year, Willis was one of twenty-five students selected nationally by the Wisconsin Program to travel to India, where she attended Banaras Hindu University in 1967 and 1968, during the Muslim/Hindi riots and anti-English campaigns (*Dreaming* 94). Returning to Cornell for her senior year, Willis discovered that the African-American population had grown to 260 students, many of whom had been recruited aggressively from New York City where they had become familiar with black nationalist thought. During the year she had been in India, racial tensions on campus had escalated considerably, especially over the administration's failure to move quickly enough to establish a black studies program on campus.

On April 19, 1969, roughly eighty Black students took over Cornell's student union, Willard Straight Hall, to protest the burning of a cross two days earlier (outside a residence in which eight Black women lived).[18] What distinguished the Straight Hall protest from others taking place across the nation was that students at Straight were heavily armed. Although the takeover ended peacefully after thirty-six hours—with the administration and faculty capitulating to most of the students' demands—the event received national attention when photographs were circulated across the country of students emerging from the building with bandoliers of ammunition across their chests and rifles held aloft. One photo shows armed students emerging from Straight Hall directly under a "Welcome Parents" banner. Another won the 1970 Pulitzer Prize. Although originally students had not taken guns into Straight Hall, weapons were smuggled into the building partly as a response to an incursion into Straight by a group of White fraternity members (Downs 1). An active member of the African American Society that had planned the takeover, Willis was one of the students who smuggled guns into the building, a role for which she was afterward named "Minster of Women's Defense."

After the Straight Hall takeover, Willis was urged by a Black Panther representative to California to meet with a key contact with the Oakland Panthers (then led by Huey Newton and Bobby Seale). That same summer,

Cornell offered Willis a scholarship to return to Nepal to study at the Buddhist monastery she had visited on her trip to India. The choice facing Willis—to study Buddhism or to join the Black Panthers—could not have been more stark. Willis decided to visit Oakland to talk to the Panthers, and on her cross-country trip, she stopped to hear Fred Hampton of the Chicago Panthers speak at the University of Wisconsin. When she met Hampton afterward, he praised the action at Cornell and complimented Willis on knowing how "to use a piece" ("Already" 32). Events seemed to be leading Willis toward joining the Panthers. But when she arrived in California, a woman close to the organization with whom she was staying confided to Willis disturbing information about factionalism within the Party and about her Panther contact's alleged abuse of female members (*Dreaming* 127). Increasingly, Willis came to question both the Panthers' tactics and those that had been deployed at Cornell. Significantly, she later tied her decision to choose Nepal over the Panthers explicitly to her earlier participation in Birmingham:

> I had learned to shoot a piece. I had even helped deliver guns to the Straight when I had to. But I had also marched, nonviolently amid violence, in Birmingham with King. . . . I didn't know where the path of Buddhism would ultimately take me, but it seemed to offer at least the possibility of peaceful transformation. I told myself that it offered the best opportunity for clarity—about personal as well as political strategies. (*Dreaming* 129)

Although the terms of Willis' choice—join the Black Panthers or accept a scholarship to study Buddhism in Nepal—were more dramatic than most, her experience captures the emotional, political, and spiritual turmoil of a time period when the daughter of a black steelworker from a small town near Birmingham could march with King, attend Cornell, travel to India, and take part in an armed student protest—all before graduating from college. Significantly, Willis' earlier participation in King's nonviolent protest played a central role in leading her to react against the violence in which she felt herself and her country becoming increasingly enmeshed—violence that would claim the life of Fred Hampton on December 4, 1969, before Willis could return to Nepal.[19]

The decision by Willis to choose studying Buddhism over joining the Black Panther Party provides a vivid illustration of the intellectual, emotional, and spiritual path chosen by several black Buddhists of her generation, who turned away from an initial attraction to the ideology and methods of Black Power toward a Buddhist practice that seemed to them to offer the possibility of recapturing the nonviolent ethos of the Civil Rights Movement as enunciated by King. Willis, hooks, Johnson, and Walker belong to a generation of black Americans who matured as King's nonviolent approach to reform became increasingly disparaged

within the black community as "Uncle Tomism." In describing the climate at
Cornell that led up to the Straight Hall takeover, for example, historian Robert
Downs reports a conversation with one former protestor who told him, "There
was no one at Cornell who took Martin Luther King seriously philosophically.
Everybody just wrote him off as—'ah, who cares' " (*Cornell* 4). Similarly, hooks
describes herself as "mesmerized" by the militant stance of black power activists
in her youth: "If we had to choose between Malcolm and Martin, my vote
was definitely going to be for Malcolm" ("Surrendered" 53). When she became
politically active in college, however, hooks found herself turning to King's writings for "inspiration and wise counsel" (53). Her effort to unlearn the lessons
of militarism, she suggests, were not completely achieved until she returned to
King's ideals twenty years later, when she found in his message "a vision not
unlike that taught during the Vietnam War by beloved Monk Thich Nhat Hanh"
(53). Like hooks, Johnson testifies to being drawn to a Black Power stance as
a college student. In "The King We Left Behind" (1996), he describes himself
as viewing "non-violence as unmanly" and listening with "greater interest to the
speeches of Malcolm X" (197). When his son was born in 1975, Johnson named
the boy Malik, partly in honor of Malcolm X (who had changed his name to
El Hajj Malik El-Shabazz). Tying his own experience to that of a generation
of Americans who "left King behind," Johnson concludes his essay with a call
for a conversion to the lost values that King represents. Significantly, today the
Buddhist writings of Willis, hooks, and Johnson frequently appear together in
issues of Buddhist publications.

    If such accounts demonstrate how difficult it can be to determine whether
it is King's vigorous moral vision that provides a pathway for some black
people to Buddhism or whether it is Buddhism that provides a pathway for
their rediscovery of King, such comments nevertheless speak to the compelling
moral resonance that some African Americans detect between the two traditions. That this identification is detected not only by the limited number of
black Buddhists that I discuss here is confirmed by studies of the Soka Gakkai
that attempt to account for the large percentage of black people who join that
particular Buddhist organization. According to David Chappell, one of the main
factors attracting blacks to the Soka Gakkai is the organization's commitment to
human rights in general and to President Daisaku Ikeda's reputation in particular
for supporting civil rights efforts worldwide (Chappell 194, 195). Whether or
not one interprets the tendency of black Buddhists to read Buddhism through
a civil rights heuristic as a legitimate appropriation of King's thought or as
something akin to those conservatives who appropriate King in order to argue
against affirmative action—an argument with which, in fact, neither Willis,
Johnson, hooks, nor Walker would agree—the emergence of black dharma in
the post-civil rights era is a historical, intellectual, and cultural phenomenon
in its own right that deserves to be taken into account.

In addition to providing an important cultural and critical context for interpreting the creative productions of such practitioners and fellow travelers as hooks, Willis, Walker, Ellis, and Johnson, taking black Buddhism into account will necessarily change the outlines of the history of Buddhism in the United States. For example, Anagarika Dharmapala's work in Sri Lanka and India as a social reformer and Buddhist advocate commonly is discussed in Engaged Buddhist scholarship in relation to Colonel Henry Steele Olcott.[20] Dharmapala's contact with Booker T. Washington and his visit to the Tuskegee Institute in June 1903, however, is not mentioned by the standard studies of Engaged Buddhism.[21] But two letters from Dharmapala to Washington can be found in The Booker T. Washington papers, one written before his visit to Tuskegee in June 1903 and another written afterward. As Dharmapala writes in his second letter:

> I have gained from my visit to Tuskegee an experience that I shall never forget and when I saw the Tuskegee Institute with its manifold branches under enlightened teachers I rejoiced that you have made all this glorious work a consummation within a generation; and I thought of the Viceroy in India who with the missions of children starving for education and bread that he should waste in sky rockets and tomfoolery and vain show to please a few loafing lords who came from England last January six million dollars in thirteen days! He is not worthy to loose the latchet of your shoe. (December 23, 1903 508)

Dharmapala visited Tuskegee after hearing Washington speak in San Francisco and meeting him in San Jose, California. The purpose of his trip is named in his first letter to Washington, dated June 20, 1903, where Dharmapala describes his intention to "stay two days with you studying the methods." Since Dharmapala's own system for reform combined the practical methods of self-help and industrial education with a reformed Buddhist practice, his visit to observe "the methods" of industrial education and self-help as they were developed at Tuskegee may well have influenced his efforts in India and Ceylon.[22] In any case, such a meeting of a well-known African-American reformer and important Indian Buddhist reformer illustrates the kind of encounters that taking account of the relationship between blacks and Buddhists will bring to light.

If the popular 2004 film *Crash* suggests that "black" and "Buddhist" are to some degree contradictory categories, the work by black Buddhists discussed here complicates that judgment by providing insight into the historical, emotional, intellectual, and spiritual complexities of black Buddhist practice in the United States. As a world religion that originated in northern India in the sixth century BCE and spread to numerous Eastern countries before its migration to the West, as the fourth largest religion in existence today (counting more than 360 million people as members), and, perhaps most important, as a philosophical religion that encourages the intellectual critique of inherited dogma, it is perhaps not surprising that Buddhism has often been judged to embody a "tradition of originality" (Thurman 8). The black Buddhists discussed here represent the latest chapter in that history of innovation, as they transform Buddhist practice from their particular location as black American minority practitioners. Deeply influenced both by the globalization of values that is one characteristic of the postmodern period and by their personal experience of racism, black Buddhists articulate a new Buddhist practice through a civil rights heuristic. In taking up Buddhist practice, black American Buddhists encounter unique cultural tensions as they attempt to fuse an ancient Eastern philosophical and religious practice with contemporary African-American religious and cultural traditions. At the same time, the multiple commitments of engaged black Buddhists work to foreground the important question of precisely how a Buddhist understanding of enlightenment relates to engaged social practice.

Notes

1. Both black and Chinese people worked on the transcontinental railroad, although blacks worked largely for the Union Pacific, and the great majority of Chinese for the Central Pacific.

2. The religions were Buddhism, Christianity, Confucianism, Hinduism, Islam, Jainism, Judaism, Shintoism, Taoism, and Zoroastrianism. For the most detailed history of the Parliament, see Seager, *World's Parliament*. Seager also collects sixty of the papers presented at the Parliament in *The Dawn of Religious Pluralism*. For a Foucauldian study of how the representation of religion at the Parliament stages and supports various colonial projects and relates to the representation of religion elsewhere at the Columbian Exhibition (such as in material representations at the midway), see Burris.

3. See John Sheldon Hunt's unpublished dissertation, *Mahayana Phoenix: Japan's Buddhists at the 1893 World's Parliament of Religions*.

4. For an analysis of the importance of Paul Carus to the Americanization of Buddhism that argues that Carus's *Monist* writings influenced the development of Suzuki's thought, see Martin J. Verhoeven, "Americanizing the Buddha: Paul Carus and the Transformation of Asian Thought."

5. In an important essay on Charles Johnson's most recent novel, *Dreamer*, John Whalen-Bridge argues that Johnson's "cross-cultural philosophical and religious exchange" is significant specifically because he has "imaginatively integrated the largely white male Beat tradition in American literature" ("Waking" 511).

6. For information on Black Buddhism, see especially *Turning Wheel*, spring 1993, fall 2000, spring 2001, and summer 2003; *Tricycle* fall 1994; and the edited collections and books by people of color listed here. Additionally, a helpful list of "Resources for and about African American Buddhists," including lists of books, audiotapes, Internet contacts, and dharma communities, is provided in the summer 2003 *Turning Wheel*, 42–43.

7. Since 1991, when William Gleason and Jonathan Little published articles on Johnson's *Oxherding Tale* ("The Liberation of Perception" and "Charles Johnson's *Revolutionary Oxherding Tale*," respectively), several critics of Johnson's fiction have discussed his work in relation to a form of Engaged Buddhism. See especially Little (*Charles*), Nash (*Charles*), Storhoff (*Understanding*), Byrd (*Charles*). See also essays by Byrd, "*Oxherding Tale* and *Siddhartha*"; Whalen-Bridge, "*Waking Cain*"; Conner "At the Numinous Heart of Being: *Dreamer* and Christian Theology"; and Nash, "The Application of an Ideal."

8. I do not mean to imply that the practice of martial arts in the United States accurately reflects traditional Asian culture—such a claim would be highly suspect.

9. Johnson would later register with Hughes' temple in Osaka. Hughes, however, died in the early 2000s on a mission working with street children in the Philippines (private correspondence August 16, 2005.)

10. See Queen's edited collections, Donald Rothberg's "Responding to the Cries of the World: Socially Engaged Buddhism," and Ken Jones's *The Social Face of Buddhism*.

11. My reading follows the distinction between Mahayana and twentieth-century understandings of engagement developed by Queen. A series of books on Western Buddhism and literature from SUNY Press, edited by John Whalen-Bridge and Gary Storhoff, will add considerably to the understanding of American Buddhism.

12. A short list of Engaged Buddhist movements in the twentieth century would include Hanh's antiwar organization in Vietnam, the human rights work of the fourteenth Dali Lama of Tibet, Dr. A. T. Ariyaratne's Sri Lanka movement on behalf of the destitute, the work of Thai Buddhist Sulak Sivaraski, and the Burmese People's Movement (for which Aung San Souky and Tein Gyatso received the Nobel Peace Prize). For a longer list of Engaged Buddhist activities in the East and West, see Rothberg, 269ff.

13. For an argument that Queen may misread the tradition in order to emphasize the West's contributions to Engaged Buddhism, see Thomas Freeman Yarnall, "Engaged Buddhism: New and Improved?"

14. See Peter Harvey, *An Introduction to Buddhist Ethics* 34.

15. As Buddhist teachings suggest, the Buddha was initially unwilling to accept women in the *sangha* until he came to the realization that his failure to include them did not follow logically from his own precepts. Even so, the rules that were established for the orders of male and female monks clearly subordinate female to male monks. See Nancy J. Barnes, "Buddhist Women and the Nuns' Order in Asia." (261).

16. John Whalen-Bridge interviews Kingston in "Now That I am Old and Have the Words for It."

17. Several critics have discussed King's importance to Johnson, whose novel, *Dreamer*, centers on King as a character. In discussing the novel's focus on what it means to "do well," Nash expertly ties the novel to a project Johnson begins in *Oxherding Tale*, arguing that the novel "completes [Johnson's] own cycle of *Oxherding Pictures*, molding his enlightenment to serve his community through this process of social and aesthetic engagement" (*Charles* 190). Whalen-Bridge's groundbreaking essay on the novel's complex engagement with the Cain and Abel myth, "Waking Cain," identifies many of the Buddhist themes in the novel; Storhoff interprets King as a bodhisattva (*Understanding*); and Byrd (*Charles*) also discusses the novel's analysis of doing well, the *Oxherding Pictures*, and the Cain and Abel biblical myth, tying each to Buddhist thematic.

18. In retelling this history, I primarily rely on Willis' own accounts in *Dreaming Me* and "You're Already a Buddha, So Be a Buddha," as well as on Donald Downs' detailed history, *Cornell '69*. According to Downs, strong evidence suggests that the cross-burning was committed by three black students (169–170), although the black women students who lived there did not know it at the time.

19. Hampton was shot to death at 2337 W. Monroe Street in Chicago—almost certainly as he slept in his bed—by a member of a special forces unit who had been provided with information about the layout of his apartment by an informant who had been working as Hampton's bodyguard.

20. This is not to imply that the relationship between Dharmapala and Olcott was not important: Dharmapala's conversion to Buddhism was inspired by Olcott, who also established the Theosophical Society in India that would provide an organizational base for many of Dharmapala's reform efforts. Nevertheless, Dharmapala's interest in Washington's "methods" should not be overlooked.

21. This includes Queen's edited collections and Ken Jones' *The Social Face of Buddhism*.

22. For more information, see the notes to Dharmapala's letters in the Washington papers.

Works Cited

Adiele, Faith. *Meeting Faith: The Forest Journals of a Black Buddhist Nun*. New York: W. W. Norton, 2004.

Barnes, Nancy. "Buddhist Women and the Nuns' Order in Asia." *Engaged Buddhism: Buddhist Liberation Movements in Asia*. Ed. Christopher Queen and Sallie B. King. Albany: State University of New York Press, 1996. 259–94.

Barrows, John H., ed. *The World's Parliament of Religions*. Vols. 1 and 2. Chicago: Parliament Publishing, 1893.

Baumann, Martin. "The Dharma Has Come West." *Journal of Buddhist Ethics* 4 (1997): 198.

Boyd, Merle Kyoto. "A Child of the South in Long Black Robes." Gutiérrez Baldoquín 101–5.

Burris, John P. *Exhibiting Religion: Colonialism and Spectacle at International Expositions, 1851–1893*. Charlottesville: University Press of Virginia, 2001.

Byrd. Rudolph P. *Charles Johnson's Novels: Writing the American Palimpsest*. Bloomington: Indiana University Press, 2005.

———, ed. *I Call Myself an Artist: Writings by and about Charles Johnson*. Bloomington: Indiana University Press, 1999.

———. "*Oxherding Tale* and *Siddhartha*: Philosophy, Fiction, and the Emergence of a Hidden Tradition." 1996. Byrd, *I Call Myself an Artist* 305–17.

Calhoun, Ramon. "Inside a Triple Parenthesis: Being a Black Buddhist in the U.S." *Turning Wheel* 12 (Summer 2003): 39–42.

Chappell, David W. "Racial Diversity in the Soka Gakkai." Queen, *Engaged Buddhism in the West* 184–217.

Chen, Viveka. "Finding True Freedom." Gutiérrez Baldoquín 111–15.

Coleman, James William. "The New Buddhism: Some Empirical Findings. *American Buddhism: Methods and Findings in Recent Scholarship.*" Williams and Queen. Curzon Press, 1999. 91–99.

———. *The New Buddhism: The Western Transformation of an Ancient Tradition.* Oxford University Press, 2001.

Conner, Marc C. " 'At the Numinous Heart of Being': *Dreamer* and Christian Theology." Conner and Nash 57–81.

Conner, Marc C., and William R. Nash, eds. *Charles Johnson: The Novelist as Philosopher.* Oxford: University Press of Mississippi, 2007.

Cooper, Carol. "About Black Folks and Buddha Dharma: An Interview with bell hooks." 2001. www.carolcooper.org/iview/hooks-01.php.

Deitrick, James. "Engaged Buddhist Ethics: Mistaking the Boat for the Shore." Queen, Prebish, and Keown 252–69.

Dharmapala, Anagarika. "Criticism and Discussion of Missionary Methods." Barrows, *The World's Parliament of Religions* 2:1093.

———. Letter to Booker T. Washington. June 20, 1903. *The Booker T. Washington Papers Online.* Vol. 13. 507–8. www.historycooperative.org/btw/info.html.

———. Letter to Booker T. Washington. December 26, 1903. *The Booker T. Washington Papers Online.* Vol. 13. 508. www.historycooperative.org/btw/info.html.

Downs, David Alexander. *Cornell '69: Liberalism and the Crisis of the American University.* Cornell University Press, 1999.

Fields, Rick. *How the Swans Came to the Lake: A Narrative History of Buddhism in America.* Boston: Shambhala Publications, 1981.

Foye, Addie. "Buddhism in America: A Short, Biased View." *Tricycle: The Buddhist Review* Fall, 1994. 57.

Gleason, William. "The Liberation of Perception: Charles Johnson's *Oxherding Tale.*" *Black American Literature Forum* 25 (1991): 704–28.

Gutiérrez Baldoquín, Hilda, ed. *Dharma, Color, and Culture: New Voices in Western Buddhism.* Berkeley: Parallax Press, 2004.

Hanh, Thich Nhat. *Going Home: Jesus and Buddha as Brothers.* New York: Riverhead, 2000.

———. *Living Buddha, Living Christ.* New York: Riverhead, 1997.

———. *Peace Is Every Step.* New York: Bantam, 1991.

Hanson, Niel. *The Custom of the Sea.* New York: John Wiley, 1999.

Harvey, Peter. *An Introduction to Buddhist Ethics.* New York: Cambridge University Press, 2000.

hooks, bell. "bell hooks Speaks to John Perry Barlow." *Shambhala Sun* 13: 1 (September 1955). www.shambhalasun.com/index.php?option=content&task=view&id=2089.

———. *Rock My Soul.* New York: Atria Books, 2003.

———. "Surrendered to Love: King's Legacy." *Shambhala Sun* 13.3 (January 2005): 51–53.

———. "Waking Up to Racism." *Tricycle: The Buddhist Review* 13 (Fall 1994): 42–45.

Hurst, Jane. "Nichiren Shoshu and Sokka Gakkai in America: The Pioneer Spirit." Prebish and Tanaka 80–97.

Jeffreys, Derek S. "Does Buddhism Need Human Rights?" Queen, Prebish, and Keown 271–85.

Jenkins, Stephen. "Do bodhisattvas relieve poverty?" Queen, Prebish, and Keown 38–49.

Johnson, Charles. *Dreamer.* New York: Scribner, 1998.

———. "The King We Left Behind." *Common Quest* (Fall 1996). Byrd, *I Call Myself an Artist* 193–99.

———. "The King We Need: Teachings for a Nation in Search of Itself." *Shambhala Sun* 13.3 (January 2005): 42–50.

———. *Oxherding Tale.* New York: Grove, 1982.

———. "Reading the Eightfold Path." 2003. Gutiérrez Baldoquín 127–55.

———. "A Sangha By Another Name." In *Turning the Wheel: Essays on Buddhism and Writing,* 46–57.

———. *Turning the Wheel: Essays on Buddhism and Writing.* New York: Scribner, 2003.

Jones, Ken. *The New Social Face of Buddhism: An Approach to Political and Social Activism.* Somerville, Mass.: Wisdom Publications, 2003.

Jones, Marlene. "Moving toward an End to Suffering." Gutiérrez Baldoquín 43–45.

Lee, William Poy. "Black on Black: Interview with Lawrence Ellis with Introduction by William Poy Lee." 2002. 1–7. www.spiritrock.org/html/diversity_Blackon-Black_Ellis.html.

———. "Black on Black: Interview with Ralph Steele." 2001. 1–4. www.spiritrock.org/html/diversity_BlackonBlack_Steele.html.

Levine, Lawrence. *Black Culture and Black Consciousness.* New York: Oxford University Press, 1977.

Little, Jonathan. *Charles Johnson's Spiritual Imagination.* Columbia: University of Missouri Press, 1997.

———. "Charles Johnson's Revolutionary *Oxherding Tale.*" *Studies in American Fiction* 19 (1991): 141–51.

Nash, William R. "The Application of an Ideal: *Turning the Wheel* as Ontological Program." Conner and Nash. 171–81.

———. *Charles Johnson's Fiction.* Urbana: University of Illinois Press, 2003.

Nash, William R. and Marc C. Conner, eds. *Charles Johnson: The Novelist as Philosopher.* Oxford: University Press of Mississippi, 2007.

Nattier, Jan. "Visible and Invisible: Jan Nattier on the Politics of Representation in Buddhist America." *Tricycle: The Buddhist Review* 17 (Fall 1995): 42–49.

Perry, La Vora. "Religion Is Deeper Than Culture: On Being an African-American Buddhist." *Cleveland Plain Dealer,* August 19, 2000.

Pierce, Lori. "Buddhism and the Body Problem: A Historical Perspective on African American Buddhism." *Turning Wheel* 12 (Summer 2003): 20–22.

Pintak, Lawrence. " 'Something Has to Change.' " *Shambhala Sun* (September 2001). www.shambhalasun.com/Archieves/Features/2001/sept01/pintak.htm.

Prebish, Charles. "The Academic Study of Buddhism in America: A Silent Sangha." Williams and Queen 183–214.

Prebish, Charles, and Kenneth Tanaka, eds. *The Faces of Buddhism in America.* Berkeley: University of California Press, 1998.

Queen, Christopher S., ed. *Engaged Buddhism in the West.* New York: Routledge, 2003.

Queen, Christopher S. and Sallie B. King, eds. *Engaged Buddhism: Buddhist Liberation Movements in Asia.* Albany: State University of New York Press, April 1996.

Queen, Christopher S., Charles Prebish, and Damien Keown, eds. *Action Dharma: New Studies in Engaged Buddhism*. New York: RoutledgeCurzon, 2003.

Rabb, Christopher. "Blogging While Black." www.alternet.org/mediaculture/21301/.

Rangdröl, Choyin. "Black Buddha: Bringing the Tradition Home." *Turning Wheel 12*.

Rothberg, Donald. "Responding to the Cries of the World: Socially Engaged Buddhism in North America." Prebish and Tanaka 266–86.

Seager, R. H. "Buddhist Worlds in the U.S.A.: A Survey of the Territory." Williams and Queen 238–61.

———. *The Dawn of Religious Pluralism*. La Salle, Ill.: Open Court, 1993.

Smith, Bardwell L. "Sinhalese Buddhism and the Dilemmas of Reinterpretation." *The Two Wheels of Dhamma*. Ed. Bardwell L. Smith. Chambersburg, PA: American Academy of Religion, 1972. 79–106.

Steele, Ralph. "A Teaching on the Second Noble Truth." Gutiérrez Baldoquín 75–80.

Steinbach, Sara. "The Stories I Live With." Gutiérrez Baldoquín 89–90.

Stone, Jacqueline I. "Nichiren's Activist Heirs." Queen, Prebish, and Keown 63–94.

Storhoff, Gary. *Understanding Charles Johnson*. Columbia: University of South Carolina Press, 2004.

Thurman, Robert A. F. "The Emptiness That Is Compassion: An Essay on Buddhist Ethics." *Religious Traditions* 4:2 (1981): 11–34.

Verhoeven, Martin J. "Americanizing the Buddha: Paul Carus and the Transformation of Asian Thought." Prebish and Tanaka 207–28.

Vivekananda. "Hinduism." Barrows, *The World's Parliament of Religions* 2:968–78.

Walker, Alice. *In Search of Our Mother's Gardens: Womanist Prose*. Harvest Books, 1983.

———. "This Was Not an Area of Large Plantations." Gutiérrez Baldoquín 189–200.

Weber, Max. *The Religion of India: The Sociology of Hinduism and Buddhism*. Gencoe, IL: The Free Press, 1958.

Whalen-Bridge, John. " 'Now That I Am Old and Have the Words for It': Interview with Maxine Hong Kingston." *Shambhala Sun* 13.3 (January 2005): 60–66.

———. "Waking Cain: The Poetics of Integration in *Dreamer*." *Callaloo* 26.2 (2003): 504–21.

Williams, Angel Kyoto. *Being Black: Zen and the Art of Living with Fearlessness and Grace*. New York: Viking Compass, 2000.

Williams, Duncan R., and Christopher S. Queen, eds. *American Buddhism: Methods and Findings in Recent Scholarship*. Richmond, Surrey: Curzon, 1999.

Williams, Fannie Barrier. "What Can Religion Do to Advance the Condition of the Negro?" In Seager, *The Dawn of Religious Pluralism*, 142–150.

Willis, Jan. "Dharma Has No Color." Gutiérrez Baldoquín 217–24.

———. *Dreaming Me: An African American Woman's Spiritual Journey*. New York: Riverhead, 2001. Reissued, *Dreaming Me: Black, Baptist, and Buddhist: One Woman's Spiritual Journey*. Somerville, MA: Wisdom Publications, 2008.

———. "You're Already a Buddha, So Be a Buddha." *Turning Wheel* 12 (Summer 2003): 31–33.

Wood, Lewis. "From the Guest Editor." *Turning Wheel* 12 (Summer 2003): 2.

Yarnall, Thomas Freeman. "Engaged Buddhism: New and Improved? Made in the USA from Asian Materials." Queen, Prebish, and Keown 286–344.

PART II

THE NEW LAMP
Buddhism and Contemporary Writers

Chapter 3

Some of the Dharma

The Human, the Heavenly, and the "Real Work" in the Writings of Gary Snyder

Allan Johnston

Since the 1950s, Gary Snyder has offered one of the clearest expressions of Buddhist sensibility in American literature. A seminal figure in the "broad movement" toward Buddhism that "took off in the 1960s" (Seager 9), Snyder helped achieve a transfer of Buddhist values to the West by linking Buddhism to what he calls "the most archaic values on earth" (*Myths and Texts* viii). These values acknowledge the basis of spiritual being and political action in nature, in the pattern of deep-ecological "ethical holism" that Simon P. James finds in Zen Buddhist ethics (72–82). Thus, Snyder's work coincides with the ecological positions of Henry David Thoreau, John Muir, and others, although Snyder roots this tradition in values that predate the monotheistic, human-centered religions. He sees in Buddhism hints of ancient animistic beliefs, and explores these variations on Buddhist practice by insisting that poetry exists at the level of work. "Whatever work I've done, whatever job I've had, has fed right into my poetry . . . it's all in there," Snyder claims in *On Bread & Poetry*, the interview manifesto in which he, Philip Whalen, and Lew Welch state their commitment to the *work* of poetry (9).

The creation of poetry is for Snyder "the real work," a system of actions and attitudes that accords with natural occurrences and their spiritual significance.[1] Snyder explains that "[t]he real work is what we really do. . . . [I]f we can live the work we have to do, knowing that we are real, and it's real, and that the world is real, then it becomes right. And that's the *real work*: to make the world as real as it is, and to find ourselves as real as we are within it." Snyder continues, "the real work [is to] take the struggle on without the *least* hope of doing any good. To check the destruction of the interesting and necessary diversity of life on the planet so that the dance can go on a little better for a little longer. The other part of it is that it is always here. . . . The *real work* is eating each other, I suppose" (Snyder and Geneson 81–82).

In that it is work, poetry implies specific responsibilities. Snyder's writing is designed to maximize awareness of nature on all planes—the mundane, the political, and the spiritual. As an ecological program, work involves knowing cause and effect in human endeavor and understanding that human activity, the "human," must be identical to the "work" of nature, or the "heavenly"—a distinction made in Chuang-Tzu's "Autumn Floods":

> "What do you mean by the Heavenly and the human?"
> Jo of the North Sea said, "Horses and oxen have four feet—this is what I mean by the Heavenly. Putting a halter on the horse's head, piercing the ox's nose—this is what I mean by the human."

Political and spiritual work, however, fails if it separates humanity from the natural world. Thus, Snyder's "Real Work" offers a Dharmic practice; it acknowledges the difference between the human and the heavenly and realigns the human with the heavenly, coordinating it with Buddhist practice. This study explores Snyder's concept of "the real work."

"Real Work" in *Riprap*

Tracing the word *dharma* through different religious contexts, E. A. Burtt offers several definitions: "[r]ule of duty or of social obligation (Hinduism). The truth; the saving doctrine or way (early Buddhism). Reality; essential quality; any reality (Mahayana Buddhism)" (245). The word derives from Sanskrit roots meaning "that which has been established in the mind" or "the object of conscious-ness" (Alan Hunt Badiner, qtd. in Seager 211) and means "carrying, holding" (Fischer-Schreiber, Ehrhard, and Diener 54). *Dharma* is "central" to Buddhism and refers to "[t]he cosmic law, the 'great norm' "; "[t]he teaching of the Bud-dha, who recognized and formulated this law" (although "Buddha himself is no more than a manifestation of it"); all "[n]orms of behavior and ethical rules"; the "[m]anifestation of reality, of the general state of affairs," as well as each manifested "thing, phenomenon"; "[m]ental content, object of thought, idea"; and "the so-called factors of existence, which the Hinayana considers as building blocks of the empirical personality and its world" (Fischer-Schreiber et al. 54).

Other writers also provide distinctions. Alan Watts, speaking of the "*Dharmadhatu* ('Dharma realm') doctrine of the enormous *Avatamsaka Sutra*," joins dharma to "[t]he perception that each single form, just as it is, is the void and that, further, the uniqueness of each form arises from the fact that it exists in relation to every other form" (71). The universe, in its metaphoric manifestation as the Jewel Net of Indra, is a "realm of innumerable *dharmas* or 'thing-events' " (71), a description recalling the idea of *tathata,* "thusness," which relates to *Tathagata,* the "thusness-already" (Kerouac 142) of Buddha's manifestation as each being. Dwight Goddard ties the Twelve *Nirdanas,* or the "Chain of Simultaneous Depended Origins," to the Four Noble Truths that lead to the four *Jnanas* of compassion, joy, equanimity, and peace, and point to the ten stages of the Bodhisattva (645–56). These definitions offer an interpretation of existence that coincides with a Buddhist therapy for suffering.

Snyder's "real work" corresponds with several aspects of dharma. Practice is a way to enforce resistance and to accept the "essential reality" of the heavenly. If we here include Zen, especially the teachings of Rinzai who saw "the roots of the concept of *dharma* in the Way of Taoism" (Molesworth 79), we have a compendium of the Eastern disciplines that inform Snyder's vision. As an expression of Tao, practice connects directly to the heavenly, since for Snyder meditation is no different from the action of animals:

> At some point . . . it just hit me that I really was an animal and that all of the things that we call "human" are simply part of that, including our spiritual capacities. It's just another thing that animals can do. (Ingram et al. 4)

"Human" experience stems from the human "distinction between the see-er and the seen" that results from nature's "being seen as an object" (Ingram et al. 4). From this objectification comes power, since perceiving nature as an object leads to an attempt to control nature. By reducing nature to an object, science creates the laws that seem reductive and materialistic. These insights, transformed into the concept of individual rights, give us what Snyder calls "the mercy of the West": social revolution.[2]

The Westernized subject–object split rests on perceiving a difference between self and nature. If an order different from nature exists somewhere else (as in a Christian heaven), there is also an accompanying tendency to deny the self through a "willingness to accept the perceptions and decisions of others" (*Earth House Hold* 126)—that is, to accept an authoritarian society. Authoritarianism may permit cultural or even countercultural cohesion, but at the cost of repudiating the self's convictions and beliefs. Snyder's resistance to "the perceptions and decisions of others" appears as early as "Mid August at Sourdough Mountain Lookout," the first poem in Snyder's first published book.[3] Snyder starts the poem with a loose collection of images of place:

> Down valley a smoke haze
> Three days heat, after five days rain
> Pitch glows on the fir-cones
> Across rocks and meadows
> Swarms of new flies. (*Riprap* 1)

These lines reject an authoritative, central persona, although there is a centralized perspective. They also avoid punctuation that would, in the formal context of established 1950s poetry, have implied a linguistic linearity; the lack of the first-person pronoun combined with the associative leap between ideas in the first two lines averts normal linear processing. Lines 3 to 5 offer possible continuities of meaning, but the connections are blurred by the ambiguous "Across rocks and meadows," which reads grammatically as both "Pitch glows on the fir-cones / Across rocks and meadows" and "Across rocks and meadows / Swarms of new flies." The lines seem to move from the "grand scale" of haze in the valley to the specifics of pitch and fly swarms, but they also shift from the separated observations found in the first two lines to a merging of the speaker's perception. Recalled events—"Three days heat, after five days rain"—fade, while the phenomena of nature emerge, even flow together (ll. 3–5).

The speaker's shift from reflection to seeing, accompanied by a shift from syntactic separation to indefinite syntactic attachment, is expressed in the rest of the poem:

> I cannot remember things I once read
> A few friends, but they are in cities.
> Drinking cold snow-water from a tin cup
> Looking down for miles
> Through high still air. (1)

Snyder describes a movement from *reading* to *seeing*—from a literary and social self to one centered on the natural environment. The forgotten "things" read and the memory of a few "friends" fade; instead, Snyder enjoys "high still air" and "cold snow-water." To say that Snyder passes from literary and social modes to a release in the natural world is to state that in nature he approaches another realm, one that demands a different mode of perception from the literary world. This separation of the literary from the natural recalls Chuang-Tzu's contrast of the human with the heavenly.

The distinction between heavenly nature and human action is central to *Riprap*. For example, when Snyder describes himself on Mount Baker thinking of his need to return to Seattle to look for work ("The Late Snow & Lumber Strike of the Summer of Fifty-four"), he depicts himself as "caught on a snowpeak / between heaven and earth" (3)—a phrase both physically true and literarily reminiscent of Chuang-Tzu's conceit.[4] In "Migration of Birds," Snyder compares the "big abstraction" he studied in a book on bird migration to "Broody scrabblers pick[ing] up bits of string" and "seabirds / Chas[ing] Spring north along the coast" (17). In "For a Far-out Friend," the *natural* behavior of the girl's "calm words" contrasts with Snyder's "less sane" act of hitting her, being "stung with weeks of torment"—Snyder's violent behavior attributed to being "hooked on books" (12). The most significant of these contrasts occurs in "Piute Creek," where Snyder describes passing through meditation into an overwhelming nature that is "too much" (6) for human understanding—an experience that Tim Dean compares to the "rarefied perception" of the Kantian "mathematical sublime" (168). "One granite ridge / A tree, would be enough," Snyder tells us—enough for the senses or for contemplation, which imagines nature without ambiguous spirituality. Syntactical ambiguity appears in the first lines of "Piute Creek," since "One granite ridge / A tree" does not present grammatical distinctions but only different lines. In this way, Snyder reinforces the grammatical demonstrations of levels of connection throughout the poem. In these contrasts, Snyder implies that exposure to the heavenly affects the human sensibility:

> All the junk that goes with being human
> Drops away, hard rock wavers
> * * *
> Words and books
> Like a small creek off a high ledge
> Gone in the dry air. (6)

The "junk that goes with being human / Drops away" is confirmed in the poem's punctuation, which includes fused sentences, comma splices, fragments, and the ironic gesture toward literariness achieved through the trochaic pentameter shift to spondees. Culture, "words and books," are "Gone in the dry air"; they disappear. The image of words and books as a "small creek off a high ledge," however, implies a more fundamental failing, the wavering of "hard rock"—substance—and the failure of the "heavy present" (6), the point where self and environment meet. Grammatical and metric strategies indicate the speaker's shift of attention from physical immediacy to visionary experience. A loss of the "heavy present" that "Sourdough Lookout" suggests is *all* that remains after loss of literariness. The "heavy present" fails, and the "heart" becomes a "bubble," froth on the creek of culture which is soon "gone in the dry air." In the encounter with nature, then, the past (the "words and books" of culture) disappear; but as they do, so does the present—the solidity of earth, time, and the individual. The grammatical fusing and fragmenting of experience in this section points to a deeper fusing and fragmenting of self in a crucial though disturbing experiencing of erasure in nature.[5]

What remains after this erasure appears in the next stanza:

> A clear, attentive mind
> Has no meaning but that
> Which sees is truly seen. (6)

Snyder dramatizes "a clear attentive mind" by ambiguous language. He uses syntax to obscure whether "that / Which sees is truly seen" refers to a fact or a meaning—whether a "clear, attentive mind" has no meaning or has the "meaning" of seeing and being seen. The ambiguity, of course, rests in the meanings of mind and meaning. A meditative mind perceives itself; at this level, the mind is a tool of introspection, and the koan-like "that / Which sees is truly seen" becomes a tautology. But being seen also means being seen by others—for example, the "unseen / . . . eyes / Of Cougar or Coyote" that "Watch [him] rise and go" (6). The Cougar and especially Coyote are archetypal, and so these animals may imply the unconscious, spying on the "clear, attentive mind" from within. Yet Cougar and Coyote *are* in nature, watching and unseen, and only if we equate nature and the unconscious (as Snyder does[6]) can they be understood as metaphors. That they are unseen seems to belie the sense of seeing postulated for the "clear, attentive mind." But the speaker *has* seen them, if only as a "flick / In the moonlight" (6).

These tensions in "Piute Creek" represent an interplay of readings. In fact, the reader often confronts multiple interpretations that include self and other both observing and erasing each other. The oscillation between possibilities permits the wandering mind of the poem[7] to move away from the meditative stillness of contemplative poetry and the centrality of the speaker. This rejection of dualities points to the conundrums of sameness and difference that led Thomas Parkinson to claim that Snyder makes "the western world with its dualisms and antinomies . . . alien to himself" (*Earth House Hold* 617).

Snyder's firewatch journals reveal this distancing from antinomies as a conscientious tuning of self, a disciplining of attention to achieve direct interaction with Chuang-Tzu's "heavenly" (*Earth House Hold* 1–24). Western readings of Nature, in their evolution from medieval to modern times, express a sense of dominance. Dominance may stem from God's authorship of nature, scientific reduction of nature, nature's expression of utilitarian laws or of universal "reason"; or dominance is implied as in late eighteenth- and early nineteenth-century Idealism, nature's expression of a spiritualized "self." These "main text" (Molesworth 82) readings, with their implied dialectic of self and other, remove self from nature, but also eliminate alternative understandings of nature. Insofar as Snyder's approach to nature opposes these traditions, Snyder affirms Chuang Tzu's "heavenly," and he locates himself in it.

Snyder's Meditative Practice and Ecology

Snyder stratifies his definition of *the real work*, the term he uses to describe his effort to realign the human with the heavenly. By doing so, he suggests layers of meaning in "the real work" that show the complexities of human interactions with nature. The first layer concerns *practice* in the sense of a constant striving to make active connection so as to engage the world at all levels of life.[8] Practice refers as much to attention to what we do in daily life as it does to any special endeavor to "connect," the result of meditation in "Piute Creek." He says, "The real work is what we really do . . . [to] make the world as real as it is, and . . . find ourselves as real as we are within it" (Snyder and Geneson 81). Snyder strives for direct involvement in nature so that work as labor becomes another means of experiencing the earth. These realizations resemble the "practice" of sitting meditation.[9] Acting in nature pits humanity against nature, but meditation limits "either/or" perceptions by blending mind and environment, body and breath. The result reflects the realizations, if not the erasures, reached in meditation.

In the poem "Fire in the Hole," for instance, Snyder describes work in terms of relating it to spiritual practice or discipline. As in "Piute Creek," work permits experiencing nature similarly to, but also differently from that achieved in meditation. Snyder describes himself "Squatting a day in the sun, / one hand turning the steeldrill, / one, swinging the four pound singlejack hammer / down," while "above, the cliffs, / of Piute Mountain waver." As he describes the day, he recalls that "the mind / entered the tip of steel. / the arm fell / like breath. / the valley, reeling, / on the pivot of that drill" (*The Back Country* 21). Snyder's physical labor is like a mantra. In "Piute Creek" the "too much" of nature causes the mind to wander, but in "Fire in the Hole" attention on pounding a steel drill through granite forces the speaker's mind to solidify, so that it "enter[s] the tip of steel." The line "why does this day keep coming into mind" ("Fire in the Hole" 21), syntactically a question but punctuated as an assertion, suggests both the psychic significance of the experience and the *realization*—both as knowing and as concretizing—achieved through it. The day comes to mind because it *becomes* mind; mind becomes a tool just as body becomes rhythm or spirit, "like breath," the focus of meditation.[10] The "waver" of Piute Mountain refers literally to heat shimmers, and the parallel between this wavering and the waver of rock in "Piute Creek" needs hardly be stated. "The valley" reels "on the pivot of that drill," as Snyder's concentration on work compresses perception of the environment into an extension of task. The environment then joins with the energy released in work through its "reeling, / on the pivot of that drill." At the end of the poem, "hands and arms and shoulders" are "free" not only from the excruciating, four-hour task but also from what Snyder elsewhere calls the "ancient, meaningless / Abstractions of the educated mind" ("Logging" 5; *Myths and Texts* 7). Snyder's concentration on his work breaks down the barriers between mind and body, self and environment,[11] and thereby clears the mind.

In Snyder's poetry, work becomes an expression of the self in nature. Work and meditation differ in that meditation allows expansion of perception while work focuses on a task, but the efficacy of each depends on the worker or the meditator. Snyder emphasizes this devotion in his comments on the experience that led to *Riprap,* where Snyder discovers his voice as a poet. In writing poetry, he discovers the role poetry would play for him. Snyder makes this clear when he describes how, while working in Yosemite Park, he at first tried to "exercise [his] mind" by reading Milton, then "gave up trying to carry on an intellectual interior life separate from the work. . . . By just working, I found myself being completely there having the whole mountain inside of me, and finally having a whole language inside of me that became one with the rocks and with the trees" (Snyder and Lampe 8). "Having the whole mountain inside of me" becomes the criterion for a self that "sees [and] is truly seen," where nature and the self combine. When Snyder creates a "language . . . that [is] one with the rocks and with the trees," he assumes a fusion of humanity and nature—an identity realized in work. By turning away from Milton, as Snyder describes here and in the poem "Milton by Firelight," one comes to see that perceptions of nature often result from preconceptions rather than from nature itself.

Like meditation, work can hone the mind. In "Six-Month Song in the Foothills" (*The Back Country* 17), saws and axes are sharpened while swallows fly in and out of the barn, uniting people and birds—humanity and nature—in "seasonal activities . . . a shared home . . . pursuing separate works, separate ends without destructiveness or hostility" (Jody Norton, qtd. in Murphy 69). The poem moves from depicting "sunlight / falling through meadow" to "snow on low hills" to the "white mountains" "[b]eyond the low hills." The poem's spatial expansion parallels a perceptual expansion; the places described are loci of work and seeing, as the poem prepares the worker for these places. We see then that the *work* of meditation, or of Zen practice, resembles the connection of self and nature achieved in physical labor. In fact, Snyder describes meditation as a remnant of the primary work, the waiting in the bush for prey,[12] since both involve a manipulation of mind and matter.

Snyder depicts this manipulation in "No Matter, Never Mind," one of the more abstract poems in *Turtle Island,* in which an incestuous mix of Void, Wave, Matter and Life "Gives birth to the Mind" (11). This straightforward presentation acknowledges the Mind as a product of nature. Life recalls "The Great Mother" that Snyder later identifies as Gaia, while Matter is both brother and father to Life, its co-creator and constant companion, perhaps even a rival. As the title suggests, Mind cannot exist without Matter. The interconnection of mind and matter relieves the reader's concerns about the origin of mind. Since mind develops from the material world rather than through ideas, speculation as to its origin seems fruitless, but people always immerse themselves in the abstractions that Snyder's poetry usually counters. Humans are the creators of such abstractions as the ones in "No Matter, Never Mind," which is why Snyder downplays the relevance of his "genealogy" even as he presents it. Snyder's reaction against abstractions implies the second level of meaning in "the real work" that we might call *resistance*. The human tendency to abstract experience is the basis of the "human predicament" or the "problem of nature." Snyder suggests that when humans wrongly experience nature as an abstraction, nature is abstracted from itself and becomes a creation of the human mind—a product of the human rather than of the heavenly.[13] Yet this tendency to abstraction is the "distinction" of humanity. Such perceptions, since they represent a point of intersection in Indra's Net, retain a degree of truth. Nevertheless, any such generalization substitutes an imagined nature for phenomenal nature. The result is expressed in "Milton by Firelight" as "chaos of the mind":

> No paradise, no fall,
> Only the weathering land
> The wheeling sky,
> Man, with his Satan
> Scouring the chaos of the mind. (*Riprap* 8)

The distinction between what is and what is perceived depends on direct experience of nature rather than on interpretations of nature. Accompanying the lie of paradise is the lie of the fall, Satan, and "chaos of the mind." Nature is going about its "weathering" and "wheeling," but human beings perceive these events as consequences of natural laws. Nature's continuity and its independence from false human ordering are suggested by the poem's punctuation, the lack of syntactical separation between "the weathering land" and "the wheeling sky." If the book—Milton's *Paradise Lost*—lies, nature does not lie; for it is outside grammar and language, ordering itself beyond human conceptualization. The "clear, attentive mind" of "Piute Creek" has foregone the internalized chaos of meaning in nature and sees both itself and nature that, being in its own ways sentient, sees mind (and) (as) itself. The contrast between natural process and the "chaos of the mind" in "Milton by Firelight" suggests that the "chaos" Western society finds in nature is an illusion, a "chaos of the mind." Snyder implies this perception may be based on the belief that divine order must somehow transcend nature. "Truly seen," nature represents not a chaotic face, but a face, seen or unseen, that looks back at us: the face of nature is ultimately the face of the examined self. "Mind" and nature are the same because the "clear mind" sees nature as itself.

In "Toward Climax" (*Turtle Island* 82–85), Snyder traces mind as a feature of social evolution. "King," derived from a "central / Never-moving Pole Star," appears as a mythical creation, a human analogue of the literal "direction" given by the stars. The switch from "foxy self- / survival" to "ferocious" reason, however, results only from a human desire for order. Making "Reason" into "Law" ignores the fact that "Law" is a human institution, and therefore not congruent with "heavenly" nature. Humanity's projection of "Law" onto nature becomes the source of the idea that nature is chaos—nature, of course, does not follow human law, and so becomes "outlaw." But as the burning of the "outlaw" rooster suggests, the projection of "human" law onto nature violates what is commonly termed *natural law*. The "verdict" "Unnatural" that Snyder passes ambiguously hangs at the end of the sentence imposed on the rooster, leaving us to decide what is unnatural: the chicken or the society that condemns it. A rooster laying an egg is a natural event. In contrast, people burning an "outlaw" rooster are ludicrous, and the bizarre situation shows how far society has strayed from nature.

Work and meditation as *practices* deliberately *resist* the abstracted face of nature presented in "Milton by Firelight" and "Toward Climax." Contact with mind and matter forces us to establish a sense of relation to earth by making "the world as real as it is." Snyder does not see the mind as an evolutionary mistake, as this would be a projection of human valuation onto heavenly creation. Mind can surpass abstraction, and humanity can "break through things as they are" (*The Back Country* 87), just as humanity can break things in nature.[14] "The real work" allows contact with nature through attention to a task, but this devotedness becomes problematic when work itself is abstracted rather than attended to directly. Devotion to a task is not what most people consider important in work; in a capitalist society, work usually involves maximizing profit. Because of the profit motive, work emphasizes the human over the heavenly, even though the consequence is environmental destruction. Meanwhile, nature gets "processed" into wooden boxes that Snyder describes in "A Berry Feast":

> The Chainsaw falls for boards of pine,
> Suburban bedrooms, block on block
> Will waver with this grain and knot,
> The maddening shapes will start and fade
> Each morning when commuters wake—
> Joined boards hung on frames,
> a box to catch the biped in. (*The Back Country*, 13)

Against the work of "wrecking the world" ("Dillingham, Alaska, the Willow Tree Bar," *Axe Handles* 92), Snyder advocates the "real work" of saving the world. Snyder extends the idea of "the real work" as resistance; humanity's destruction of nature results from the human ability to self-abstract from nature, to distinguish humanity from what it destroys. Thus, Snyder calls civilization "a lack of faith, a human laziness, a willingness to accept the perceptions and decisions of others in place of your own" (*Earth House Hold* 126), and so he rejects the substitution of culture for nature, and privileging abstractions over the concrete—a process that creates "self-imposed limitations" to alternative ways of experiencing nature. Against these limitations, Snyder offers "natural" values: "As poet I hold the most archaic values on earth. They go back to the upper Palaeolithic: the fertility of the soil, the magic of animals, the power-vision in solitude . . ." (*Myths and Texts* viii).

Snyder's ecological focus reconfigures our relationship with nature. He advances the identity of nature and mind by uniting the "myths" of empowerment that constitute "the most archaic values on earth" with the "texts" of nature. The essay "Four Changes," for example, presents the "conditions" of population, pollution, and consumption, and recommends "actions" to solve these problems; yet he demands a radical "transformation" to an ecological life that acknowledges " '[w]ildness [as] the state of complete awareness' " (*Turtle Island* 99). This transformation requires development of "psychological techniques for creating an awareness of 'self' which includes the social and natural environment" (101). Revolution without "revolution of consciousness" is pointless, while "revolution of consciousness" accepts that " 'man's survival' or 'survival of the biosphere' " are part of "some kind of serene and ecstatic process which is beyond qualities and beyond birth-and-death. 'No need to survive!' " (102).[15]

Snyder's call for resistance is clear at the end of "I Went Into the Maverick Bar." But Snyder's realization also is a self-renunciation, since there is " 'No need to survive!' "[16] After dancing "fifties-style" with short-haired Americans, Snyder leaves the bar to return to "the real work, to / 'what is to be done' " (*Turtle Island* 9). The allusion to Lenin's revolutionary tract hints at Snyder's desire for revolutionary effort, and perhaps his Marxist convictions. In another context, Snyder recognizes Marx as the source of a compelling theoretical model and of many "useful insights" (Snyder and Woods 201), and he feels that "it's an easy step from the dialectic of Marx and Hegel to an interest in the dialectic of early Taoism" (*Earth House Hold* 114). But ultimately Marxism is not efficacious, since Marxism develops new abstractions rather than creating an unabstracted consciousness in which political ends become secondary to environmental needs. In contradistinction to Marxism's ideal, an industrialized state, Snyder's calls for a re-inhabitation of land and for restructuring society around ecosystems rather than biospheres.[17] This restructuring should, Snyder hopes, "check the destruction of the interesting and necessary diversity of life on the planet so that the dance can go on a little better for a little longer."

Snyder, then, defines "the real work" as the radical transformation of civilization—an end to the globalizing, consumerist, fossil fuel-based social systems—to an ecologically viable way of life that recognizes the rights of *all* beings. Snyder's countercultural stance throughout his writings, not to mention in his lifestyle, thus stands as a radical critique of civilization. Snyder, of course, is aware of the difficulty of this work. If "the real work" seems impossible to accomplish, it becomes the work of a Bodhisattva, in that it is undertaken out of compassion for all beings and surpasses lifetimes. "[T]he Bodhisattva has passed beyond all thought of individuation, or discrimination, or integration [but] retains in mind a memory of the world's ignorance and suffering, [and] untainted and undisturbed by it, his mind overflowing with compassion, he goes forth in wisdom and love for its emancipation and enlightenment" (Goddard 655). The difficulty of Snyder's goal is acknowledged as early as the *"Amitabha's vow"* section of *Myths and Texts*, where the narrator asks that he "not attain highest perfect enlightenment" if "anyone in my land gets tossed in jail on a vagrancy rap," "loses a finger coupling boxcars," or "can't get a ride hitch-hiking all directions" (45). "Real work" is ultimately emulating Buddha, who "fed himself to tigers": "a mountain-lion / Once trailed me four miles / At night and no gun / It was awful, I didn't want to be ate / maybe we'll change" (*Myths and Texts* 14). Radical effort, because it is so idealistic, is for Snyder a vehicle for spiritual as well as political liberation. "The real work" becomes a movement toward the heavenly, an alignment of human "norms of behavior and ethical rules" with the heavenly "manifestation of reality, of the general state of affairs," the Dharmic "cosmic law, the 'great norm.' " In this way work—that which must be done for nature's salvation—becomes a vehicle for spiritual liberation.

This connection between what must be done and the real work is emphasized again in the *"February"* section of "Six Years" (*The Back Country* 51). Snyder gives a meticulous detailing of daily chores and provides background for the combination of inquiry and statement. This time, however, the reference becomes multifaceted, at once alluding to political, spiritual, and mundane problems:[18]

> what will I do about Liberation.
> 6:30bath
> charcoal.black.the fire part red
> the ash pure white[.] (52)

" 'What is to be done' " as concerns *"Liberation"* seems to be simply take the bath. The question-as-statement "what will I do about *Liberation*" is answered by suggesting what would be done if liberation were not a concern. But the speaker's attention to objects or activities that often makes up a Snyder poem becomes important because these objects and activities *are* the subject of the "real work." Even the phrase "what is to be done" suggests a possible dual reading of all activity, assuming that any "real work" is to be done at all. " 'What is to be done" as question, like the question "what will I do about *Liberation*," becomes, simultaneously with its imperative for radical action, a declaration that *nothing* need be done, since " 'what is to be done' " is being done now: "Knowing that nothing need be done, is where we begin to move from" (*Turtle Island* 102). As Snyder says in "Why Log Truck Drivers Rise Earlier than Students of Zen," "There is no other life" (*Turtle Island* 63).

This aspect of "the real work" is Snyder's view of *resignation* or *acceptance*. In "The Real Work," Snyder describes what he sees while boating in the San Francisco Bay around Alcatraz and Angel Island: "sea-lions and birds, / sun through fog / flaps up and lolling, / looks you dead in the eye" (*Turtle Island* 32). Again, Snyder combines elements as he did in the poems in *Riprap*, so that a literal reading cross-references sea lions and sun, making it seem that "sun through fog" (as well as the sea lions) "flaps up [and] / looks you dead in the eye." Snyder's linking the sea lions and the sun foreshadows the linkage of human and animal activities at the end of the poem, where Snyder offers us another definition of "the real work"—one that seems as applicable to animals as it is to humans: "the real work. / washing and sighing, / sliding by" (32). The "real work" is simply "sliding by," doing what we do whether we be gull, seal, or human; and accepting the moment for what it is. "What will I do about *Liberation*" is to take a bath. The fire functions symbolically, since the ash is burning: "charcoal. black. the fire part red / the ash pure white." Snyder's meaning is that the present moment, "the fire part," lasts only as long as the coal burns, and that with each instant everything burns away. In contrast, the processes of nature, the heavenly, go on, and entry into the ways of the heavenly consists of doing what we are doing. In turn, such entry provides no insight beyond what is actually present, but only offers a series of images or experiences, since "The Way is Not a Way":

> scattered leaves
> sheets of running
> water.
> unbound hair.loose
> planks on shed roofs.
> stumbling down wood stairs
> shirts un done.
> children pissing in the roadside grass. (*Regarding Wave* 51)

"The path is whatever passes" (*Turtle Island* 6); the vehicle of liberation, the " 'what is to be done,' " is acceptance of whatever happens. The nondirectiveness of the Zen approach to enlightenment aims to eliminate intention from action; enlightenment is not achieved through intentionality because intention itself is human projection. Even if an individual engages in radical political action, he or she must recognize the need for resignation and acceptance, and "take the struggle on without the *least* hope of doing any good." The real work involves taking the world for what it is. As such, it also involves knowing that all human tasks are doomed to failure—failure in the human sphere because people are mortal, and possibly failure on the heavenly sphere, because radical work on earth's behalf has no guarantee of success. Yet the tasks of survival that shape human life are the only ones that have any significance. To the extent that modern life is based on rapidly disappearing resources, these tasks will survive if humanity survives: "all of us will come back again to hoe in the ground, or gather wild potato bulbs with digging sticks, or hand-adze a beam. . . . [W] e're never going to get away from that work, on one level or another" (Snyder and Geneson 81–82).

Gathering food and providing sustenance are all we must do to survive. They are real because "the real work is what we really do" (Snyder and Geneson 82), and they offer the fullest alignment of human behavior with "the cosmic law, the 'great norm,' " the "manifestation of reality, of the general state of affairs" that constitutes the *dharma*. This is the real work of Chuang-Tzu's "heavenly": "The *real work* is eating each other, I suppose."

Notes

1. Charles Molesworth, in his book *The Real Work,* uses this phrase to describe Snyder's "establishment of an alternative vision, especially a vision of the role of the poet" which ultimately aims to "[correct] the values of multinational capitalism" by pointing humanity back toward "a total process of nature to which the human species must submit" (3, 9, 6). However, Snyder's articulation of "the real work" also surpasses these political or artistic meanings. The "real work" for Snyder includes a comprehensive practice designed to maximize awareness at all levels—the mundane, the political, and the spiritual. It conveys patterns of intention or attention that link it with spiritual *practice,* with a *resistance* to preconditioned perceptions or understandings, and with ultimate *acceptance* of the First Noble Truth—that existence is suffering.

2. "The mercy of the West has been social revolution; the mercy of the East has been individual insight into the basic self/void. They are both contained in the traditional three aspects of the dharma path: wisdom (*prajna*), meditation (*dhyana*), and morality (*sila*). Wisdom is intuitive knowledge of the mind of love and clarity that lies beneath one's ego-driven anxieties and aggressions. Meditation is going into the mind to see this for yourself—over and over again, until it becomes the mind you live in. Morality is bringing it back out in the way you live, through personal example and responsible action, ultimately toward the true community (sangha) of 'all beings'" (*Earth House Hold* 92).

3. According to Patrick D. Murphy, Snyder had actually completed his second book, *Myths and Texts,* before the first, *Riprap.* For Murphy, however, this very fact demonstrates the extent to which the poems in *Riprap* represent Snyder's finding of his true voice, because *Myths and Texts* displays a Modernist style that recalls Pound and Eliot more than Asian or Amerindian influences (Murphy *Understanding* 22).

4. According to Snyder, the image of being "caught . . . / between heaven and earth" actually reflects the end of Tu Fu's last poem. However, the trope is a common Chinese formulaic description of the human condition. Personal interview with Gary Snyder. April 22, 1988.

5. Snyder defines meditation as "one kind of erasure of the self," referring to it as a state "where the conscious mind temporarily relinquishes its self-importance" ("Craft Interview" 34).

6. See Snyder's comments on the shaman in "The Yogin and the Philosopher": "The shaman speaks for wild animals, the spirits of plants, the spirits of mountains, of watersheds. He or she sings for them. They sing through him. . . . In the shaman's world, wilderness and the unconscious become analogous: he who knows and is at ease in one, will be at home in the other" (*The Old Ways* 12).

7. For a sense of the poems in *Riprap* as "wandering," see Robertson 52–59. Robertson claims that some of the poems written at this time "take us along on a trail in the quite literal sense of narrating a hike" and points out that at least one of the poems "narrates a 'hike' that takes place wholly within the mind" (55). This sense of wandering and discovery seems applicable to most of the poems in *Riprap*, since they all seem to involve discovery of the unknown.

8. For an in-depth discussion of practice as spiritual discipline in Snyder's life and work, see Murphy (*Literature, Nature, and Other* 97–110). Murphy links practice to process and describes Snyder's evolving practice in relation to Dogen's "Mountains and Waters Sutra."

9. Cf. Snyder's description of practice as "Meditation, devotion, dharma-studies, cause-and-effect studies, chopping wood and carrying water, and more meditation yet" (Ingram et al. 25).

10. In "Poetry and the Primitive" Snyder defines breath as "the outer world coming into one's body" and "With pulse . . . the source of our inward sense of rhythm" (*Earth House Hold* 123).

11. Murphy points out that "Fire in the Hole" shows how "[e]xertion leads to liberation," but adds that "the freedom is relative, a pause before the resumption of labor. Both are part of universal energy transfer" (*Understanding Gary Snyder* 79).

12. For comments connecting *zazen* and hunting, see Snyder and Chowka 107.

13. From this perspective, one must recall the Zen Buddhist perception that "[e]arth, water, fire, wind, space *and consciousness* are the elements out of which everything is traditionally said to be composed" (italics added) (Hoshin 67).

14. In this light it is interesting to view Snyder's poem "T-2 Tanker Blues" (*Riprap* 27–28) as a poetic argument with Robinson Jeffers, a poet who provided an early significant impetus to Snyder's own writing. In fact, Robert M. Torrance includes Jeffers as one of the "Western" poets that "[e]choes" in Snyder's writings (268). In "T-2 Tanker Blues" Snyder presents the typically Jeffersian perspective of "inhuman" nature and "man, inhuman man" and decides that "I will not cry Inhuman & think that makes us small and nature great, we are, enough, and as we are." Along with the philosophical argument, we see Snyder experimenting with Jeffers' prosody, while also parodying it through interjections of personal catastrophe more appropriate to Ginsberg's style than to that of Jeffers.

15. Snyder elsewhere explains this statement as bearing on the perceptions of the functions of human work discussed earlier. Snyder explains the origin and significance of this phrase:

Nanao Sakaki once said, "No need to survive"—just as we were bundling our leaflets and lacing our boots to do some ecological political excercises [*sic*]. Why this apparent paradox? Quite simple—it's the same as Dogen's instructions 'Cast body away, cast mind away.' The human world is brought to this pass by an all-too-effective survival consciousness, which breeds anthropocentrism, ethnocentrism, nationalism, parochial localism, and other assorted self-centered uselessly narrow notions of identity. Throwing away these narrow notions of membership helps us to join the mammal world, the vertebrate world, the world of all animals, the world of plants and lichens as well, the world of rocks, sand, clouds, and glaciers, the world of space, the world of emptiness" (Snyder and Woods 201).

16. In his discussion of this poem, Whalen-Bridge describes both its "anti-dualistic dualism" and its "undualistic dualism," meaning by the first that the poem "takes a stance against duality or dualistic thinking," and by the second that the poem recognizes that "dualism is part of this world no less than anything else" (206–7). For Whalen-Bridge, these characteristics indicate the poem's failure as "right speech," or "not lying or not saying true things out of an intent to harm" (202). The rightly illustrated dualities of the poem point to the difficulties of poeticizing political resistance in a context of nonduality, especially considering Snyder's own closeness to the short-haired "1950s-style" world of the bar. Perhaps the issue here is the seductiveness of the simplicity of presumably unthinking acceptance of the redneck status quo, and the subsequent need Snyder feels to resist this familiar world.

17. The terms *ecosystem cultures* and *biosphere cultures* appear in Snyder's "The Politics of Ethnopoetics," where he attributes them to Ray Dasmann. "Ecosystem cultures [are] those whose economic base of support is a natural region, a watershed, a plant zone, a natural territory. . . . Biosphere cultures are the cultures that begin with early civilization and the centralized state; are cultures that spread their economic support system out far enough that they can afford to wreck one ecosystem, and keep moving on" (*The Old Ways* 20–21).

18. The "mundane" issue at hand is renewal of a subscription to the journal *Liberation*. Personal interview with Gary Snyder, March 25, 1988.

Works Cited

Burtt, E. A., ed. *The Teachings of the Compassionate Buddha*. New York: Mentor, 1955.

Chuang-Tzu. "Autumn Floods." *The Complete Works of Chuang Tzu*. Trans. Burton Watson. *Terebess Asia Online*. http://terebess.hu/english/chuangtzu.html. June 21, 2004.

Dean, Tim. *Gary Snyder and the American Unconscious*. New York: St. Martin's Press, 1991.

Fischer-Schreiber, Ingrid, Franz-Karl Ehrhard, and Michael S. Diener, eds. *Shambhala Dictionary of Buddhism and Zen*. Trans. Michael H. Kohn. Boston: Shambhala, 1991.

Goddard, Dwight, ed. *A Buddhist Bible*. Boston: Beacon, 1994. Orig. pub. 1938.

Hoshin, Anzan, Sensei. Mountains and Rivers: Zen Teachings on the San Sui Kyo of Dogen Zenji. 2nd ed. Ottawa: White Wind Zen Community, 1990.

Ingram, Kathrine, Barbara Gates, Wes Nisker, and Gary Snyder. "Chan on Turtle Island: a Conversation with Gary Snyder." *Inquiring Mind* (1988) 4.2: 1, 4–5, 25.

James, Simon P. *Zen Buddhism and Environmental Ethics*. Aldershot, UK: Ashgate Publishing Ltd., 2004.

Kerouac, Jack. *Some of the Dharma*. New York: Viking, 1997.

Molesworth, Charles. *Gary Snyder's Vision: Poetry and the Real Work*. Columbia: University of Missouri Press, 1983.

Murphy, Patrick D. *Literature, Nature, and Other: Ecofeminist Critiques*. Albany: State University of New York Press, 1995.

———. *A Place for Wayfaring: The Poetry and Prose of Gary Snyder*. Corvallis: Oregon State University Press, 2000.

———. *Understanding Gary Snyder*. Columbia: University of South Carolina Press, 1992.

Parkinson, Thomas. "The Poetry of Gary Snyder." *The Southern Review* (1968) 4.3: 616–632.

Robertson, David. "Gary Snyder Riprapping in Yosemite, 1955." *American Poetry* (1984) 2.1: 52–59.

Seager, Richard Hughes. *Buddhism in America*. New York: Columbia University Press, 1999.

Snyder, Gary. *Axe Handles*. San Francisco: North Point Press, 1983.

———. *The Back Country*. New York: New Directions, 1968.

———. *Earth House Hold*. New York: New Directions, 1969.

———. "Craft Interview." *The Real Work: Interviews & Talks 1964–1979*. Ed. Wm. Scott McLean. New York: New Directions, 1980. 31–43.

———. *Myths and Texts*. New York: New Directions, 1978.

———. *The Old Ways*. San Francisco: City Lights Books, 1977.

———. *Regarding Wave*. New York: New Directions, 1970.

———. *Riprap, & Cold Mountain Poems*. San Francisco: Grey Fox Press, 1965.

———. *Turtle Island*. New York: New Directions, 1974.

Snyder, Gary, and Paul Geneson. "The Real Work." *The Real Work: Interviews & Talks 1964–1979*. 55–82.

Snyder, Gary, and Keith Lampe. "*The Berkeley Barb Interview.*" The Real Work: Interviews & Talks 1964–1979. 7–14.

Snyder, Gary, Lew Welch, and Philip Whalen. *On Bread & Poetry: A Panel Discussion with Gary Snyder, Lew Welch & Philip Whalen*. Ed. Donald Allen. Bolinas, CA: Grey Fox Press, 1977.

Snyder, Gary, and Phil Woods. "An Interview with Gary Snyder." *Northwest Review* (1984) 22.1–2: 200–6.

Torrance, Robert M. "Gary Snyder and the Western Poetic Tradition." *Gary Snyder: Dimensions of a Life*. Ed. Jon Halper. San Francisco: Sierra Club Books, 1990. 263–74.

Watts, Alan W. *The Way of Zen*. New York: Vintage, 1957.

Whalen-Bridge, John. "Gary Snyder's Poetic of Right Speech." *Sagetrieb* 9: 1–2 (1990): 201–14.

Chapter 4

"Listen and Relate"

Buddhism, Daoism, and Chance in the Poetry and Poetics of Jackson Mac Low

Jonathan Stalling

"Poetry expresses the emotional truth of the self. A craft honed by especially sensitive individuals, it puts metaphor and image in the service of song. Or at least that's the story we've inherited from Romanticism, handed down for over 200 years in a caricatured and mummified ethos—and as if it still made sense after two centuries of radical social change." With this statement, Craig Dworkin begins his introduction to the *UBU Web Anthology of Conceptual Poetry*,[1] but Dworkin asks, "what would a non-expressive poetry look like. . . . One in which the substitutions at the heart of metaphor and image were replaced by the direct presentation of language itself, with "spontaneous overflow" supplanted by meticulous procedure and exhaustively logical process? In which the self-regard of the poet's ego were turned back onto the self-reflexive language of the poem itself?" Dworkin and his co-editor Kenneth Goldsmith are themselves well-known "conceptual poets," known for resituating, recycling, or re-purposing expended language forms (past online chat rooms, newspapers, etc.) as poetry in order to challenge the romantic foundations of contemporary poetry nearly a century after the art world first encountered the conceptual artworks of Marcel Duchamp.[2] Yet most poets who work out of the conceptual tradition would recognize Jackson Mac Low as the father of these strains of experimental poetry, since he was the first American poet to explore the dynamic possibilities of chance operations in the composition of poetry.[3] Difficult, disjunctive, always unexpected, his body of work reveals a sustained and complex engagement with varieties and levels of chance that range from randomized textual production to intuitively composed works. Mac Low also developed one of the most sophisticated and influential Buddho-Daoist poetics of the twentieth century. Indeed, Mac Low's critique of the lyrical, expressive "I" is a precedent for so-called LANGUAGE poetry years before the rise of poststructuralist theory.

Of course, Mac Low was by no means the only poet experimenting with Buddhism and poetry after World War II. After all, the American occupation of Japan, combined with the gradual lifting of the various anti-Asian immigration laws, not only increased immigration and travel across the Pacific, but also marked a new period of intense cultural migrations. As Buddhism and Romanticism both influenced the "Beat Generation" of poets, concepts like "emptiness" and "no self" began to erode the naturalization of the "expressive self" and the autonomous "I" in the work of many other poets of this period. Snyder's use of classical Chinese aesthetics (as understood vis-à-vis Japanese Zen) to alter and ultimately minimize subjective expression in many of his poems; Joan Kyger's dry wit and complex self-reflexivity to challenge the "self" and gender roles, predating post-structuralist feminism; and Phillip Whalen's notion of poetry as that which "wrecks the mind" or "graphs the mind in motion"—these poets' aesthetic strategies and those of others transform what it means to be a poet. Poetry for this generation of Buddhist practitioners is a deliberate philosophical praxis. Yet none of these interventions can claim to be more radical in their challenge to the expressive "I" than the work of Mac Low. Many of his experiments generate texts through chance operations that largely bypass the writer altogether in order to transform poetry itself into a realization of "no-self."

Mac Low often explicitly points to "the Zen Buddhist motive for use of chance (&c) means" as a method to "generate series of 'dharmas' (phenomena/events, e.g., sounds, words, colored shapes) relatively 'uncontaminated' by the composer's 'ego' (taste, constitutional predilections, opinions, current or chronic emotions)."[4] In his short essay, "Buddhism, Art, Practice, Polity," he writes, "Being 'choicelessly aware' is perceiving phenomena—as far as possible-without attachment and without bias. Artworks may facilitate this kind of perception by *presenting* phenomena that are not chosen according to the tastes and predilections of the artists who make them" (177). In the essay, Mac Low traces the origin of Buddhist influence in his work to the early 1950s. At that time, he first encountered Zen in the writing of and personal instruction under Dr. Daisetz Teitaro Suzuki. Throughout the 1940s, he had studied Daoism and the *Book of Changes*, which also played a central role in the chance-generated music of John Cage. In this chapter, I explore the convergence of Buddhism and Daoism in Mac Low's work, and I pay special attention to the way Mac Low uses Buddhist notions of nonduality to achieve a coherent "poetics of no-mind."

Mac Low's Daoism

After 1991,[5] Mac Low tends to emphasize the importance of Buddhist concepts such as "no self" or "choiceless awareness" in his chance-based composition

methods and "non-egoic" poetics. Yet Mac Low's turn toward aleatoric procedures cannot be reduced to his engagement with Buddhism alone, because it
is his earlier engagement with Daoism—specifically the notion of *wuwei* (無
為, nonintervention or noninterference), which he later reinterprets through a
Buddhist viewpoint—that forms the principal philosophical and ethical foundations of his work. In order to understand this particular configuration of
Buddhism and Daoism, however, it is important to understand the singular
Daoist elements that undergird his poetics.

The writer Paul Goodman introduced Mac Low to Daoism around 1945,
and Mac Low introduced Goodman to the anarchist-pacifist group then publishing the magazine *Why?* (called *Resistance* from 1947 to 1954). This was not
a coincidence because Mac Low writes that he and many other anarchist poets
and theorists became increasingly interested in the Daoist principle of *wuwei*.[6]
Mac Low describes *wuwei* in sociopolitical dimensions: "Wu-wei in society
was taken to mean the same as the absence of a central institution exercising
power over the individuals and groups constituting a society, and competing for
power with the central institutions of other societies through such procedures
as diplomacy, covert and open warfare, and economic and political imperialism"
("Some Ways Philosophy has Helped Shape My Work" 3–4). That Mac Low's
reading of *wuwei* as a primarily ethical and sociopolitical concept is notable,
for it is historically accurate that the *Daodejing* (one of the foundational texts
of Daoism) was intended as a political treatise on rulership. And when read as
a sociopolitical text, the *Daodejing*'s two central terms—*ziran* (自然, natural /
self-so) and *wuwei*—assume ethical meanings. *Ziran* means the way in which
the macrocosmic nature of the Dao mysteriously unfolds or becomes (micro-
cosmically) the "itself" of all things, or that all things "become themselves
naturally." This natural unfolding implies that nothing needs additional guidance
or contrivance to become "itself," and, therefore, humans must learn to "step
aside" (*wuwei*) to allow the *ziran* of both themselves and others to "self-become"
without interference.

In his essay " 'It-self-so-ing' and 'Other-ing' in Lao Zi's Concept of Zi Ran,"
Qingjie Wang, by contrasting positive and negative aspects of *ziran*, offers a
more exact reading of the ethical dimension of *ziran*" (237).[7] Wang correlates
the mysterious "self-so-ing" with the positive aspects of *ziran* because it results
in all things "emerging, growing, flourishing, ripening, declining, demising"
naturally; in contrast, he correlates negative aspects with "any kind of coercion,
interference, or oppression of the 'it-self-so-ing' should be reduced, eliminated,
and morally blamed, and that the sphere of 'other-ing' and the other must
be established and respected" (237). For Wang, *wuwei* is nothing more than
a concept to express an ethical, "live-and-let-live" dimension of *ziran*. Wang
writes, "We should understand the true philosophical spirit of Lao Zi's *wuwei*
not only as something refraining or even eliminating the action or the desire of
the action from the agent, but . . . something requiring the agent to recognize

and to have respect for the existence and the distinctness of the recipients of that action, i.e., the existence and distinctness of *the other*" (italics added, 233). It is clear why Mac Low and others supporting a "hands-off," anarchist society would be drawn to such a concept, even if they did not read the ancient Chinese text within its own complex historical context. Framing *ziran* in terms of the mysterious unfolding of both the "I" and the "other" provides insights into the prominent role of both chance and the performer's/reader's autonomy in Mac Low's works.

Regarding his poetry, prose, and performance works composed after 1953, Mac Low writes,

> wu-wei has been exemplified [in my own work] in two principle ways: through aleatoric or chance procedures operative during composition, performance or both; and through composition of works requiring performers or readers to exercise personal choice. Ideally, performances of works of the latter type exemplify or at least act as analogies for libertarian communities in that performers make independent choices throughout each performance while paying close attention to everything they can hear—both the sounds produced by other performers and ambient sounds—and relating very consciously with this perceived aural plenum as well as with the other performers themselves. ("Some Ways" 4)

Mac Low concludes that "the principle of wu-wei amounts in practice to standing out of the way (at least to a significant extent) of processes conceived either as natural or as otherwise transpersonal" ("Some Ways" 4). For Mac Low, there are four different degrees of "standing out of the way" in the writing process: "randomization," "chance generation," "translation," and "reading through."[8] As an expression of Daoist ethics, Mac Low's poetics attempts to relinquish authorial expression. If not entirely bypassing the ego's desire to assert itself, Mac Low at least diminishes the ego's ability to "make choices" by allowing others (such as performers encouraged to improvise) or an otherness (such as various aleatoric mechanisms) to create poetry. The varying degrees of *wuwei* deployed by Mac Low transform poetic praxis from a romantic "expression of the emotional truth of the self" to an emptied space receptive to the unfolding mystery of its own mysterious unfolding (*ziran*) among the *ziran* of others.

Not long after Mac Low studied Buddhism under D. T. Suzuki at Columbia in the early 1950s, he begins to describe his non-egoic work in a more clearly Buddhistic context, which regards the ego as an illusory formation. Possibly, after his exposure to Buddhism, he chose Buddhist rather than Daoist language to undergird his poetics; nevertheless, such a simple explanation does not do justice to the subtle and complex convergence of Buddhism and Daoism in Mac Low's thinking. Suzuki's writing was seminal for many mid-century poets (and long into the 1960s and 1970s).[9] Yet for Mac Low, Suzuki not only introduced him to Buddhism, but as Mac Low tells Allen Ginsberg in a letter, Suzuki remained his principle Buddhist teacher throughout his career, even after having taken refuge under Kalu Rimpoche . . . ("Jackson Mac Low to Allen Ginsberg" 3). Perhaps his continued attachment to Suzuki, long after most poets had moved on to other gurus and teachers, can be traced to Mac Low's close identification with Suzuki's heterocultural presentation of Buddhism, and to his dislike of the "church polity" of most religious organizations (*Beneath a Single Moon* 180). No later teacher would possess the same admixture of Daoism, Chinese Buddhism (Chan and Huayan), and Jungian psychology that became the foundation of Mac Low's aesthetic of "egoless" composition.

When I began my archival research for this chapter, the first thing I wanted to look at in the boxes of his papers held at the University of California, San Diego, was the notebook he used during his classes with Suzuki. The small notebook is still intact but has been burned around the edges, making it quite fragile and (because of his cursive script) fairly difficult to read. Luckily, Mac Low wrote an extensive essay in 1956 based largely on these notes and Suzuki's books, which reveals with great specificity how he came to integrate Daoism and Buddhism. The still unpublished essay, "The Taoist Principle of Wu-Wei as exemplified in Zen Buddhism," was likely written for Suzuki's Columbia class, and despite the fact it reads a bit like a term paper, it shows how Mac Low struggled to create his own synthesis of Daoism and Zen.

The essay begins with Mac Low's discussion of correspondence between himself and Ezra Pound, who had told Mac Low that "Waley's translation of Laotze is a thoroughly dirty book," and "I haven't studied the original text and won't speak of it: the translations show him full of rot in most subversive form." Pound wrote, "The hell of Lao is that some good in his soup conceals the poison" (Mac Low, "The Taoist Principle" 1). Mac Low, who calls Pound a modern Confucian, points to his rejection of Laozi as being fundamentally the same as Han Feizi's (韓非子, 280–233 BCE, Watson), one of the founders of "Legalism" and a famous critic of Daoism and the *Daodejing*. However, Mac Low takes both critiques as a misinterpretation of *wu-wei* meaning "the sapping of the will to action." Mac Low supplies a corrective: "Taken crudely," Mac Low writes, "this condemnation means: 'the believer in Wu-Wei just sits and does nothing' " (1). Mac Low's essay rebuts Pound's criticism and argues that *wu-wei* can be an "active" (yet receptive) rather than a "passive" (and inert) practice. Mac Low follows closely Suzuki's argument in Suzuki's essay "The Zen Doctrine of No Mind." Suzuki bifurcates meditative practices into "dust-wiping" quietism and a "*prajna* producing" or wisdom-producing schools, which unlike "quietism," is capable of leading the practitioner into a powerful realization of *satori*, a Japanese Buddhist term for "lasting awakening" gained through a direct experience of sunyata, or emptiness.[10]

The term *dust-wiping* is an allusion to the *Platform Sutra of the Sixth Patriarch*, where Hui Neng, the Sixth Patriarch of Chan, demonstrates a profound understanding of nonduality and is rewarded with the mind-transmission from the Fifth Patriarch Hong Ren. Mac Low uses the same deconstructive logic as is demonstrated in the sutra. The sutra focuses on a poetry contest between Hui Neng and Hong Ren's most senior student, Shen Xiu, to transform the Daoist notion of *wuwei* into a Buddhist concept of nonduality. When Hong Ren instructs his monks to write a verse (or gatha) encapsulating their understanding of Buddhism, Shen Xiu writes,

> The body is a Bodhi tree,
> the mind a standing mirror bright.
> At all times polish it diligently,
> and let no dust alight.

Hui Neng responds,

> There is no Bodhi-tree
> Nor stand of mirror bright
> Since all is void
> Where can the dust alight?[11]

Upon reading these gathas the next morning, Hong Ren saw that while Shen Xiu's poem demonstrated a strong foundation in Buddhist practice, Hui Neng's dehypostatization (i.e., undoing the tendency to make abstract concepts into seemingly concrete "things") of Shen Xiu's language revealed a still deeper understanding of sunyata. When Hong Ren made Hui Neng the next patriarch, he asked him to move South to teach his understanding of "sudden enlightenment" (*dunwu*). This led to the schism known as the Southern School, which advocated a direct and abrupt engagement with emptiness, in contrast to the Northern School of "gradual enlightenment" (*jianwu*), which placed a greater emphasis on persistent and diligent meditation.

For Shen Xiu, the practice of cleansing the mind is hypostatized by a clear subject–object dichotomy, because both "mind" and "body" are rendered as discrete "things" (a mirror on a stand or a Bodhi tree) as perceived by an external observer. Hui Neng's verse negates these apparent things by abandoning the position of the external observer and speaking from the position of "Suchness" itself. This term in Chinese—*zhenruxing* (真如性, "the real which is like itself") demonstrates that "suchness" merely designates the nature of emptiness itself. All "things" are empty, including the external observer, and therefore nothing can be separate from or be the other to this emptiness. Hence, we have only suchness itself.

Mac Low develops this argument in an original way. He writes,

> when he begins, the Zen student, like anyone else, thinks of real- ity as being fundamentally—outside world and inner "soul" world. To the discriminative intellect, this distinction is fundamental and cannot be over-passed. Therefore a method has to be used whereby the discriminative intellect will wear itself out and a higher intui- tive wisdom (Prajna) comes into action. . . . In this way Wu-Wei becomes an actuality. For where there is no distinction of subject and object, "I" act not at all, and yet I do indeed many actions. I eat breakfast, I rake the courtyard, I break sticks, but not "I" does this, but the underlying Buddha-nature. (13–14)

In this passage, Mac Low transforms *wuwei* from an ethical charge to abstain from interfering with the *ziran* of otherness into an expression of Buddhist non- duality. "I" cannot act because, from the position of ultimate reality, there is no "I" to act. In this way, he blends two radically different philosophical concepts into a single heterocultural foundation; he reveals the illusory nature of self (*wuwo*) while retaining *wuwei* as his ethical foundation. Furthermore, Mac Low refutes Pound's charges by showing how nondualism can turn *wuwei* into both an ontological concept of nonduality and an ethical form of receptive action.

Chance in Mac Low's Work

We now need to explore the idea of chance as an element of Mac Low's aesthetic. Regarding chance, Mac Low writes, "Nonintentional methods both diminish the judgmental activities of the ego and open one to many of the possibilities that one's ego would exclude. . . . They teach one to put one's intentions in abeyance and to accept what is not-I" ("Writing and Practice" 9). Clearly, there are ample intuitive connections between chance, the anarcho- Daoist ethics of *wuwei*, and the Buddhist insistence on the illusory state of the "I." However, there is another common factor that would have brought them together: Carl Jung. For Mac Low, the primary source text and philosophy of chance can be traced to the *Yijing* (*Book of Changes*), and for most Americans (Mac Low included) this book was synonymous with a single edition: Cary F. Bayne's English translation of Richard Wilhelm's German version of the text. The most popular edition (published by Pantheon) has a "Foreword" written by Jung, who explains his notion of "synchronicity" as a key feature of what he refers to as the "Chinese worldview" ("Some Ways" 4). Mac Low apparently accepts this reading of the *Yijing*, pointing out that "events happening at the same time are meaningfully, though 'acausally,' connected" (4). Mac Low believes that composing and performing his poems through chance-generated procedures would make these "acausal" relations apparent. Jung's thinking had already influenced Mac Low's understanding of Buddhism through the work of Suzuki, who uses the Jungian notion that our individual egos are connected to a single collective unconscious—what Suzuki renamed as "no-mind."[12] For both Suzuki and Jung, synchronistic thinking provided an aperture into the "no-mind" or the "collective-unconscious" by revealing the interconnectedness of all consciousness(es).

Mac Low synthesizes these concepts, writing that the *wuwei* he had previously described is the process whereby one replaces the "superficial layers of the psychological unconscious" with "this No-Mind, this Unconscious, which is identical with the Tao itself, . . . the greatest paradox of Taoism and Zen alike." He explains, "by making the No-Mind conscious, one attains to a point of rest in the midst of the flux from which the most direct, spontaneous actions continuously flow" ("Taoist Principle of Wu-Wei"). So important is this discovery of a "conscious no-mind" that Mac Low links it to his most important influences, Duchamp and Cage:

> Allowing this [chance] to happen in works is important. And this has something to do with what in Zen is called the "No Mind," that layer of mind below the Unconscious, the impulses, the instincts, the Id, the deepest deep layer, which is common to all people: the No Mind. [what he calls *Sunyata* viewed as an aspect of mentality]. From the no-mind or from Emptiness, everything arises. And if one can step aside a little bit, one can allow it to manifest itself: that is the important discovery made by people who began working with chance operations, such as Duchamp and especially Cage. (" 'Poetics of Chance' " 8)

Mac Low's Poetry

A series of Mac Low's poems entitled "gathas" demonstrates how he integrates chance, Buddhism, and Daoism. These poems, composed as a series from 1961 through the 1970s of mostly transliterated Buddhist mantras, are arranged on heavy-lined quadrille paper in configurations dictated by chance procedures.[13] Of all of the "gathas," the "Mani Mani Gatha" (Figure 4.1) is the only one to feature the entire mantra (rather than a series of A's, U's, and M's) along the middle horizontal axis, despite the fact that this position and all of the other crossing vertical lines were determined by chance procedures. In this way, Mac Low emphasizes the illusory nature of the "expressive, creative ego."[14]

Although certainly interesting as visual pieces, the "gathas" principally are performance pieces and are published (as is much of Mac Low's work) with detailed performance guidelines, intended to be collectively performed as a "happening." The indeterminacy of Mac Low's chance-based compositional procedure is expanded even further by the freedom Mac Low gives to the performers—to make interpretive choices "in relation" to the choices of others and to the ambient textures of the piece. Although each "gatha" has its own unique compositional method and performance instructions, generally each set of instructions would ask performers to "listen and relate." In a talk given at Naropa in 1975, Mac Low describes the instructions for the "gathas" in some detail:

> I ask the performers simply to "move" from any square to any other square that is adjacent to one of its sides or corners (that is they can move in any direction, horizontal, vertical, or diagonal). Thus each performer follows a path on the plane of the quadrille paper. They can say letter names, such as "M" letter sounds such

Mani-Mani Gatha   1975

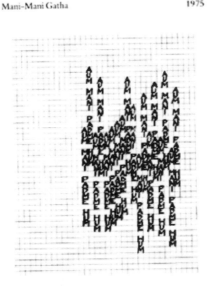

Fig. 4.1. "Mani Mani Gatha."

as "mmmmmmmmmm"; syllables formed by letters adjacent in any
direction(s); or they can say the whole mantram [a familiar variant
of mantra] (they can do that at <u>any</u> time, no matter where they are
on their path). By each person's producing all of these possibilities
at different times in their performance, and by listening very hard
to what everybody is doing (as well as to any other sounds that
are audible where they're performing), any number of people can
perform one of these. . . . A great deal is thus left up to the performers' choices-not only whether to produce letter sounds, letter
names, syllables, words, or whole repetitions of the mantram, but
<u>how</u> to produce or treat these sounds. ("Poetics of Chance" 20)[15]

In the case of the "Mani Mani Gatha," Mac Low directs the performers to
first intone the mantra "two or more times before each jump to a new path, as
well as at the beginning. When not spoken as mantra words, the letters may be
pronounced or named as in any language" (236). In this piece, therefore, the
visual layout and especially the performance guidelines emphasize the mantric
nature of the poem, a fact Mac Low stresses by carefully detailing the different Sanskrit and Tibetan pronunciations of each phoneme: "The Mani Mani
Gatha" is based on "AUM MANI PADME HUM (pronounced in Sanskrit
Ohm Mahnee Pudmay Ho¯om, and in Tibetan *UM Mahnee Paymay Ho¯ong*),
the mantra of the Boddhisattva Avalokiteshvara [Ch: Guanyin, Tib: Chenrezig,
Ja: Kannon], the Great Compassionate One" (*Representative Works* 236). His
request—that performers use these pronunciation guidelines when intoning the
Mantra or any letter as "mantric sound"—accentuates how for Mac Low these
particular sounds hold specific, psycho-physiological significance "as sounds":
"AUM embodies the indwelling principle of all being—the Tao. . . . [16] HUM
is 'limitless reality embodied within the limits of individual being.' "[17] These
"meanings" are not merely representational but more importantly "performative"
in that Mac Low and other Buddhists believe that mantric sounds "enact" or
activate various energies and effects beyond referential signification. In fact,
some sounds point to the absence of referential signification as the source of
their power: this absence, a marriage of "emptiness" and sound. "Mantra" is
derived from two Sanskrit words: "man-" is derived from "*manas*" or "mind";
and the second syllable, "-tra," is derived from "*trail*," meaning "free from."
Thus, "mantra" can be interpreted as "to free from the mind." As sounds and
not signs, these "seed syllables" often are not translated, as one cannot translate
a particular, physically distinct configuration of sound waves into another.[18] In
Mac Low's "gathas," any notion of semantic value is thereby subordinated to
the language's visual and aural texture (its fundamental materiality).

Mac Low emphasizes the sonorous over the semantic quality of each "seed
syllable" to actualize these meanings as so-called pure sound. He does this by

disrupting the conventional clustering of letters (into words) and words (into sentences) through the use of the quadrille paper's atomizing effect and the disruptive potential of multidirectional writing. Moreover, asking the performers to focus on each letter as a "sound" after having completed a reading of the mantra further liberates the sonorous from its customary subordination to signification. Yet Mac Low takes this liberation of sound from the phrase even further by requesting instrumentalists and trained vocalists to "translate" each letter as tones in the following pitch classes:

A=AbE=EbI=Db O=Gb/F# S=Eb/D#D=Cb
D=DbH=BbM=GbP=Fb (*Representative Works* 237)

Assigning notes to letters promotes what Mac Low continually calls "bare attention" to the ambient sounds. The term *bare attention* often is paired with "choiceless awareness" by Mac Low. "Choiceless awareness" is linked to the chance-based procedures in composing much of his poetry, whereas "bare attention" is usually reserved for his performance works. Both of these terms refer to key concepts associated with vipassana, or "insight meditation" (a form today more commonly referred to as *mindfulness*[19]). Vipassana focuses on the twofold process known in Pali as *satipatthana,* where *sati* is a prelingual (i.e., nondiscriminatory) mindfulness and *patthana* is the foundation that makes this mindfulness possible. Thus, "bare attention" reflects all phenomena, including the mind encountering the phenomena, without leading to speculation, discriminatory thoughts, or judgments (what Mac Low calls "choices").[20]

However, giving our "bare attention" to language is derailed by our automatic sorting through the interplay of phonemic differences that, through untold layers of contextualization, give rise to discriminatory meanings. "Discrimination," in this sense, is how language functions, but makes "nondiscriminatory" mindfulness of language difficult if not impossible to attain. Although one can bring attention to the sonorous quality of the voice, the sounds that physically constitute it are almost immediately absorbed, even lost, by the moment of meaning-making that renders sounds unnoticed by the listener. Yet Mac Low's gathas do not allow the voice to fall away into what is "said" in terms of content.[21] In this way, sonorous language/ the "voicing of poetry" mobilizes stimuli (e.g., physical, psychological, emotional) that cannot be stated through referential language but must be felt or experienced. In the gathas and many of the other radically disjunctive works, the sounds-letters and words point us toward places where words cannot follow.

Mac Low's nonreferential language offers the reader aesthetic qualities unmatched by other discursive poems: language as pure sonorous excess, inviting the audience to dissolve the "I" into a space in which listening occurs. Speaking of Cage's belief that sounds unhinged from their referential meaning can be a "skillful means"[22] that aids one toward enlightenment, Mac Low writes, "I think he views the experience of composing, performing, and hearing such works as being equally conducive to the arousal of *prajña*—intuitive wisdom/ energy, the essence/seed of the enlightened state—by allowing the experience of sounds perceived in themselves, 'in their suchness,' rather than as means of communication, expression, or emotional arousal or as subordinate elements in a structure" ("Writing and Practice" 2).[23] Clearly, Mac Low's gathas are an attempt to do just this. Mac Low's insistence that performers not only to "listen" (the directive of "bare attention"), but also to "relate" to the phenomena encountered by adjusting to rather than interfering with "otherness" recalls his Anarcho-Daoist ethics of *wuwei*. So although the gathas are certainly "Buddhist" poems, they nevertheless reveal a unique combination of chance, Buddhist metaphysics, and Daoist ethics.[24]

In order to really "get" these gathas, I perform them with my students at the University of Oklahoma by strictly following Mac Low's guidelines. Neither the "bare attention" given to sound itself nor learning to integrate the self into a group of "more than I" requires a direct experience of both. Jerome Rothenberg describes his experience performing a gatha:

> I got the "idea" early along, but really *got* the idea sometime mid-60's in a performance of one of the "gathas." . . . The text, as I remember, was the Japanese Buddhist prayer or mantra, *namu amida butsu* ("praise Amida Buddha"), a repetitious, quite familiar formula of Pure Land Buddhism. Mac Low's directive, as it would be thereafter, was to *listen! Listen! Listen!* & to observe & interact while "listening intensely to everything in the performance & in the environment"—though our inclination back then was more likely to take his "anarchism" in the colloquial sense as each man/ or woman for him/or herself. It didn't matter that night. The old Japanese words, resonant from earlier readings, & the recognizable *aum* as mantric axis line that held the piece together, appeared & then disappeared as phonemes & syllables began to move around the space in which we had dispersed ourselves. I had never so clearly heard or felt my own voice or Voice Herself as carried by the others—the separation & recombination of sounds that related back to a fixed string of sounds & to a meaning that I didn't reach but that I knew was there. It was something very old & very new: Jackson's arrangement & innovation but vibrant with the source itself. (*Representative Works* X)[25]

Rothenberg's idea of something both new and ancient is important, as Mac Low's work is not simply a public performance of Buddhist mantra, but a transformation of mantra into something new through a fresh application of his heterocultural Buddhist and Daoist principles.

Quasi-Intentional Poetry

In a letter to Allen Ginsberg in 1991, Mac Low writes that he had combined Ginsberg's "First Word Best Word" idea (based on a spontaneous mindfulness of one's thoughts) with his own chance-based procedures. The product of this welding creates what Mac Low calls an "intuitive method" of inscription that mixes computer-generated automations with his own writing. He gives the examples of DIASTEXT & DIASTEX4, which are "automations of my own diastic text-generation method, developed in 1963," the outcomes of which he edits to make his "intuitive" poems. He writes, "Thus as in the nucleic poetry[26] and the performance pieces composed since 1960, I carry on & encourage (in the case of other performers) a dialog between the nonintentional and the intentional: I not only use my own intuitive poetry as a source; I also edit (following certain limiting rules that prevent nullification of the nonintentionality of the mediating methods) the result of the computer programs" ("Mac Low to Ginsberg" 3).

Mac Low explains to Ginsberg that "this dialog between the intentional and the nonintentional has been encouraged by my understanding of Kegon Buddhism, as taught in his books and classes by D. T. Suzuki, which emphasizes the interpenetration of the individual and the universal (*Dharmakāya*) and the transparency and interpenetration of all dharmas" (2). The interdependent origination of all phenomena understood through the metaphor of "Indra's Net" grants Mac Low an ontological basis for working with or through the individual ego while simultaneously revealing the illusory nature of the ego forms themselves. The *wuwei* ideal of wholly "getting out of the way" thus gradually is phased out in Mac Low's work the longer he studied Buddhism. In a lecture Mac Low gave in 2001 at the University of Arizona, entitled "My Writingways," he describes his shift away from chance and deterministic procedures as a growth in his Buddhist awareness. He writes,

> It was only later, after years of studying and irregularly practicing Buddhism, as well as years of utilizing such artmaking methods, that I realized that using those methods is as egoic as other ways of making artworks—that, in short, there are no shortcuts to "enlightenment" . . . an understanding of a self—even though the term is ultimately meaningless—is only attained by working *through* what each of us thinks of as "my self," not by attempting to evade or abolish it. . . . Buddhism had led me to them but no longer provided me with justifications or motivations for utilizing them. (xvii)

The convergence of Buddhism, Daoism, chance; his later, mixed compositional methods, which include a mixture of intentional or "direct" writing; and non-intentional or procedural practices (e.g., "Pieces o' Six" and the "Twenties" and "Forties")—all these elements should be read not as a refutation of his Buddhist poetics, but as an evolution in his career. Mac Low undergoes a fundamental shift in the configuration of East-Asian philosophies that make up his transpacific poetics. In short, Buddhism was not the impetus to "get out of the way" or "evade" the ego from the beginning—Daoism was. These two systems of thought could not be separated early in his career, given the hybrid Buddho-Daoist nature of Suzuki's Buddhism and Mac Low's own interpretive frame, saturated by Anarcho-Daoist ethics. As Mac Low's work shifted from a pure expression of *wuwei* toward an investigation of the illusory nature of ego, he grows as a Buddhist, but becomes increasingly uneasy about the contradictions of the Buddho-Daoist convergence in his early work. Although notions of "non-egoic" composition may have fallen away throughout Mac Low's career, the undergirding Daoist ethics that energized his first adoption of *wuwei* did not. He finally found a way to unify the two in his constant request that we "listen and relate": "listen" to bring nonjudgmental attention to phenomena; "relate" without interfering with the *ziran* of otherness.

By exploring the Asian nexus at the base of Mac Low's critique of "lyrical I" decades before the advent of postmodern theory, we can give proper credit to the influence of East Asian philosophy on avant-garde poetry and poetics of the last quarter of the twentieth century. The historically specific notions of "no self," "*wuwei*," and "mantric sound" can be seen as another chapter in the ongoing American transformations of Asian philosophical concepts as well. Mac Low never settled into a Buddhist community during his lifetime because he had a fundamental disagreement with the hierarchy of most Buddhist communities. He writes, "I understand that knowledge confers authority in the context of teaching, but its extension to the political constitution of the groups within which it is exercised seems entirely uncalled for. . . . Religious authoritarianism is all but ubiquitous, it is especially painful to experience it within the religion of compassion and wisdom" ("Buddhism, Art, Practice, Polity" 180).[27] Mac Low's fusion of Daoist ethics and Buddhist metaphysics is unique. Although Daoist elements are often at play in American poetry, Mac Low's fusion arrives by way of his own search for an ethical poetics capable on the one hand of creating more generous and open social engagements, while on the other, of serving as a soteriological aid in the pursuit of enlightenment.[28]

Notes

1. This online anthology and its introduction can be found at http://ubu.com/concept/.

2. Of course, the work represented in the *UBU Web Anthology* is by no means the only poetry to challenge the romantic, expressive confines of what Charles Bernstein calls "Mainstream Verse Culture," as we can point to a long tradition of radical American poetics that foreground the materiality of language in ways that problematize the notion of poetry as a transparent window into the soul of the poet (one could point to poets as early as Gertrude Stein and Luis Zukofsky). But the methods most often associated with "conceptual poetry" can be primarily traced back to the work of radicals like John Cage and Jackson Mac Low. The so-called Language School here in the states and the *L'Ouvoir de littérature potentielle* (The Workshop for Potential Literature, or OuLiPo for short) in France also owe a debt to these writers.

3. In Mac Low's essay/talk "Poetics of Chance and the Politics of Spontaneous Simultaneity, or the Sacred Heart of Jesus," he writes that "Duchamp was also the first 'conceptual artist' in the present sense, and many of his pieces were the ideas themselves of making such works. There is an element of concept art in my own work, although I'm usually as much or more interested in the actual sounds and sights than in the generative ideas" (6–7). Furthermore, he differentiates his "chance" derived work from other traditions: "Dada and Surrealists called this 'objective hazard.' I call it 'systematic chance' to distinguish it from the kind of chance that's directly related to human impulse, such as that used by Jackson Pollock, the painter (which he described as using 'impulsive chance'). He then goes on to describe the difference between his work and William Burroughs' method of 'cut-up' which he called 'unsystematic chance.' "

4. Mac Low, "Museletter," The L=A=N=G=U=A=G=E Book 26-7.

5. After the publication of the anthology *Beneath a Single Moon* and the volume *Talking Poetics From Naropa Institute: Annals of the Jack Kerouac School of Disembodied Poetics,* both of which included essays on his Buddhist poetics, Mac Low tends to foreground his Buddhist practice a great deal more than his previous engagements with Daoism.

6. Mac Low goes so far as to say that the concept of wu-wei "came to permeate the thinking of New York anarchists and pacifists in the late 1940's and early 1950's" ("Philosophy" 3). Mac Low's earliest reference to Daoism appears to be in a review he wrote of Goodman's book *The Facts of Life* in which he mentions Goodman's interpretation of the *Daodejing*. See "Fastidiousness and Love, a Review of *The Facts of Life, by Paul Goodman*. Box 68, Folder 29. Early correspondence between Goodman and Mac Low dates to the early 1940s. See Box 17, folder 1.

7. He locates the positive examples of *ziran* in Chapters 25 and 51 of the Daodejing and negative readings of the concept in Chapters 17, 23, 64.

8. For those not familiar with his work it might be helpful to briefly define these different compositional methods: Mac Low defines "randomization" as compositional methods where all probabilities are equal (which he would construct using computer-generated randomizing programs). "Chance-generated" works use things like the *Yijing*, coins, dice, or other chance-based tools to compose works. "Translation" for Mac Low did not usually mean an attempt to transfer meanings from one language to another but methods whereby "the possibilities in one universe of discourse are selected among by the occurrence of certain features in another universe of discourse." He gives the example of pitches, for instance, being translated into words. The compositional methods he calls "reading through" entails reading through a source text and "finding successive words, phrases, or other linguistic units that have the letters of a certain word, phrase, etc, in specific places. (The latter is called a "seed" or "index" string.)" Mac Low breaks

these methods into two further categories called acrostic (which began using in May 1960) and Diastic methods (which he began using three years later). When composing an acrostic, one reads through the source text until one finds certain kinds of linguistic units that begin with the seed string as their initial letters. In Diastic works (or spelling-through) methods, one finds "linguistic units that have the letters of the seed string in corresponding places." (For example, the first letter of the seed string will be the first letter of the first linguistic unit taken from the source, the second letter of the seed will be the second letter of the next source unit, etc.) Mac Low distinguishes between these groups of practices based on the degree to which "choice" is involved in the writing and performance processes, but also states that "what both reading through and translation methods have in common with chance operations and randomization is that both involve a large degree of nonintentionality: They all diminish the value-judging activity of the ego and increase the activity that accepts the rest of creation." These notes and others can be found in the unpublished essay "Writing and Practice."

    9. Interestingly for many American poets (especially Joanne Kyger, Diane DiPrima, and Phillip Whalen), Suzuki Roshi, the abbot of the San Francisco Zen Center, played a still greater role. The two Suzuki's introduced two different schools of Japanese Zen: Suzuki Roshi brought the Soto lineage to the West Coast with its emphasis on "just sitting," and although Suzuki was not a priest or monk, his work leaned far closer to the Renzai tradition, with its emphasis on koans and language play. See Fields.

    10. Suzuki would go on to state that "Satori is the raison d'être of Zen, without which Zen is no Zen. Therefore every contrivance, disciplinary and doctrinal, is directed towards satori" (*An Introduction to Zen Buddhism*, Rider & Co., 1948). Mac Low quotes this line in his essay "Taoist Principle of Wu-Wei."

    11. Mac Low quotes Suzuki's translation. See Suzuki 157.

    12. If not ironic, there is a lovely cyclical nature to this transpacific synergy, for Jung's notion of a collective unconscious is itself largely a reformulation of the Hindu notion of Brahman, Atman, and Maya. In the Hindu worldview (specifically Advaita Vedanta), our individual egos are like waves on the surface of the sea; we appear as separate autonomies, when our true reality—hidden by Maya or a veil of illusion—is none other than the sea itself, Brahman. Of course, this notion, called in recent Buddhology "gharba" or "womb matrix," is a key concept of Yogacara Buddhism, which forms the basis of the monistic notion that all phenomena are none other than manifestations of "Buddha Nature" or "Thusness," a concept central to much East-Asian Buddhism including Suzuki's Zen. Therefore, it is easy to see why Jungian principles would appeal to Suzuki and vice versa. In terms of Mac Low's poetics, however, it is important to note nexus because it can help explain how paying greater attention to "synchronistic": Privileging so-called "chance" over causal logic might help liberate oneself from the confines of ego by revealing the untold connections that permeate us in and through the illusory membranes of the egoic "waves" we call our "selves." For more on the connections between Jung and Indic thought see Jung. For more on Yogacar Buddhism see Lusthaus.

    13. In Mac Low's essay "The Sacred Heart" he describes the procedures he used to compose this poem: "Since one of these three A's must coincide with each of the A's in the Aum-Axis, I used a die to determine which one would do so in each case (a "one" or a "four" would determine that the A of "AUM" woud coincide with an A on

the axis; a "two" or "five," the A of "MANI"; a "three" a "six," the A of "PADME"). And he threw dice for the remaining letters as well choosing odds or evens to decide the placements of the U's, M's, etc."

14. The first drafts of the "Mani Mani Gatha" from 1961 have a base cord of "AUM," whereas the one published in *Representative Works* (shown in text) we have the full mantra. See box 47 folder 15.

15. He discusses both the composition and performance of the "Mani Mani Gatha" in great detail from pages 18–21 of this talk.

16. We might take notice of the appearance of the word "Tao," which creeps into not only Mac Low, but also Blofeld's description of Buddhism. For a good introduction to and deconstructive critique of John Blofeld's Buddhist writings see Wright. Wright re-enters Blofeld's transpacific imaginary through a self-reflexive reading practice. While liberating Zen from Blofeld's romantic Orientalism, Wright has, perhaps too tightly contained Blofeld's transpacific imaginary under an unnecessarily narrow sign. Implicit in Western literary criticism's deployment of deconstructive readings is a search for a kind of truth, the more correct reading. And although often such re-readings are "better" in the sense that they are more textured, open, and capable of further meaning productions, this is not always the case. Wright's analysis is a bit too theoretically "clean," too few loose ends to be chucked back into translation's alchemical furnace.

17. There also is one "Gatha" that is composed wholly of "AUM." See box 47 folder 16. In the collection *Representational Works,* Mac Low also offers a translation of "MANI PADME" as "the jewel of the lotus," which he says signifies "the eternal in the temporal, the Buddha within each sentient being," but often he does not offer the semantic meanings of his mantric Gathas (237). Because this is one of the most popular mantras in Asia, there are many different interpretations of the various affective power or energy of each syllable, but these are not necessarily pertinent to my discussion (e.g., see http://dharma-haven.org/tibetan/meaning-of-om-mani-padme-hung.htm).

18. See Frits Staal's *Rules without meaning: ritual, mantras, and the human sciences.*

19. The rise of "mindfulness" (sati) as an important aspect of Western Buddhist practice can be traced to the work of Hanh. Hanh is the Dharma Teacher of the Lâm Tế Dhyana school (Japanese: Rinzai) school of Zen, but has combined "insight meditation" methods from Theravada Buddhism, and ideas from Western psychology to form his own Westernized form of Buddhism, but he is not alone. Other Western teachers like Jack Kornfield, Jon Kabat-Zinn, Joseph Goldstein, and Sharon Salzberg all have helped popularize "mindfulness" as an aspect of their practice and teachings.

20. To quote from the Pali, "*Sati paccu patthita hoti yavadeva nanamatthaya patisatimatthaya*" (in order to reflect, we have to establish mindfulness and in order to understand things clearly as they are we have to establish mindfulness, which is bare attention). Venerable Dhammasami "*Mindfulness Meditation Made Easy,* 1999, Ch. 6 par 1. http://web.ukonline.co.uk/buddhism/dmasam2a.htm.

21. Levinas' distinction between the "saying and the said" can be very useful here to understand not only the difference between sound and the semantic significations they initiate, but to the ethics of hearing sound, and of offering sound to the Other, without having to redomesticate all language into "meanings" mastered by the subject, but left in the pure vocative as a call to the Other. An ethical language for

Levinas, then, is one of antecedence and address: "While language cannot touch the Other, it reaches the Other by calling upon, commanding or obeying him" (Levinas 62). He continues, "The other is maintained and confirmed in his heterogeneity as soon as one calls upon him, be it only to say to him that one cannot speak to him, to classify him as sick, to announce to him his death sentence; at the same time as grasped, wounded, outraged, he is 'respected.' The invoked is not what I comprehend: he is not under a category" (68).

22. *Skillful Means* or *Upaya* (full Sanskrit: *upaya-kaus*halya) is a term in Mahayana Buddhism that emphasizes a practitioner's use of a specific methods or techniques in order to aid in the cessation of suffering and introduce others to the dharma.

23. On an interesting note, the "Platform Sutra" discussed earlier mentions that the Sixth Patriarch of Chan, Hui Neng, actually became enlightened prior to his entering the monastery just after hearing the resonating sound of his knife hitting a hollow bamboo tree. It was this sound that "woke him." See the "Platform Sutra." One of the standard translations is Yampolsky's.

24. Although I see the influence of Daoism in the socio-ethical sphere of the Gathas, Mac Low turns to his understanding of Tantric Buddhism as a source of inspiration for these works. He writes, "Another Buddhist consideration that influence the move to performers' decision making during performances comes from Tantric (e.g., Tibetan) Buddhism: that highly conscious work with and through the ego (as against its uncritical "expression") can lead to enlightenment. Attentively making choices in a communal performance situation seems such a conscious working with and through the ego" ("Writing and Practice" 7). In the end, I do not see any reason why both Buddhism and Daoism could play a role in this element of his poetry.

25. The reader can listen to an MP3 of Mac Low's "Black-Tarantula-Crsswrd-Gatha" being performed at http://media.sas.upenn.edu/pennsound/authors/Mac-Low/Mac-Low-Jackson_8-Voice-Blck-Tarantula-Crsswrd-Gatha_NY_11-25-73.mp3.

26. Of nucleic poetry, Mac Low writes in an interview with Gil Ott: "I began using the 'Nucleic Method' in 1961, In making the FROM NUCLEI poems, the NUCLEI FOR SIMONE, and some other 1961 texts. . . . I just used aleatoric means to draw words from their lists, which was in one of my dictionaries. That's when I began working freely between chance-given pivotal points ("nuclei"). Starting with Ogden and Richards' list, I'd let random digits draw a large list, and then often make a smaller list from the larger one, also by means of random digits, for use in any particular poem." http://nineteen-sixty.blogspot.com/2007/11/most-basic-words-in-english.html. Also see the essays in THE PRONOUNS for more on his "nucleic poems."

27. Of course, one might look again to the authoritative nature of Mac Low's "performance guidelines" as a strange paradox in his thinking: to bring bare attention to phenomena and to not intervene on the alterity of otherness, we must be told to "listen and relate" to prohibit our habitual desire to express our "selves."

28. Although I can find little to suggest a direct link between Allen Ginsberg's notions of matric sound or the influence of specific works like "Wichita Vortex Sutra" on Jackson Mac Low's work, nevertheless, reading these American Buddhist poets in relation to one another would be both an important and worthwhile exercise. For more on Allen Ginsberg's Buddhist poetics see Tony Trigilio's excellent pioneering book.

Works Cited

Dolar, Mladen. *A Voice and Nothing More*. Boston: Massachusetts Institute of Technology Press, 2006.

Dworkin, Craig, and Kenneth Goldsmith, eds. *UBU Web Anthology of Conceptual Poetry.* http://ubu.com/concept/ October 29, 2008.

Fields, Rick. *How the Swans Came to the Lake: A Narrative History of Buddhism in America*. Boston & London: Shambhala, 1981.

Huang, Yunte. *Transpacific Displacement: Ethnography, Translation, and Intertextual Travel in Twentieth-Century American Literature*. Berkeley: University of California Press, 2002.

———. *Transpacific Imaginations: History Literature, Counterpoetics*. Cambridge, MA: Harvard University Press, 2008.

Jung, C. G. *The Psychology of Kundalini Yoga*. Princeton, NJ: Princeton University Press, 1996.

Levinas, Emanuel. "Language and Proximity." The Collected Philosophical Papers. Trans. and ed. A. Lingis. Pittsburgh, PA: Duquesne University Press, 1986.

———. *Totality and Infinity*. Pittsburgh, PA: Duquesne University Press 1969.

Lusthaus, Dan. *Buddhist Phenomenology: A Philosophical Investigation of Yogacara Buddhism and the Ch'eng Wei-shih lun*. London: Routledge, 2002.

Mac Low, Jackson. "A Talk about my Writingways, University of Arizona, Tucson, January 24 2001." Written in New York, early December 2000–January 24, 2001. [Unpublished manuscript] Quoted in Anne Tardos's "Foreword" to *Thing of Beauty*. Berkeley: University of California Press, 2008. xvii.

———. "Black-Tarantula-Crsswrd-Gatha" being performed at http://media.sas.upenn.edu/pennsound/authors/Mac-Low/Mac-Low-Jackson_8-Voice-Blck-Tarantula-Crsswrd-Gatha_NY_11-25-73.mp3 October 29, 2008.

———. "Buddhism, Art, Practice, Polity." *Beneath a Single Moon*. Kent Johnson and Craigaulenich, eds. Boston & London: Shambala Press, 1991, 177.

———. "Fastidiousness and Love, a Review of *The Facts of Life, by Paul Goodman.*" Jackson Mac Low Papers 1923–1995 MSS 0180, Mandeville Special Collections Library, Geisel Library, University of California, San Diego. Housed in Box 68, Folder 29.

———. "Jackson Mac Low to Allen Ginsberg 9/30/91." MSS 180, Box 17, Folder 8.

———. "Mani Mani Gathas." MSS 0180, box 47 folder 15.

———. "Museletter," *The L=A=N=G=U=A=G=E Book*. Carbondale: Southern Illinois University Press, 1984. 26–7.

———. " 'Poetics of Chance' and the Politics of Spontaneous Simultaneity, or the Sacred Heart of Jesus." MSS 0180 Box 69, Folder 5.

———. *THE PRONOUNS*. 3rd edition. Barrytown, NY: Station Hill Press, 1979.

———. *Representative Works*. New York: Roof Books, 1986.

———. "Some Ways Philosophy has Helped to Shape my Work." MSS 180, Box 68, Folder 15.

———. "Taoist Principle of Wu-Wei as Exemplified in Zen Buddhism." 1956–1957. MSS 0180, Box 68, Folder 19.

———. "Writing and Practice," 1991, Box 69, Flder 13 from the Jackson Mac Low Ppaers, MSS 180, Mandeville Special Collections Library, University of California, San Diego.

Staal, Frits. *Rules Without Meaning: Ritual, Mantras and the Human Sciences*. New York: Peter Lang, 1989.

Stalling, Jonathan. *Poetics of Emptiness: Transformations of Asian Thought in American Poetry*. New York: Fordham University Press, 2010.

———. The Emptiness of Patterned Flux: Buddhism and Ernest Fenollosa's "The Chinese Written Character as a Medium for Poetry." *The Emergence of Buddhist American Literature*. John Whalen-Bridge and Gary Storhoff, eds. Albany: State University of New York Press, 2009.

Sharf, Robert. "The Zen of Japanese Nationalism." *Curators of the Buddha: The Study of Buddhism under Colonialism*. Ed., Donald S. Lopez, Jr. Chicago: University of Chicago Press, 1995.

Suzuki, D. T. *An Introduction to Zen Buddhism*. London: Rider & Co., 1948.

Suzuki, D. T., Erich Fromm, Richard De Martino. *Zen Buddhism and Psychoanalysis*. New York: Harper & Brothers, 1960.

———. "The Zen Sect of Buddhism," *Journal of the Pali Text Society*, 1906.

The Platform Sutra of the Sixth Patriarch: The text of the TUN-HUANG manuscript. Trans. Philip B. Yampolsky. New York: Columbia University Press, 1967.

Trigilio, Tony. *Allen Ginsberg's Buddhist Poetics*. Carbondale: Southern Illinois University Press, 2007.

Waldman, Anne and Marilyn Webb, eds. *Talking Poetics From Naropa Institute: Annals of the Jack Kerouac School of Disembodied Poetics*. V. I. Boston & London: Shambhala, 1978.

Wang, Qingjie (James). " 'It-self-so-ing' and 'Other-ing' in Loa Zi's Concept of Zi Ran," *Comparative Approaches to Chinese Philosophy*. Ed., Bo Mou. Burlington, VT: Ashgate, 2003.

Venerable Dhammasami. *Mindfulness Meditation Made Easy*. http://web.ukonlinen.co.uk/bhuddhism/dmasam2a.hthm.

Watson, Burton, *Han Fei Tzu: Basic Writings*. New York: Columbia University Press, 1964.

Wilson, Rob. *Inside Out*. New York: Rowman & Littlefield Publishers, Inc., 1999.

———. *Reimagining the American Pacific*. Durham, NC: Duke University Press, 2000.

Wright, Dale. *Philosophical Meditations on Zen Buddhism*. Cambridge: Cambridge University Press, 1998.

Chapter 5

A Deeper Kind of Truth

Buddhist Themes in Don DeLillo's *Libra*

Gary Storhoff

Does he have to be a Buddhist to be taken seriously?

—DeLillo, *Cosmopolis*

We need a Japanese monk.

—DeLillo, The Names

Raised as a Catholic by Italian immigrant parents, Don DeLillo acknowledges that he is a "spiritual person," one whose writing "brings [him] closer to spiritual feelings than anything else. Writing is the final enlightenment" (Moss 158). DeLillo's use of the word "enlightenment" is suggestive of an Asian philosophical lens, specifically Buddhism, for interpreting his work. DeLillo's iteration of "enlightenment" is probably not Buddhist in intent, and it must be conceded that his spiritual thematic is neither literal nor obvious. Nevertheless, DeLillo's fiction consistently challenges the reader with the notion that there *is* an elusive spiritual enlightenment, and if writing itself is the "final enlightenment" for the author, what path exists for the reader? Reading can also be a path toward enlightenment—"final" or otherwise—and reading DeLillo's work through a Buddhist thematic can help clarify this enigmatic writer in surprising ways. If we see DeLillo's fiction within a Buddhist framework, we not only understand his work from another angle; we also add another aesthetic dimension to the view that the literature expresses fundamental truths about how we live.[1] Of course, my approach in this chapter does not dogmatically foreclose other useful religious avenues to DeLillo; rather, my intention is to elucidate an understanding of DeLillo not usually developed—to uncover, as it were, another level of his novel *Libra*. As the narrator of *Libra* states, beneath the literal plot, "there is always another level, another secret, a way in which the heart breeds a deception so mysterious and complex it can only be taken for a deeper kind of truth" (260).

My model for this chapter is John A. McClure's superlative study of spirituality in postmodern fiction, *Partial Faiths* (2007). McClure argues that in many "postsecular narratives," the author does not embrace conventional religion in an unquestioning, dogmatic way; instead, the narratives "affirm the urgent need for a turn toward the religious even as they reject (in most instances) the familiar dream of full return to an authoritarian faith" (6). On the one hand, then, the authors McClure discusses find a spiritual vacancy in pure secularity and renunciation of religion; on the other hand, the confident religiosity of American evangelicals, worldwide fundamentalists, and other conventional religious leaders offers no alternative to secularity, since these religious leaders insist on an absolutist sense of certainty that most contemporary American writers cannot accept. A postsecular author instead "inhabits the border zone between the secular and the religious . . . producing new, complexly hybridized forms of thought and life" (*Partial Faiths* 10). In McClure's treatment, DeLillo is a postsecular author. In his discussion of DeLillo (63–99), he demonstrates how DeLillo dramatizes "a choice of how secular-minded peoples will approach that complex of intuitions and impulses identified with the religious" (75). It is my goal in this chapter to demonstrate how an understanding of Buddhist ideas contributes to DeLillo's religious postsecularism—not to categorize DeLillo's religion definitively, but to expand our understanding of his work beyond interpretations oriented toward Catholicism. DeLillo's religious pluralism and ambiguity guide his work, resisting the representation of any one faith as an exclusive source of spirituality.

"Being versus Nonbeing": DeLillo and the Struggle for Self

At the center of Buddhist teachings is a therapeutic motive, which would appeal to DeLillo as a writer whose works measure American malaise.[2] *Libra* analyzes a pivotal point in American history, President Kennedy's assassination. DeLillo's novelistic concern would be a self-evident problem to a Buddhist reader. For a Buddhist, the fundamental spiritual problem is human suffering (*dukkha*). Suffering in the Buddhist sense is not to be confused with pain, which all human beings necessarily experience; instead, suffering is a mental state that arises from craving (*tanha*) that leads to attachment: attachment itself the inevitable result of the wished-for acquisition of the object(s) one craves. Craving is essentially a psychic possessiveness—a stubborn, emotional denial of the impermanence of all things, and the failure to understand that transience of all things motivates one to covet these entities.

Libra is about many kinds of craving: the desire to know who killed Kennedy, a wish that the assassination had never happened, and most of all a desire to assimilate the shock of history through narrative retelling. Craving and attachment can take many forms, many of which are conventionally thought (from a Western perspective) to be commonsensical if not noble. There is craving for external things—one's possessions, career, reputation, achievements, friends' and family's success and health, and so forth. One may also be attached in more a subtle manner to internal entities: one's opinions, hopes, particular mental and emotional states, even remembered and anticipated experiences, and—perhaps most important of all—a sense of a coherent self. From a Buddhist perspective, human beings are inattentive to the impermanence of all things (although all people may cognitively understand this radical transience), and in a day-by-day unmindfulness of impermanence, craving and attachment are the inevitable consequences.

Although DeLillo's religious affiliation cannot be ascertained definitively from either his literary works or his interviews,[3] the sometimes abstract or vague elements of religious experience become clearer and more concrete when reading his fiction. The spiritual dimension of his work has been recognized by several critics. In recent criticism there has been a division among his readers: Although such critics as John Duvall argue that DeLillo represents the best of contemporary deconstructionists, such critics as McClure, Paul Maltby, and Jonathan Little assert that "DeLillo is reenchanting our world" (Little 301) by reintroducing to contemporary fiction an animating spirituality. Daniel Born, for example, insists, "the realm of the sacred in DeLillo's work—and in postmodern work more generally—needs preliminary attention rather than receiving treatment as an afterthought or appendage to the linguistic whole" (219). Little has demonstrated convincingly in his exhaustive article on *Ratner's Star* that DeLillo is thoroughly conversant with Kabbalism, Gnosticism, and various mystic traditions (303). David Cowart discovers in DeLillo's use of language "a religious feeling" (96),[4] and he also asserts that in *Libra*, "DeLillo allows . . . a curious religious dimension to emerge in his essentially historical and political novel" (92).

The aforementioned critics have drawn from theistic religions, but Buddhism has a part to play in this dialogue, since DeLillo's work expresses a Buddhist criticism of Western ideal of individuality and self-identity. McClure has already demonstrated DeLillo's familiarity with Tibetan Buddhism in a discussion of DeLillo's *Running Dog* (*Partial Faiths* 72–75), and the range of DeLillo's religious pluralism can be seen in his treatment of the concept of self as dramatized in *Libra*. For philosopher David Loy, an obsession over identity is the West's abiding spiritual problem: "Our most problematic duality is not life against death but self versus nonself, or being versus nonbeing. . . . 'Forgetting' ourselves is how we lose our sense of separation and realize that we are not other than the world" (7).[5] The remedy Loy recommends for alleviating this problem is to develop a Buddhist outlook toward the self. Although DeLillo charts the many ways that human beings fall victim to their own desires and cravings, he also recommends paths away from self-defeating craving and directs his reader toward a greater, more expansive sense of reality than Western religion typically offers. Buddhist attitudes toward the self have not been addressed directly by DeLillo himself or by his critics, yet Buddhist therapeutic prescriptions very closely resemble the spiritual solutions that we may extrapolate from his fiction.[6]

Western metaphysics has assumed the existence of some single, underlying, presocial reality that we term *the self*, whereas Buddhist thought concedes that such a reality may exist but rejects the assumption that human reason can mirror it. Buddhism differs sharply from Judeo-Christian approaches to the self, in that the human "being" is not immutable and innate but rather is thoroughly contingent on specific behavior performed in the context of social occasions. In contrast to the idea of immortal, permanent, and immutable human selves, T. P. Kasulis writes that the Buddhist ideal is "to act spontaneously in the situation without first objectifying it in order to define one's role" (132). For a Buddhist, insisting on a consistent, static, substantialist, and absolutist self produces anxiety, since the world's transience ensures the inevitability of change. This contrast between Buddhist and Judeo-Christian attitudes in regard to the self provides a critical basis for understanding DeLillo's own spirituality and psychology.

DeLillo's work enacts key Buddhist themes that clarify the nonexistence of the self. His most deluded characters, particularly in *Libra*, are planners, never acting spontaneously. His positive characters, in contrast, are able to lay aside their individual selves, even if only temporarily, but their disavowal of the self leads to their appreciation of the moment and to their profoundly gracious acts to others. Unlike the deluded characters who cling to the self, these positive characters seem to understand intuitively the seminal Buddhist concept of dependent origination (*partityasamutpada*), which explains how all things derive their transient identity and how things eventually become what they fleetingly are. Dependent origination holds that all people, thoughts, and objects are incessantly changing because they depend, at the very moment they come into existence and from that point thereafter, on other things, which also are changing because they too are dependent on other things—and so on ad infinitum. All things are what they are at any given moment not because it is their essential nature to be such and such—the basis of Cartesian dualistic metaphysics that confirms the individual self—but because other things (also changing) have influenced, shaped, or partially determined whatever exactly they are at the present moment. Because of dependent origination, all things exist in a relational matrix. No one thing has an essential nature, nor is any thing self-determining: Any thing depends on a complex of relations with other evolving things to derive its own evolving identity.

Because of this radical contingency, Buddhism recognizes that social roles work very much like dramatic roles, dictating action and determining an individual's identity; and that a rational analysis of events is often merely an effort to write more scripts. As Kasulis explains, "We go through life thinking that our words and ideas mirror what we experience, but repeatedly we discover that the distinctions taken to be true are merely mental constructs" (55). The most we can know of ourselves, then, is who we are within abstract and generalized social boundaries. So it is that Lee Harvey Oswald, insisting on the primacy of the self, can never discover a place in society, whether it be the Soviet Union or the United States. Perhaps Lee is the best example of self-delusion in DeLillo's canon, for given the ample opportunities to affirm his humanity with other people, he consistently refuses; his purpose is to substantiate his illusory self even if this requires the murder of another person. He cannot accept that his identity beyond social boundaries is an illusion. This Buddhist principle is a favorite topic of koans, conundrums that present a paradoxical truth arrived at through mediation. For example, a Zen master may ask his disciple, "What is your face before you were born?"—a demand that the disciple meditate on the nonexistence of a presocial identity.

"There is much here that is holy": The Search for Refuge in *Libra*

At the narrative level, *Libra* is ostensibly an effort to explain the assassination of Kennedy, and DeLillo offers a bizarre and somewhat implausible theory that the assassination was not to have been an assassination at all, but rather a purposely botched attempt that would inspire hatred for the Cuban regime that should ultimately have led to the destruction of Fidel Castro and reclamation of Cuba for the United States.[7] DeLillo makes it clear in his author's note that it is not his intention to "furnish factual answers to any questions raised by the assassination."[8] Instead, "readers may find a refuge here—a way of thinking about the assassination without being constrained by half-facts or overwhelmed by possibilities."[9] As implied with his use of the word *refuge*, DeLillo's primary purpose is to point the way to a spiritual relief from the ongoing effects of the tragedy that Kennedy's assassination brought the nation. DeLillo asks readers to put the novel's characters on the libran scales and reweigh them, to see in the tragic event of Kennedy's assassination a spiritual dimension that most of his characters (and many of his critics) ignore, although even the most deluded characters have an intuition of the religious nature of the event. As Nicholas Branch says, "There is much here that is holy" (15).

Libra's aesthetic organizing principle can be understood as an attempt to provide a readerly refuge from the sense of purposelessness in postmodern society.

As Loy writes in his Buddhist history of the West, "When the world becomes what's in the newspapers or on television, to be unknown is to be nothing" (69). Oswald, like the other characters, needs refuge from his sense of lack, from his sense of unreality—for DeLillo and Loy, the quintessentially spiritual condition of our time. To be sure, the novel does not exonerate or excuse Oswald, but it suggests that most people, because they share the characters' traditional conceptualization of the self, experience suffering (in the Buddhist sense) because they lack wisdom. Their alienation and insatiability for recognition ends in agony, in an intractable feeling of there being something missing in their world: their own substantive identities. DeLillo suggests that this craving for a substantialized self is a major factor in the tragedy.[10] Libra's characters are lost because they feel they are indistinguishable from one another, and each character is on his or her own quest to affirm a stable, consistently enacted self—a critical spiritual mistake from a Buddhist perspective. All the characters, especially but not only Lee Harvey Oswald, are frustrated—even to the point of rage—with their anonymous conditions, and they desperately seek acknowledgment from world history as unique individuals. Although they ironically mouth DeLillo's own stated intention of providing "refuge" for Americans, even as they plot murder, this stated goal is only their effort to rationalize their egocentric behavior. They collectively aspire to their own sense of individuality by figuratively setting themselves above and beyond the "normal" range of human experience; they each seek to become shining examples of vision, commitment, and courage.[11]

Central to their goal of affirming their uniqueness is maintaining secrets, known only to them and those whom they include in their small circle. As José Liste Noya writes, "Secrecy . . . becomes a shoring up of the self" (243). They seek this status neither symbolically nor anonymously, but each in his own name, concocting scripts in which they are heroic actors in their own dramas. If DeLillo believes that his writing provides the "final enlightenment," then the self-deluded group of scriptwriters in Libra finally discover that their "writing" leads only to greater spiritual bondage to their own desire. These are men who create dramas, self-contained structures that, they believe, are immune from transience and all unanticipated events of life. As Branch says, "If we are on the outside, we assume a conspiracy is the perfect working of a scheme. . . . A conspiracy is everything that ordinary life is not. It's the inside game, cold, sure, undistracted, forever closed off to us. . . . Conspirators have a logic and a daring beyond our reach" (440).

Perhaps because he is the conspirator who instigates the assassination plot, the most important writer in the novel is Win Everett. A man of "all principle, all zeal" (18), Win, a renegade CIA agent, believes he can distinguish himself from the rest of humanity by exposing to the public the immoral undercover plots of Kennedy's administration regarding Castro's Cuba. Like a writer himself, Win would "put someone together, build an identity, a skein of persuasion and habit, ever so subtle" (78). He concocts a plot where a failed assassination attempt on Kennedy—a "spectacular miss" (51)—would justify re-instating him as an active CIA operative in charge of an invasion of Cuba. In broader terms, Win considers his plot his own patriotic duty to instruct the American public through his own theatre in the deceptions of federal government, thereby creating for himself a role that would rescue him from the unglamorous identity of instructor at a women's college:

> Let them see what goes on in the committee rooms and corner offices. The [physical evidence of the attempt] must allow investigators to learn that Kennedy wanted Castro dead, that plots were devised, approved at high levels, put into motion, and that Fidel or his senior aids decided to retaliate. This was the major subtext and moral lesson of Win Everett's plan. (53)

Scrupulously phrased as written discourse with "subtext and moral lesson" for the nation, Everett's plan seems to him to be the essence of patriotism. If his plan works, not only will he have exposed the moral corruption of Camelot, but he also will have masterminded the plan that would eventually liberate Cuba, righting Kennedy's wrong in failing to support the Bay of Pigs invasion. Even beyond the nationalistic benefits to be gained by his plan, he also would, from his own perspective, have made a major contribution to resisting the communist advance threatening the entire Western hemisphere. Thus, Win acts as if his name is the perfect eponym for his plotting; in his imagination, he is the triumphant writer establishing a better world through his action. His plan creates a refuge not only for his contemporary America but for all people for all time.

What makes Win feel even more exalted is that he chooses for himself the perfect martyrdom: His plan must remain clandestine throughout his own lifetime, and for the time being, he will have to be satisfied with the knowledge that only a few other virtuous men know about his own vision, imagination, courage, and selflessness. But he believes that once sufficient time has passed, future historians—other writers, studying his work long after his death—will be able to piece together the paper trail he will bequeath them:

> He would not consider the plan a success if the uncovering of its successive layers did not reveal the CIA's schemes, his own schemes in some cases, to assassinate Fidel Castro. This was the little surprise he was keeping for the end. It was his personal contribution to an informed public. (53)

At that distant time beyond his death, he will be marked down publicly and permanently as a courageous, committed patriot, a charismatic hero of the West.

Win's ultimate goal, then, is to control events from beyond his grave. For Win, "history was in [his] care" (127). It is as if Win cannot live for the moment; instead, his perspective is Janus-like, one side of his imagination facing only his personalized past, where he feels he suffered an injustice from the almighty in Kennedy's administration; and his other side, facing an imagined future in which all injustices (toward him) will be rectified by that scrupulous future historian's discovery of his "little surprise."

Ironically, the future historian Win hopes who will "read" his work and vindicate him turns out to be Nicholas Branch, the second major scriptwriter of the novel. And he turns out to be Win's adversary. Branch assumes the duty of writing the secret history of the assassination, to be studied by the CIA in some time in the distant future when it can be revealed to the nation. Branch's secret goal is also to exalt his self. A retired CIA analyst, he hopes to claim a unique historical role to be recognized in the future, but Branch's quest for securing selfhood depends on discrediting Win, not reinterpreting and vindicating him. Branch hopes that he, Branch, will be the writer who goes down in history as the covert historian of the assassination, the one who helped America finally "regain our grip on things" (15)—not Win, whom Branch would like to consign to oblivion. Branch's Herculean chore—overwhelmed by evidence, recognizing connections that seem to go nowhere, scarcely knowing where to begin—is to write "the megaton novel James Joyce would have written. . . . This is the Joycean Book of America, remember—the novel in which nothing is left out" (181–82). But Branch's redemptive purpose (like Win's) is only a pretext; recording the truth about the assassination is not as important to Branch as his vision of himself as the great chronicler of America's concealed contemporary history. His projected, never-to-be-completed work has a similar purpose to Win Everett's carefully concocted murder plot: to lift himself out of anonymity.

Both writers, however, end not with the world's gratitude and acclaim but with their own frustrated hopes and desires. Like Win, Branch ends his quest for his unique individuality "frustrated, stuck, self-watching, looking for a means of connection, a way to break out" (181). Branch's writing has led him to realize the mystery of infinite connections and spiritual interdependence— what Buddhists call *partityasamutpada*—but Branch interprets this revelation as a nightmare that threatens his loss of control. Rather than discover meaning and fulfillment in his sense of infinite connectiveness, Branch mistakes—as a Buddhist proverb has it—the pointing finger for the moon itself. He becomes lost in the welter of transcripts, photos, polygraph reports, the Zapruder film, and other detritus of the assassination; instead of discovering what is real in the terrible event—his own mortality, and the mortality of all people—his unwritten history becomes lost in "the surrounding blurs, patches and shadows" (441). He ends with a sense of his own failure: "The case will haunt him to the end. Of course they've known it all along. That's why they built this room for him, the room of growing old, the room of history and dreams" (445). Branch's horror is of disintegration and alienation—he does not conceptualize an infinite connection of human beings and events that is spiritual consolation in itself. Looked at from a Buddhist perspective, Nicholas' room is not a nightmare chamber of chaos and coincidence, as many critics interpret it, but a spiritual symbol of Buddhist dependent origination. Like Win (and DeLillo's critics), turns away from a religious context. If the novel, as DeLillo says, is written to provide an emotional and spiritual refuge for his readers, Branch ironically seeks "refuge in notes . . . [which] are becoming an end in themselves" (301).[12]

In their mirror quests for a unique sense of selfhood, Win and Nicholas prepare the narrative way for the book's ultimate failure: Lee Harvey Oswald. As John Johnston writes, "Everett, Oswald, Branch, and by extension DeLillo the author form a series of men in small rooms who are both aligned and differentiated" (331). Like Win and Branch, Lee attempts to consolidate the self by reference to future roles in the social world. At first, his actions are pathetically modeled on the choices of others. He tries to become a Marine, like John Wayne; Lee is impressed with Wayne's laugh and with his masculinity. When he fails as a Marine, he dabbles at being a spy like Francis Gary Powers, whom Lee observes in a cell, by offering to pass classified information to communist undercover agents. But as a spy Lee is only "some kind of Chaplinesque figure" (194). Still dissatisfied and frustrated in his own attempts to transcend contingency, he assumes the role of a Marxist idealist, one who continues to meet disillusionment and further disappointment:

> It was this blankness that caused his terror. No one could distinguish him from anyone else. . . . He'd made plans, he'd engineered a new life, and now no one would take ten minutes to understand who he was. A zero in the system. (151)

Perhaps DeLillo finds Lee more admirable than either Win and Nicholas because he steadfastly confronts "his own incompleteness" (211), a courageous willingness to acknowledge himself as a "zero in the system"—or perhaps Oswald's fearful apprehension of his own contingency is also a form of cowardice. For Oswald in this sense, the Libran scales balance evenly.

Lee's unwavering belief in his own self has several times made itself manifest, most especially in his attempt to control life through language. Learning the Russian language, "he could almost believe he was being remade on the spot" (113); and in an attempt to transform the world single-handedly, Oswald pictures himself as an author, his goal to expose his notion of the truth about the two superpowers. Like the other two authors, Win and Nicholas, his salvific mission is only a pretext for his self-aggrandizement. By writing a "Historic Diary" about his life in the former Soviet Union, he is re-creating himself to claim greatness by laying bare the illusions proffered by both superpowers. He invests himself in distant future readers who will ennoble him as the incarnation of the oppressed working class: "Even as he printed the words, he imagined people reading them, people moved by his loneliness and disappointment, even by his wretched spelling, the childish mess of composition. Let them see the struggle and humiliation . . ." (211).[13] He never lives in the present moment, but always a future time of imagined endless glory and future public acclamation: "He was never fully there" (202).

Oswald too feels a need to establish himself as a solid self, but he goes further than even Win or Branch, for Lee's yearning for a substantialized self ultimately becomes all-consuming, even psychotic. As Christopher M. Mott writes, Lee finally "begins discovering himself in everything"(239). For example, one instance of Lee's narcissism is that shortly before he murders Kennedy, he is invited to his own birthday party at the Paine house where Marina is staying after their separation. A beaten wife, Marina is now ready to attempt reconciliation, trying to make the marriage a success, and she and the Paines plan a surprise party and cake. After the party, Oswald watches the television movie *Suddenly* as Marina falls asleep beside him, "her head in his lap," but instead of reconciling with Marina, Lee "felt connected to the events on the screen" (369). And the television movie's plot does involve him on his own imaginative level. Produced in 1954 and starring Frank Sinatra, *Suddenly* is about an attempted assassination. Sinatra plays John Baron, a former sniper in World War II, who is now a professional assassin intending to shoot the president from a window when he stops in a small California town to change trains. As Baron says of his Army experience, "They taught me to kill and I liked it." Such a statement marks Baron, of course, as a monstrous psychotic, and Sinatra's performance is unexpectedly convincing, especially for Oswald.[14] Oswald guesses the film's predictable ending: The film's assassination attempt is not successful, the conspiracy foiled by an honest local sheriff and an earnest housewife, but Oswald notices inevitably his coincidental involvement in this filmic fantasy, for he, like Baron, would be somebody if he were to kill the president.

Clearly, Oswald is depicted in this scene as having alternatives. Rather than identify with a television fantasy, Lee could have been alert to competing sources of meaning around him: his wife, his daughter, and his friends the Paines, who support the Oswalds' reconciliation. He has just celebrated his birthday party, and if he were to view the television movie with detached judgment, he would perceive the tranquility of the Paine household that juxtaposes Baron's insanity and megalomania, and Marina's forgiveness of his abuse. This moment could be pivotal for his life if he could accept its mundanity—"Marina next to him, asleep, softly breathing" (370)—but such is Lee's obsession with his future fame, his own actual surroundings do not capture his imagination.

Caged in a jail cell after the assassination, his prognostication of future fame is ironically confirmed, since "everybody knew who he was now" (435). The ironic end of these three plots is that they all converge and intertwine, as various commentators have pointed out. For example, Bill Millard writes that "each conspirator, seeing no further than his own interests, fears, or desires for revenge, moves in a private direction; the resultant vector of all these individual movements is something no individualist interpreter dares call conspiracy" (216). The characters do not perceive, however, what the reader is intended to see: that individualistic, self-confirming assumptions are misguided and lead to death or despair. Instead, the novel affirms that despite our most conscious efforts, we are intimately connected with each other in an interdependent web. In Buddhist terminology, we "originate dependently."

"Six Point Nine Seconds of Heat and Light": Illumination in Dependent Origination

"I think my work has always been informed by mystery," said DeLillo in an interview: "the final answer, if there is one at all, is outside the book" (DeCurtis 63). The mystery for each of these characters is not who killed President Kennedy, but how to achieve selfhood, an immortal entity to be recognized by all—the only imagined antidote for them to being "a zero in the system." What is the end of this unfulfilled human desire for a permanent self? If the individual self is unreal, a fiction devised by authors in search of their own humanity, where does refuge reside in the novel?[15] For Buddhism as well as the Judeo-Christian tradition, meditation on death and the various stages of the body's decomposition is intended to foster a detachment from worldly things, including (for Buddhists) an insistence on the impermanence of self. In his comments on *White Noise*, DeLillo explains his intention in that novel to evoke a sense of death in the same manner that death becomes an object of meditation for Buddhists: "I think it is something we all feel, something we almost never talk about, something that is *almost* there. I tried to relate it in *White Noise* to this other sense of transcendence that lies just beyond our touch. This extraordinary wonder of things is somehow related to the extraordinary dread, to the death fear we try to keep beneath the surface of our perceptions" (DeCurtis 71).

DeLillo employs the *memento mori* theme as he offers his grim answer as to where reality may be found. Branch discovers reality when he examines a gruesome autopsy photo of Oswald, where his "left eye is swiveled toward the camera, watching," now silently awaiting the examination of others—the clinicians who will destroy his remains for their purely materialist answers to his being, as if discovering how much his liver weighs will illuminate his inner life (299). DeLillo's emphasis on death is repeated later, when Branch examines a goat's head that has been shot for a ballistics test on Oswald's rifle. As Branch gazes at the shattered carcass, the goat's head speaks to Branch, reiterating the answer previously discovered in Oswald's autopsy photo: "Look, touch, this is the true nature of the event. . . . Not your roomful of theories, your museum of contradictory facts. There are no contradictions here. Your history is simple. See the man on the slab. The open eye staring. The goat head oozing rudimentary matter" (300).

Furthermore, DeLillo does not shield the reader from the horror of the assassination itself. Indeed, Kennedy's death is presented as the most incontrovertibly real event in the novel, as the nation's hero is shown to be an ordinary mortal. Although the novel generally paints a quite positive—even somewhat sentimental and nostalgic—picture of his administration, President Kennedy is not presented as a political naïf, a righteous king whose Camelot is about to be destroyed. On the contrary, Kennedy himself is presented as a plotter of assassination conspiracies himself, a fact corroborated by history and generally accepted even by Kennedy devotees. To a certain extent, DeLillo even implies that the historical Kennedy may have created for himself his own "world of blood and pain" (302). Thus, Kennedy is complicit in his own assassination plot, insofar as Kennedy's personal bloodlust has inadvertently inspired the plotters in their own desire for revenge against him: "They all knew that JFK wanted Castro cooling on a slab" (21). In acknowledging Kennedy's unknowing complicity in his own assassination, DeLillo emphasizes ironically the Buddhist doctrine of dependent origination that underlies the novel.

In underscoring Kennedy's common humanity, DeLillo emphasizes the horror of Kennedy's death: "the third shot sent stuff just everywhere. Tissue, bone fragments, tissue in pale wads, watery mess, tissue, blood, brain matter all over them" (399). This ghastly scene is DeLillo's commentary on the quest for self-affirmation. DeLillo emphasizes the awful and ghastly gore of the event again and again in the event. Bobby W. Hargis, the escort in the death car, sees "blood and matter, the unforgettable thing, the sleet of bone and blood and tissue struck him in the face. . . . He kept his mouth closed tight so the fluid would not ooze in" (399). Jackie, crying that she has "his brains in my hand" (399), tries to "retrieve part of her husband's skull" (402). A bystander feels "bloodspray on her face and arms" (400–01). As Daniel Born remarks about DeLillo generally, "one of DeLillo's gifts is that he can always discover yet another layer of death we didn't think existed" (217). By the power of DeLillo's mimetic writing, the reader is shocked by perhaps the most famous murder in twentieth-century America.

Yet the novel is spiritually affirmative, despite its emphasis on death and our shared mortality. Frank Lentricchia, opposing this view, argues that there is no refuge possible in this novel. He writes, "The disturbing strength of *Libra*—DeLillo gives no quarter on this—is its refusal to offer its readers a comfortable place outside of Oswald" (204). But as DeLillo himself has asserted about his work, he affirms

> a kind of radiance in dailiness. Sometimes this radiance can be almost frightening. Other times it can be almost holy or sacred. . . . I think that's something that has been in the background of my work: a sense of something extraordinary hovering just beyond our touch and just beyond our vision . . . [an] extraordinary wonder of things. . . . (DeCurtis 70–71)

Weird Beard, in his radio station baffling his audience, expresses in the novel his author's sense of spirituality that undergirds life: "Some things are true. Some things are truer than true" (382). Nothing in the novel is "truer than true" than death itself. Death for Buddhists should bring the individual a closer understanding of the transient moment, and increase the radiance of the everyday, of the mundane.

Because no character escapes suffering, as the Buddhist First Noble Truth claims, what posture should one take in relation to personal suffering, not only one's own but that of other people? Although some suffering is the consequence of vast, impersonal forces in *Libra*—for examples, the Cold War, the reemergence of radical American conservatism, the secret funding of covert agencies—suffering is also the result of individual actions, whose actions work together and intertwine although unbeknownst to the actors. Each character seeks desperately to shape his life, yet each suffers as a result of his choices and actions that almost always lead to the opposite of what he intends. Win, for example, believes that he desires to advance the welfare of the United States, but his own "character" that he has been constructing sets in motion forces that lead to national chaos, division, and suspicion. For setting the assassination plot in motion, then, Win is morally responsible.[16] Win, like the other characters, fails to foresee that his choices will inevitably act in tandem with all other events throughout history. Events "arise dependently," as Buddhism argues in its doctrine of dependent origination. Thus, Win's plot both fails and succeeds because of the infinity of events and characters acting both in concert with and opposed to him: for example, Oswald, the perfect dupe, designing plots of his own; or T-Jay, the embittered Bay of Pigs veteran, "forgetting" to tell Raymo and Frank that "they were supposed to miss" (123). Even the placement of the Texas School Book Depository, the weather, and the quality of sunlight in Dallas on November 22, 1963, were all essential in the murder of the president. Branch believes that "the conspiracy against the President was a rambling affair that succeeded in the short term due mainly to chance" (441). But "chance" is another way of saying that there is a mutual causality generated by the totality of phenomena—the essence of the doctrine of dependent origination.

DeLillo's dramatization of interdependence leads the reader to question his or her basic perception of the world. The reader may be led to identify with the conspirators in many ways: the reader may share with the conspirators their quest for certainty, their philosophical dualism, their hopes for the future, their disregard of contingency, their fear of death. Yet a Buddhist understanding of dependent origination, in the words of the Buddhist monk Matthieu Ricard, should "demolish the wall of illusions that our minds have built up between 'me' and 'the other' " (71). The conspirators' desire to construct their unique and self-sufficient identities on another person's pain is not simply immoral: It is also unrealistic, since their lives are tied together in ways they cannot possibly see or immediately understand. As Ricard implies, the understanding of life's interdependence should lead instead to a compassion and understanding for others.

This understanding is intuitively grasped by many of the women in the novel. In contrast to the plotters who desire future fame, the women characters maintain admirable ideals by living emphatically in the present. Their ordinary human virtues have a redemptive, although a necessarily limited, thematic meaning, for it is they in the novel who infuse the ordinary world with a sense of sacredness that is the reader's option for refuge. If the nation is changed irrevocably by "six point nine seconds of heat and light" (62) that comprise the Kennedy assassination, the women characters in their modest recognitions point to a way beyond suffering. These characters, by and large, renounce the desire for a permanent self and a wish for a future affirmation of greatness. Instead, the women characters choose a Zen-like appreciation of the moment, with no real concern for what the next day might bring them in fame and fortune.[17] They seem to intuit a more profound conception of the self, present in Christianity as well as Buddhism, that can arise from an encounter with the other person in which the separate and individual self is negated. This is true even for several women who barely appear in the novel. Nellie Connolly, Governor Connolly's wife, holds her wounded husband while President Kennedy dies in the car; given her gruesome situation, the reader could readily sympathize with her if she were to think only of herself. Yet DeLillo imagines that her sympathy goes out to the horrified crowd watching the presidential limousine: "Nellie thought how terrible this must be, what a terrible sight for people watching, to see the car speeding past with these shot-up men" (399).

Many women in the novel seem to achieve these moments of insight primarily in the context of their families. Win's wife, Mary Frances, for example, observes her husband's preoccupation with the Kennedy assassination with skepticism and dread because he alienates himself from his family and his friends: "Deprived of real duties, of contact with the men and events that informed his zeal, he was becoming all principle, all zeal. She was afraid he would turn into one of those men who make a saintliness of their resentment, shining through the years with a pure and tortured light" (18). As DeLillo writes, "She knew how to use the sound of her own voice to bring him back to what was safe and plain, among the breakfast dishes" (16). Instead of Win's ambition and resentful sense of being ignored by the CIA, Mary Frances understands that "happiness [is] lived minute by minute in the things she saw and heard" (135)—including such mundane chores as running the vacuum cleaner and shopping for groceries, all the day-to-day activities they could enjoy together and with their daughter Suzanne, whom Mary Frances calls an "ordinary mystery" (76). Unlike her grim husband, Mary Frances asks rhetorically, "Isn't it one of the best things there is, feeling the air on your body on a night like this?" (77). Indeed, Suzanne's birth seems to be an example for Mary Frances of the wondrous sense of the moment: "Because they'd wanted a child but had given up hope, she was a sign of something unselfish in the world, some great-hearted force that could turn their smallness to admiring awe" (18). In a moving moment in the novel, little Suzanne tries to capture her father's attention by drawing him close, ready to tell him a childhood "secret" and enjoy an intimate moment together; Win, however, consumed with his own sense of destiny, criticizes her because she is "generous with secrets" (26).

Mary Frances' role is mirrored in the novel by Oswald's wife and child, Marina and little Junie. Marina, perhaps of all the characters in this novel, comes to understand what DeLillo describes in an interview as the "radiance in dailiness." As Douglass Keesey writes, "Marina and June offer Lee the possibility of a world where secrets are shared and mystery can be benign" (162). In the beginning of her relationship with Lee, she offers even him "a sense of what it was like to be a child again" (220). Filled with a sense of "ardor and trust" in Lee (371), Marina, like Mary Frances, disavows any claim to fame and greatness but discovers in the ordinariness of their simple lives the "preciousness" of each moment: "They [Marina and Lee] were the same as anyone, completely ordinary, saying what people say. *Every fact about their lives was precious*" (italics added, 202). Indeed, Marina takes joy in the ordinary circumstances of their relationship, never expecting that their marriage would transcend a momentary appreciation for the common and routine: "They seemed to shine together at the center of things. They made things theirs. A certain bench in the park, near the chess players, ordinary things, not unusual in any way. They fell in love the way anyone does" (201). Like Mary Frances, Marina enjoys simple tasks like "doing the laundry or mopping the floor" (202), buying groceries, choosing wallpaper, and preparing dinner for her family. A famous Buddhist verse that mirrors Marina's commitment to the ordinary world of work wherein enlightenment is found is the following poem: "How wonderful, how marvelous! / I fetch wood, I carry water!"

As with Suzanne's birth for Mary Frances, Marina hopes that Junie's birth will provide Lee with her sense of the joyousness of their family. Marina rather naively believes that Lee will inevitably commit himself to their family unit, since "a father took part. He had a place, an obligation" (206). This hoped-for happiness in the family is made even more pathetic because Marina is an abused wife. Her abuse is a consequence of Lee's cynicism about his wife, who seems to him to become "an American in record-breaking time" because from Lee's perspective she seems to covet material wealth that he cannot provide for her, and his cynicism about her desire is consistent with his distrust of anything outside of his own obsessive and self-centered desires. The reader must indeed be skeptical of Lee's understanding of his own wife's attitude toward American consumerism. In a much-studied passage in the novel, the Oswalds shop in Fort Worth stores, and Marina's love for her family—rather than her lust for consumer items—is dramatized poignantly. Although Lee is frustrated because Marina, he thinks, wants more consumer goods than he can provide, Marina is "happy just to walk the aisles of the Safeway," taking pleasure in the colors of the packaged food (226). When the family visits a department store, Marina watches a television screen showing her image appear and reappear. When Oswald watches television, he sees only himself, but Marina sees herself with her family: "She was on television. Lee was on television, standing next to her, holding Junie in his arms. . . . She didn't know anything like this could ever happen" (227). Many commentators focus on the descriptive paragraph's last sentences in order to emphasize the destructive nature of consumerism in America: "She kept walking out of the picture and coming back. She was amazed every time she saw herself return" (227).[18] A close reading of this passage, however, reveals that Marina is *not* self-absorbed; nor is her behavior dictated by media representations of the self; nor is she fixated on the consumer items in the shelves around her. Instead, she is preoccupied with the togetherness of her family. The image she watches again and again in the television screen is Lee, "holding Junie in his arms" (227). But Lee misunderstands what the reader perceives: What absorbs Marina is not so much having goods, affluence, and a "postmodern American self," as various critics believe, but her pleasure in enjoying each moment with her husband and daughter, and her pathetic hopes for a future with them.

It is her final gesture at Lee's gravesite that illuminates the world's mystery and beauty for the reader:

> Now Marina came forward and picked up a handful of dirt. She made the sign of the cross, then extended her arm over the grave, letting the dirt fall. Marguerite and Robert had never seen anything like this. The beauty of the gesture was compelling. It was strange and eloquent and somehow correct. (454)

Marina's intentions for a happy life with her husband and child are, of course, tragically defeated, and the reader cannot be oblivious to Marina's dire straits at the end of the novel. Alone in a foreign country, impoverished, unable to speak English, a widowed and unemployed mother whose dead husband will go down in history as the assassin of a beloved and heroic president—Marina knows too well, the reader understands, the perilous road before her, created by her self-deluded husband and by so many other forces. Yet the authorial voice implies that hers is an "eloquent," "correct," but altogether "beautiful" gesture. Marina making the cross over Lee's grave redeems the bleakness and pessimism critics often discover in the novel. As Paul Maltby writes in a different context (about a different DeLillo novel), "The passage is typical of DeLillo's tendency to seek out transcendent moments in our postmodern lives that hint at possibilities for cultural regeneration" (261). Whoever Marina Oswald was in history, this scene depicts her as a figure of love, forgiveness, and redemption. Marina's spontaneous gesture at Lee's grave is explicitly religious; however, whatever her conscious intent (DeLillo withholds her own consciousness at this point, referencing the gesture from Marina's and Robert's points of view), Marina points toward a spiritual meaning under girding the historical grief that the novel dramatizes. In Marina's final gesture, we witness love, forgiveness, and an acceptance of the world that passes beyond our understanding of individuals caught in historical circumstance. She seems here to understand Lee as he never understood himself: a "zero in the system," but a human being nevertheless who also needs forgiveness.

DeLillo's novel seems to respond to Loy's assumption that the fundamental need for the Western culture lies in a spiritual liberation from our radical sense of lack of grounding. The characters constantly planning the deaths of others—be it Kennedy or Castro—all suffer from their own lack; they represent for the reader, in the words of Jack Ruby, "what it means to be nothing, to know you are nothing, to be fed the message of your nothingness every day for all your days, down and down the years" (445). The release, as the reader discovers in the women characters discussed in this chapter, is, in Loy's words, "the option of a here-and-now liberation from our lack. The Buddhist denial of a substantial self opens up the possibility of a this-worldly transcendence of self, in realizing the nondual interdependence of a no longer alienated subject with a no longer objectified world" (213). To be whole, DeLillo implies, is to accept the nothingness that horrifies Ruby, to be willing to accept being a "zero in the system," but in so doing welcome our profound connection with the universe.

Notes

1. For one of the first justifications of employing Buddhism as a critical approach to Western art, see Archie J. Bahm. For a much more recent discussion of the Buddhist aesthetic in literature, see Tony Trigilio's excellent study of Allen Ginsberg.

2. According to Frank Lentricchia, DeLillo is the kind of writer "who conceive[s] of their vocation as an act of cultural criticism; who invent[s] in order to intervene; whose work is a kind of anatomy, an effort to represent their culture in its totality; and who desire[s] to move readers to the view that the shape and fate of their culture dictates the shape and fate of the self" ("The American Writer as Bad Citizen" 2).

3. Of course, it is possible to discover in DeLillo's work Christian themes, especially in his latest novel, *Underworld*. In general, however, I would qualify but essentially agree with Pearl K. Bell's sweeping assertion that "his ethnic background and Catholic upbringing are entirely absent from his work" (138); his work certainly does not identify him as a Catholic apologist. Yet DeLillo has speculated that the "mystery" in his work may be attributed to his "Catholic upbringing" (DeCurtis 63); however, DeLillo also told LeClair that "It's my nature to keep quiet about most things" (2).

4. Cowart's analysis of the novel's religious dimension is centered on "the primal slaying of the father" that gives rise to "primitive ideas of the sacred"—a narrative that leads to the "breakdown" of religious myth (107, 109). Through an analysis of imagery he suggests a connection with the Crucifixion.

5. Loy's thesis in this book—that "since our lack is basically a spiritual problem, any solution must also have a spiritual dimension" (213)—provides the paradigm for my approach to DeLillo's novel.

6. For a discussion of DeLillo's earlier work *End Zone*, where he examines the fruitless effort of creating games to give life a stable structure and individuals a static sense of self within the context of the game, see my discussion, "The Failure of Games in *End Zone*." In this novel, the characters create games that are played so frantically that they are taken more seriously than the life on which it is dependent as a concretized function. Buddhism calls this self-serious absorption "*avidja*" and identifies it as the central human dilemma. Bondage ("*samsara*") is the result of taking the game more seriously than life itself, which each of the characters do.

7. DeLillo's plot is not *entirely* implausible. A recent book on the Kennedy assassination, *Ultimate Sacrifice*, argues that the assassination was carried out by the Mafia, with Oswald fingered as the patsy. Lamar Waldron and Thom Hartman, the book's authors, reveal for the first time the Kennedy's top secret plan to overthrow Castro on December 1, 1963, code-named AMWORLD. The Mafia discovered this plot and used parts of it in the assassination to circumvent their prosecution by Attorney General Robert Kennedy, since Robert Kennedy would have had to reveal AMWORLD's existence in any prosecution of conspirators.

8. It is important in this regard to note, however, that DeLillo seems to have firm ideas about what actually happened in Dallas and that he does not seem to think the assassination was an entirely unknowable event. Unlike his deconstructionist critics, DeLillo obviously believes that we are justified in believing partial truths even if we cannot discover the complete and absolute Truth. In visiting Dallas while researching *Libra*, DeLillo visited the famous Texas School Book Depository, and he reviewed many times the Zapruder film. His judgment is as follows: "The strongest feeling I took away from that moment is the feeling that the shot came from the front and not from the rear. Of course, if that's true, there had to be more than one assassin" (DeCurtis 61).

9. DeLillo, "Author's Note," unnumbered page.

10. Political columnist George Will famously called *Libra* "yet another exercise in blaming America for Oswald's act of derangement," and Jonathan Yardley has written

that "DeLillo would have us believe . . . that [Oswald's] course is beyond his control." Their mistaken argument is that DeLillo excuses Oswald's actions; however, the real burden of change is on the entire cast of characters and their self-conceptions. That is, Oswald differs from the other characters only in degree. Although he does not place the novel within a religious context, Frank Lentricchia somewhat anticipates my argument when he asserts that Oswald should be conceived as a "negative Libran" that discloses the "nonidentity of sheer possibility—of the American who might play any part. The negative libran is an undecidable intention waiting to be decided . . . [there is] the presiding tone of the postmodern absence of substantial and autonomous selfhood" ("*Libra* as Postmodern Critique" 201). Lentricchia's emphasis on the theme of anonymity and the deterministic nature of postmodern America, however, does not parallel the Buddhist conception of "no-self." Furthermore, Lentricchia's argument primarily concerns DeLillo's "unsettling vision" of America's "charismatic environment of image" that at least partly determines the actions of his characters (198).

11. Maltby opposes the critical consensus that DeLillo is a representative postmodernist novelist. He emphasizes DeLillo's connection with Romantic writers such as Blake or Wordsworth. However, as I argue, the Romantic confidence in the individual imagination is a spiritual danger in the novel.

12. Nicholas Branch has often been mistakenly seen as a surrogate for DeLillo himself. For example, Paul Civello argues that Branch "comes to represent the impossibility of the objective observer and, by extension, of the experimental novelist" (16). This reading, however, ignores DeLillo's ironic treatment of Branch, DeLillo's qualified faith in his own meditations on the assassination, and DeLillo's skepticism about the primacy of the self's imagination.

13. Ironically, however, Oswald is not now seen as an avatar of class-consciousness, but as the progenitor of later warped, misfit assassins and would-be assassins like James Earl Ray, Sirhan Sirhan, Mark David Chapman, Arthur Bremmer, and John Hinckley. As DeLillo writes, Oswald was the "first of a chain of what we might call instances of higher violence—violence with its own liturgy of official grief, its own standards of newsworthiness, with its built-in set of public responses" ("American Blood," 24).

14. DeLillo recirculates the legend that Oswald had seen *Suddenly* shortly before the assassination, and that Sinatra, understandably worried that the film had partly motivated Oswald, supposedly pulled the film from circulation, as he may have done with his other film about conspiracy and assassination, *The Manchurian Candidate*. However, recent research proves these legends to be false. *Suddenly* was not shown on Dallas networks at the time alleged, and *The Manuchurian Candidate* was in fact one of Sinatra's favorites. See Anthony Summers, 498–99.

15. Historically, criticism of DeLillo has emphasized his aesthetic project as an entirely postmodernist deconstruction of reality. For example, Frank Lentricchia, in a powerfully influential essay, describes *Libra* as "an entire charismatic environment of the image" (198). Lentriccha's lead is followed by Paul Civello, who contends that the book "undermines . . . the theoretical foundation of the naturalistic novel" (33). Glen Thomas goes even further, and argues that the novel demonstrates that history is only a set of "verbal fictions" (121). Patrick O'Donnell, employing Baudrillard's theory, writes, "the dominance of the orders of representation . . . suggests that the perceptual variations of de-totalization—essentially, parodies of representation—will be quickly reincorporated into another image connected with other images" (195). David Cowart partly echoes

this view: "The only reality knowable is the one shaped by endlessly self-referential sign systems, and by an art committed to replication, pastiche, and the commodified 'mechanical reproduction' . . . in short, the age of the simulacrum" (3–4). Joseph Kornick insists that "we are consistently told in the book that the facts have no value or meaning in themselves" (121). Joseph S. Walker takes the most extreme position, and writes about *Libra*, "there is no real; indeed, there can be no real" (446).

However, as Stuart Hutchinson points out, critics who insist on the novel's surrealist, postmodernist perspective ignore its central horror: the bloody slaughter of President Kennedy: "*Libra* is offered confidently as 'coherent history,' and as a representation of reality we are not invited to question" (119).

16. Paul Civello argues that "The self must now exist in a universe of 'no control,' a universe of looping systems that defies man's mastery" (55): but such a reading ignores the novel's moral urgency that my reading insists on.

17. Although Michael's concerns in are different from mine, her article on political themes and paradoxes in the novel also touches on the women characters, who, she argues, "seem to counter the novel's pull toward the vision of a chaotic world ruled by chance and coincidence" (8). However, similar to many deconstructionist critics, Michael ultimately asserts that DeLillo's political vision is negative, focusing on "the breakdown of the Western tradition, of the certainties on which it depends, and of its version of political agenda and individual agency" (13).

18. For example, Lentricchia reads this scene as Marina's futile self-assertion, more evidence of an American life determined "totally inside the representations generated in the print and visual media": "What is shocking to Marina is also seductive: she can't keep herself from walking back into the picture in order to give audience to her own charismatic self" (207).

Works Cited

Bahm, Archie J. "Buddhist Aesthetics." *Journal of Aesthetics and Art Criticism* 16.2 (1957): 249–52.

Bell, Pearl K. "DeLillo's World." *Partisan Review* 59.1 (Winter 1992): 138–46.

Born, Daniel. "Sacred Noise in Don DeLillo's Fiction." *Literature & Theology: An International Journal of Theory, Criticism, and Culture* 3 (1999): 211–21.

Civello, Paul. "Undoing the Naturalistic Novel: Don DeLillo's *Libra*." *Arizona Quarterly* 48, no. 2 (1992): 33–56.

Cowart, David. *Don DeLillo: The Physics of Language.* Athens: University of Georgia Press, 2002.

DeCurtis, Anthony. " 'An Outsider in This Society': An Interview with Don DeLillo." In *Conversations with Don DeLillo*, 52–74.

DeLillo, Don. "American Blood: A Journey through the Labyrinth of Dallas and JFK." *Rolling Stone* (8 December 1983): 21–22, 24, 27–28, 74.

———. *Libra.* New York: Viking, 1988.

———. *The Names.* 1982. New York: Vintage, 1989.

DePietro, Thomas, ed. *Conversations with Don DeLillo.* Jackson: University Press of Mississippi, 2005.

Duvall, John. *Don DeLillo's Underworld: A Reader's Guide*. New York and London: Continuum Publishing, 2002.

Hutchinson, Stuart. "DeLillo's *Libra* and the Real." *The Cambridge Quarterly* 30.2 (2001): 117–131.

Johnston, John. "Superlinear Fiction or Historical Diagram? Don DeLillo's *Libra*," *Modern Fiction Studies* 40 (Summer 1994): 319–42.

Kasulis, T. P. *Zen Action/Zen Person*. Honolulu: University of Hawaii Press, 1981.

Keesey, Douglass. *Don DeLillo*. New York: Twayne Publishers, 1993.

Kornick, Joseph. "*Libra* and the Assassination of JFK: A Textbook Operation." *The Arizona Quarterly* 50.1 (1994): 109–32.

LeClair, Thomas. "An Interview with Don DeLillo." In *Conversations with Don DeLillo*, 3–15.

Lentricchia, Frank, ed. *Introducing Don DeLillo*. Durham, North Carolina: Duke University Press, 1991.

———. "Libra as Postmodern Critique." In *Introducing Don DeLillo*, 193–215.

Little, Jonathan. "Ironic Mysticism in DeLillo's *Ratner's Star*." *Papers in Language and Literature* 35.3 (1999): 301–32.

Loy, David R. *A Buddhist History of the West: Studies in Lack*. Albany: State University York Press, 2002.

Maltby, Paul. "The Romantic Metaphysics of Don DeLillo." *Contemporary Literature* 37.2 (Summer 1996): 258–77.

McClure, John A. *Partial Faiths: Postsecular Fiction in the Age of Pynchon and Morrison*. University of Georgia Press, 2007.

Michael, Magali Cornier. "The Political Paradox within Don DeLillo's *Libra*." *Critique* 35 (Spring 1994): 146–55.

Millard, Bill. "The Fable of the Ants: Myopic Interactions in DeLillo's *Libra*." In *Critical Essays on Don DeLillo*, 213–28.

Moss, Maria. " 'Writing as a Deeper Form of Concentration': An Interview with Don DeLillo." In *Conversations with Don DeLillo*, 155–68.

Mott, Christopher M. "*Libra* and the Subject of History." *Critique* 35 (Spring 1994): 131–45, rptd. in *Critical Essays on Don DeLillo*, 229–44.

Noya, José Liste. "Naming the Secret: Don DeLillo's *Libra*." *Contemporary Literature* 45.2 (2004): 239–75.

O'Donnell, Patrick. "Engendering Paranoia in Contemporary Narrative." *Boundary 2* 19.1 (1992): 181–204.

Ricard, Matthieu and Trinh Xuan Thuan. *The Quantum and the Lotus*. New York: Three Rivers Press, 2001.

Ruppersburg, Hugh and Tim Engles, eds. *Critical Essays on Don DeLillo*. New York: G.K. Hall & Co., 2000.

Stor[h]off, Gary. "The Failure of Games in Don DeLillo's *End Zone*." *American Sport Culture: The Humanistic Dimensions*. Ed. Wiley Lee Umphlett. Lewisburg: Bucknell University Press, 1985. 235–45.

Suddenly. Dir. Lewis Allen. United Artists, 1954. With Frank Sinatra, Sterling Hayden, and James Gleason. Screenplay by Richard Sale. Produced by Robert Bassler.

Summers, Anthony and Robbyn Swan. *Sinatra: A Life*. New York: Alfred A. Knof, 2005.

Thomas, Glen. "History, Biography, and Narrative in Don DeLillo's *Libra*." *Twentieth-Century Literature* 43.1 (Spring 1997): 107–24.

Trigilio, Tony. *Allen Ginsberg's Buddhist Poetics.* Carbondale, IL: Southern Illinois University Press, 2007.

Waldron, Lamar and Thom Hartman. *Ultimate Sacrifice: John and Robert Kennedy, the Plan for a Coup in Cuba, and the Murder of JFK.* New York: Carroll & Graf, 2005.

Walker, Joseph S. "Criminality, the Real, and the Story of America: The Case of Don DeLillo." *The Centennial Review* 43.3 (1999):433–66.

Will, George. "Shallow Look at the Mind of an Assassin." *Washington Post,* 22 September 1988, A25, rptd. in *Critical Essays on Don DeLillo,* 56–57.

Yardley, Jonathan. "Appointment in Dallas." *Washington Post Book World,* 31 July 1988, 3.

Part III

Speaking as Enlightenment

Interviews with Buddhist Writers

Chapter 6

"The Present Moment Happening"

A Conversation with Gary Snyder About *Danger on Peaks*

Julia Martin

Julia Martin (JM): In *Danger on Peaks* there is so much awareness of suffering and destruction at many levels, yet the collection also is deeply concerned with healing. So reading the poems brings to mind for me the great question of how to work with integrity as a writer in the late modern world. At the same time I've been thinking about how this view of suffering and healing might relate to your idea of the female Buddha Tārā; how it connects with what she represents. In *Mountains and Rivers Without End*, you describe the whole epic poem as a sort of sutra for Tārā. Now, although she isn't mentioned explicitly in the new collection, there seem to me to be some continuities in what you're doing. Perhaps we can approach these questions through the poems.

I'd like to start by talking about the vow which you made as a fifteen-year-old, and now return to near the beginning of the book. The young Snyder has just come down from his first ascent of Mt. St. Helens and reads the reports of Hiroshima and Nagasaki. He makes a vow: "By the power and beauty and permanence of Mt. St. Helens, I will fight this cruel and destructive power and those who would seek to use it, for all my life" (9). Of course that was sixty years ago now. Although you put it in the book, you are clearly no longer that fifteen-year-old, wanting to fight. And yet in another sense you have never stopped engaging with the powers you identified then, although the focus has changed over the years. So I am interested in how from a Buddhist point of view, or from your point of view, one takes on the problem, the disease which you recognized as a teenager. If "fighting" it in an oppositional, dualistic way could be a way of replicating it, what alternatives are there? More particularly, could you say something about what has happened to that early vow?

Gary Snyder (GS): That's a very large question. I'll just say a few words about the idea of the vow. I was moved at that age of fifteen, to express a vow to fight against, to oppose, governments and powers, scientists, politicians, whoever would dare use, hope to use, nuclear weaponry in any way on earth. The shock and outrage that had provoked that was the destruction of Hiroshima and Nagasaki, not only the suffering of human beings, but realizing that these bombs could destroy much of nature itself.

One could take such a vow literally and try to act on it for a whole life. What I found over the years was a growth in my understanding of what had happened and why it happened. I also had to learn what is actually possible in the world. But most important, I learned more about what it means to take a vow. I could say, "Well I tried. And it didn't work, did it? I've been living my life by this and I guess it didn't come to anything *[laughs]*—In fact it's worse than ever!" *[laughs]*

JM: But?

GS: Well, I came to realize, no use being so literal. So I've measured my original intention against my ignorance and my gradual great understanding, all these years. I had no answers either. But I had questions. How did we get here? How can I not contribute to more war? And why is it, how is it, that so many fellow human beings on earth are apparently comfortable with it? I realized that there is also a war against nature. The biosphere itself is subject to a huger explosion by far than anything nuclear—the half-million-year long slow explosion of human impact.

One of my tools has been my poetry, my art. My guide came to be Shakyamuni and all the other Buddhas. And my ally, my critic, is old Doctor Coyote, who is not inclined to make a distinction between good and evil.

JM: I suppose that by the end of *Danger on Peaks* the vow has become the Bodhisattva's vow to save all sentient beings.

GS: The primary vow, the primal vow, is to save all sentient beings. Or to help all sentient beings. Or, as Dōgen says, "I take a vow to help all sentient beings take a vow to save all sentient beings." And I'd add, "let myself, let us, be saved by all beings."

JM: The extra layer?

GS: Yes, we don't take it because *we* can do it. All we can do is take the vow to help *others* also take it. So the vow turns over on itself and rolls onward in its karma. In the Shin Buddhism of Japan it's called the *Hongwan*, the primary—the original—cosmic vow. There are two huge temples in Kyoto called

Hongwanjis, the East Hongwanji and the West Hongwanji. That is, the East Temple of the primary vow, and the West Temple of the primary vow.

Now the primary vow was taken eons ago, absolutely eons ago, by some wandering girl or boy who was eventually to become Amitabha Buddha, and who said, "I take a vow to save *all* beings, however many lifetimes it takes." So that is the story of Amitabha, Amida, whose primary vow is still at work in the world: to save all beings, regardless of how long it takes. Then Dōgen says, "Well—to help them save themselves. [*laughs*]

This is the amazing Mahayana vision, which ultimately does not shrink from the disappearance of this universe either. Such a huge view. So, let's have a cup of tea and take note of the falling leaves. Whatever else I have to say on that is in a poem or two.

JM: In my own writing I keep returning to questions about impermanence and continuity. What is impermanent? What continues? In one sense everything is changing into everything else and is impermanent, falling leaves. But in another sense there is continuity.

GS: Well, there's continuity of impermanence. We know that. [*laughs*]

JM: There are a couple of moments in the book when you hint at the possibility of a sense of continuity that seems different from what one has come to expect in your work. I'm thinking of two beautiful poems, "Waiting for a Ride" and "The Acropolis Back When." In the past you've tended to write away from the habitual big focus on "self" which is such a feature of modern culture. So instead of lots of "I," you'll situate personal experience in relation to the Big Flow, the big living system, the nondual world and so on, and there are plenty of Buddhist and ecological reasons for doing so. But here I'm noticing something a bit different among the familiar. Both poems imagine the idea of some long continuity, perhaps even personal continuity, beyond this particular life. Words like: "Or maybe I will, much later / some far time walking the spirit path in the sky" (56), or else "Lifetimes ago . . . I climbed it" (88). What sort of continuity might this suggest?

GS: When Allen, Peter, and Joanne and I were traveling together in India I let myself imagine my way into the view of literal reincarnation. There's a faint glimpse you catch once in a great while of ancient relationships, of eras come round again, deep déjà vu. One can play with these, but it's dangerous to take them too lightly. Those are risky poems.

JM: I suppose the idea of continuity in your writing is more often to do with the continuity of the wild, and our participation in it. In *Danger on Peaks* there is that poem toward the end where you reflect on the human impact on the planet that you spoke about earlier: "we're loose on earth / half a million years / our weird blast spreading" (103). But then the poem goes on to remember that in the long view, wildness is ineradicable and that wilderness inevitably returns, grows green again. That's the long view.

GS: That's not actually terribly long. But there is a question about the long-term impact of the particular variety of human civilization we have right now, the developed world variety of civilization. Truth is, human beings probably had little impact up till 20,000 or 30,000 years ago, when they started setting fires everywhere to improve the landscape.

JM: And the developed world variety of that trend is a very recent experiment.

GS: Yes. And as Tonto says, "Speak for yourself, white man." It is not that everybody on earth is involved in that. There are many cultures and societies and peoples on earth who stand aside from the recent destructive side of civilization. Many are not doing it even now. They're suffering from it as much as nature herself is suffering from the effects of it.

JM: You see it as something that has a fairly limited period of duration?

GS: Not that I hope for it, but it's very likely that the present energy-intensive high-population society will have to crash from key shortages and from garbage-glut. People will go on, keep a lighter technology going, and bring back the walking routes. Tell stories and meditate. Grow lots of garlic.
      Another approach is Robinson Jeffers, who said, "I am an *in*humanist. Not an antihumanist, just an inhumanist. In the inhuman perspective humans are a passing problem." We might ask "Well what's lost? When human beings are gone, what's lost?" Is that something we should concern ourselves with?

JM: Well what *is* lost? When you're writing in the last section of the book about the bombing of the Buddhas of Bamiyan by the Taliban. it seems to me that you're looking at a sense of the loss of those human artifacts that have been destroyed.

GS: Yes, I'm seeing it as deep art. It is what some bold builders tried to do, making a human figure into rock. What a culture.

JM: Making big things, beautiful things.

GS: Yes, there are some cultures who make bold things, as the Chinese did on quite a scale, for a long period of time. All the rich high civilizations tried it.

In my Bamiyan poem I don't want to make more of it than to say, "Honor the dust." Dōgen somewhere says, "The whole planet is the dust of the bones of the ancient Buddhas."

JM: So what's the difference?

GS: So, honor the dust.

JM: If it's all bones of Buddhas, then surely we are thinking in a pretty vast timescale. I hear your point that it doesn't need a very long view to think about the end of our Western industrial civilization, but in terms of what you're calling inhumanism you're also situating things in a geological perspective, a very long time.

GS: Truth is, it's not too useful to calibrate on too large a time scale for human affairs.

JM: What sort of scale would you want to use?

GS: A useful scale is the present moment. The present moment starts about 11,000 years ago, probably has about the same time to go into the future.

JM: Beginning with agriculture?

GS: Holocene. Post Pleistocene.

JM: Post the last Ice Age.

GS: That's a Northern Hemisphere perspective, that the Holocene is about 11,000 years old. I'm not sure how it applies in other parts of the world. This is the moment in planetary time of our present climate, the flora and fauna in their combinations just for now. It's the world in which we live. Are we living it well? Or are we not—in terms of what it is now?

JM: That is interesting, because in the Southern Hemisphere where I come from there was no glaciation at that time. So it's more diverse and the plants are older, and the continuities go back a lot further.

GS: More continuous, probably. Different portions of the globe have their own sort of present moment, assuming that things are constantly changing, but also knowing that there's a certain stability there for a while. And that finite world is also where we challenge ourselves: What do we know?

JM: Our finite capacities? The limits of what we are able to do?

GS: The limits of who we are, and the limits of what our world is.

JM: We personally, or we as a species?

GS: Individually, personally—also whoever we are, as a family. But the very last two poems in *Danger on Peaks* push it to the point where you "go beyond" that. Like, you asked about Tārā. Tārā is not another version of the Earth Mother. She's not the mother of all beings. She's the mother of the Buddhas. She is the mother of beings who see *beyond* being. The Earth Mother, the mother of all beings, is the mother of birth and death. The mother of the Buddhas is the mother of those beings who see through birth and death. Some people would like to see a little bit toward what is *through* birth and death. And Tārā is represented as a virgin.

JM: But a mother of those beings.

GS: As I understand it, only the mother of the Buddhas, not the mother of beings. She's a different kind of mother. She's the mother of Wisdom, the mother of Wisdom and Compassion. She's not giving birth to beings. She's not even the mother of God, like Mary. She is also the same as Prajñā. The goddess Prajñā is represented exactly the same in the iconography. And Prajñā is also called the goddess "Wisdom who is the mother of the Buddhas."

JM: And it's the Wisdom that goes beyond, *Mahāprajñāpāramitā*.

GS: Yes, I'd say she is the mother of nondual insight, beyond birth and death. So she can look like a virgin if she wants. It doesn't matter. [*laughs*]. Or like a young woman, actually, she's just portrayed as a very young woman in the iconography.

JM: Or even like the world, the nondual world? The other day when I was walking with a friend from San Francisco up Steep Ravine on Mt. Tamalpais through that wonderful green forest, I imagined we were walking in the body of Tārā. But perhaps you'd say it's more like the body of Gaia—if we're going to talk in archetypes at all.

GS: Yes? Dōgen would also say it's the body of all the old dead Buddhas. [*laughs*]

JM: All those bones.

GS: Sort of archaeological, geological. Or it is just the present moment happening.

JM: We don't need to turn it into a metaphor.

GS: Mt. Tamalpais is a very fine place.

JM: And so close to the city. We have the same sort of situation where I live in Cape Town.

GS: What's that mountain called?

JM: Table Mountain. It really changes the sense of a city to have the wild mountain in the midst.

GS: Tom Killion and I are working on a book on Mt. Tamalpais. He's a woodblock artist and he's been doing some blocks of the Mt. Tamalpais area. He and I are doing some writing to go with that, and then there's the "Circumambulation," the older stories, the native Miwok stories about it, and so forth. We're really focusing on its closeness to the city.

JM: And the sea, sea and mountain and city, that combination. It's extraordinary, and its something I recognize from home.

GS: Yes, it's wonderful.

JM: Gary, to go back to Tārā or Prajñā as mother of nondual insight, of Wisdom and Compassion. Could you connect these Buddhist images with Coyote? You said at the beginning that Coyote was your ally and so on. He's also nondual, isn't he? He isn't interested in those dualisms either.

GS: No, he's not. How Doctor Coyote fits into this is a good question. In fact that is one of the things about the Trickster figure: the Trickster manages to stand outside of all these discourses. Indefinitely. [*laughs*] We'll have to work on that eventually.

JM: Could you say something more about it now? We don't have Coyote in Africa so I always feel that I'm missing some resonances.

GS: In West Africa isn't Spider a Trickster figure? I know there is or was a San Trickster, Mantis. At any rate, it's the Trickster we're looking at—Coyote is just one incarnation (and one of the most remarkable). Jehovah is playing Trickster when he gets Abraham to almost sacrifice Isaac, and then slips a ram into the bushes. Let's not try to do more than this with Trickster for now.

JM: Sure. But to take it sideways slightly, there's that poem in *Danger on Peaks* about Doctor Coyote consulting his turds, and then a couple of others about consulting the "old advisors." You describe a feeling of not knowing what to do, like "despair at how the human world goes down." And then, in the poem, you do this thing, you consult the fallen trees or the mountain or whoever it is, and some kind of response comes, some kind of healing insight, returning you to the present moment. Reading this makes me wonder about how one writes about nonhuman things in ways that seem to be telling a human story.

GS: You just have to try. You can't be sure if it's fair or not. It takes a lot of nerve to do this stuff.

JM: I'm not asking you to explain the poems. But when you appeal to Mt. St. Helens for help and there is a sense of a response, what is happening?

GS: There are mysteries that come to us. I could give a kind of reasonable answer to your question, but that would make it slighter than it is.

JM: Yes, I know. It's just that those are obviously key moments in the book.

GS: It stands better as a question: "How is it that, if you ask for help it comes, but not in any way you'd ever know?" Many people who read that have said to me, "That's *true*." I don't ask them "How do you know it's true?" I believe they know. It's true for them. There is a truth there, but it's not a truth that everybody recognizes until it happens to them. Some people never have the necessity, or the nerve, to even *ask* for help. [*laughs*]

Works Cited

Snyder, Gary. *Danger on Peaks*. Washington, D.C.: Shoemaker & Hoard, 2004.
———. *Mountains and Rivers without End*. New York: Counterpoint, 1996.

Chapter 7

Embodied Mindfulness

Charles Johnson and Maxine Hong Kingston on Buddhism, Race, and Beauty

John Whalen-Bridge

This interview was conducted on May 29, 2004 at the American Literature Association (ALA) Conference in San Francisco. Charles Johnson and Maxine Hong Kingston each gave readings at the ALA that year and generously agreed to meet with me for the interview. Also in attendance were fellow members of the Charles Johnson Society: Marc Conner, Will Nash, Linda Furgerson Selzer, and Gary Storhoff. In 2009, I reorganized the material and asked Charles and Maxine if they would like to review the interview to emend or update any of the points made five years earlier.

—JWB

Linda Selzer (LS): I'd like to begin by asking about selfhood and representation, about cross-representation. How do each of you feel about representing someone who is supposedly "other"?

Joh Whalen-Bridge (JWB): Yes, and Maxine's Wittman Ah Sing is a very lively male character. But when you represent another gender or race, you have problems both at the level of composition and reception. Critics might not like what you're doing. So maybe you guys could respond to that idea a little bit.

Charles Johnson (CJ): I tend to be very cautious with sexual descriptions because, as we know, it's a powerful subject. It's a bomb that can blow up on you if you're not careful—but I want to know what Maxine says.

Maxine Hong Kingston (MHK): When I wrote Wittman Ah Sing, I was seeing that as a big artistic challenge for myself. I saw my career of forty years before as selfish—not ethnocentric but *ego*centric, just writing from a woman's point of view. If I could—if I could write a male character, then it would be a great artistic breakthrough. And I believe I was seeing myself as such a limited person and as a limited writer if I could only stay within the bounds of the feminine. There's the other half of existence and I am—I'm not even trying to create male characters, a male fiction character.

Actually, this struggle started when I was writing *China Men*. One of the ways that I approached this was to give myself permission. I had to have the faith that any one of us is free to be looked at from the point of view of any other human being on this earth. I struggled against the critical argument in which, you know, that you have no right to presume that you can inhabit the body and mind of a person of another race or culture. So I thought, well, I'm not going to listen to that. It's restricting my freedom. To write a character that's not me is almost like an out-of-body experience—what we can do is fly out of our own body and inhabit the body of another. That's already very magical. We can choose any person and write from their insight. At Berkeley in my writing classes, I just gave the students permission. You know? "You, white person, you go ahead and write about black people. I give you permission to do that." You know? I don't care what your background is.

CJ: At a panel recently with Octavia Butler and some other science fiction writers last fall in Seattle, somebody asked about writing outside your race. Octavia said, "Well, you're going to get it wrong. But you can try." She said, "You're going to get something wrong." I think I realized after writing *Faith and the Good Thing* that there are just too many subtleties that I would just never be able to get perfectly.

I've been married thirty-four years. I know my wife pretty well. But when we first got married, she was going to be a teacher, an elementary school teacher. And then, you know, she had our first kid and she decided to be a homemaker. A little later she went back to school and did a bachelor's and master's in social work. At that time—this after she had cancer actually and wanted to get back into the world, 1993. And she said something I thought was really interesting. She said she had never wanted to be a teacher. She had wanted to be a social worker before we met. But she had nursed her grandmother through her death and was so emotionally involved with that that she didn't feel she'd make a good social worker. Her second choice was being a teacher.

All of a sudden I discovered, you know, after the gap from 1970 to about 1993, this one piece of information that she'd never had occasion to talk about before. In my view as writers we have this obligation to create a social world that looks a little bit like the one outside our window. All kinds of people walking around out there that we bump into, right? You can only have usually one major character. It's either first- or third-person limited overlooking this person's shoulder, male or black or white or whatever the case might be. But that role can have other people whose heads we have to enter. We have to do that as writers.

Philosophically and certainly in a Buddhist sense, I think the Other is an unending mystery. And I *like* it like that, to write without making assumptions. Literature is not a game. Art is one of the most important things that we do. But we've got to put it in its proper context.

JWB: Well, that's fine, but when you say, "I can't expect to get the Other exactly correct," I am reminded of Jesse Jackson's presidential run. Someone asked Jimmy Carter, "Is he qualified?" Remember, this was when Ronald Reagan was in the White House. Jimmy Carter said, "Compared to who?"

CJ: Good point.

JWB: So if you're talking about representing the other and you don't know this about your wife and you're surprised by your daughter, one could say the same thing about the self. Lama Surya Das, that, you know, after all these years of meditation, you know, what have you figured out? Have you figured out "I'm not who I think I am."

JWB: In *Middle Passage*, you comically present "the dance of love." Rutherford Calhoun goes to sea to flee from marriage: "Ah, there it was, revealed at last, the one thing inside at the door that made me shudder. This is what you heard all your—

CJ: "—blessed life from—"

JWB: "—black elders and church women in flowered gowns: comb your hair. Be a credit to the race. It made my insides clench."

CJ: Yeah! He's in reaction against the black bourgeoisie, so to speak. Doesn't want to be one. He was young. He was a free man, but he really doesn't understand what the meaning of freedom is. He doesn't know his responsibility, in flight from what he says he doesn't like. Like an Englishman dusted over with cinnamon—so there's a little bit of the "trying to escape from the bourgeois" element.

But go on. You were—you didn't get to the end of your question.

JWB: Well, I'm curious about the tension between bohemian freedom and responsibility across your career. You start writing in the 1970s, after the sexual revolution. There is a celebration of sexual freedom in much of the literature of this era, but many readers complain that freedom without responsibility has been a specifically *male* movement. People often talk about the 1960s as, well, in retrospect, being kind of a—it was kind of a *man's* game in a nice way because it was a celebration of freedom apart from responsibility. So is this a shift in your career? How would you describe it?

CJ: I've got to zero in on the one thing and this is terribly important as we talk about American history, when we talk about the 1950s and the 1960s. I know the 1960s quite well. And friends of mine from the 1960s remember it quite well from *their* perspective. When they remember it, it's Woodstock. It's the Beatles. It's rock-n-roll. When *I* remember it, it's the Civil Rights Movement. When we sit down and talk, I suddenly realize we were looking at different things. The assumption is that across the board somehow in America, the Beats and other liberators affected everybody the same way. It isn't the case. I grew up in a community in Evanston in which I was acutely aware of the history of my people, and of my parents and of my grandparents. And I kind of knew where I fit in.

I'm the first one in my family to go to college. I thought you went to college to gain *wisdom*. That's what I thought until I got there. And then I thought, "WHAT is going on?" [*laughter*] This is why I wound up in philosophy. But I was acutely aware of all the people who had their heads busted, killed, bodies dumped in rivers just so I could be on that damn campus. I was *never* forgetful of that. There was always a weight that you carry as a black person, at least prior to, you know, the 1970s in respect—you know. I mean I'm joking about it with Rutherford, "Be a credit to the race." But I grew up with that. I grew up with that. The moment I went outside my door, I represented my people in what I did and what I didn't do. I tried to raise my kids that way as well. They have to be clearly, perfectly aware that: *yeah*, we're Americans. *Yeah*, we've been here since 1619. We built this place and we could—we have evidence all the way back to the Colonial period. However, in a predominantly white society we don't have an awful lot of control. We always have to be on guard, just like somebody who comes here from another country. You don't know the language. You can read things two ways.

Going through elementary school, I'm reading the same books as my white friends. These are all white characters and some of them are even saying negative things about black people. This was riddled throughout the literature prior to 1960. And so I've got to do a double-take. I've got to say, "I'll blank that part in this great writer's work and I'll empathize totally, as much as I can, with his situation." Why? I've got to write a paper about this. I've got to get an "A" just like this guy over there. So I'm doing a double-take on *everything*, you see, as I move through this particular society. Now, that's a complexity that I don't think we recognize about black experience as we do with people who were new immigrants to America. This is absolutely true of my experience.

JWB: Yes. Maxine, if I could ask about your understanding of the 1960s in terms of race in this sense, because you have—you have some commentary on this in *Trip Master Monkey* where you have Wittman Ah Sing as a critical reader of culture. Now, you've got Beat ancestors in your work. Wittman has Beat bohemian ancestors, but it's not uncritical, and he kind of hits the pause button now and then and has to then ask what Kerouac would say about an old Chinese man. What was your feeling about that? "Hey there, little Chinese man—you're so beautiful, you are just WOW!" I'm paraphrasing—

MHK: ". . . with your little twinkling feet." [*laughter*] I think that we people who are non-black, non-white, we have a very special sight because the whole discussion during the 1960s was about black and white. And our—from our point of view, "Where am I in this?" The answer was so complicated because you have to make your place in the artistic, literary life of America. You *know* that the question is not black and white. It's not *only* black and white. And so it's making your own place, but also making your vision known. And it's a vision of nonduality. Wittman and I were aware, yes, of the Beatles and Woodstock—*and* the Civil Rights Movement. We were there. And Vietnam. And then, I was in Berkeley, and so there is that Berkeley experience in my life and fiction.

Wittman is critical of *all* of it. Wittman contemplates his literary heroes and realizes that Jack Kerouac doesn't have the true vision. He knows that the Beatles do not have the true vision. I think that Asian-American writers and also Asian Americans generally did look to the blacks for solutions. Martin Luther King Jr., was talking about what we needed to hear when he spoke of the "beloved community." I knew that the beloved community included us. The artistic challenge has been to create this inclusiveness.

I don't like it when critics label my work, "Asian American" or worse than that, it's "Chinese." You know. "She's written about China." I'm writing America. And when they put this China label on it, it means that they have denied what they have read. And they say, "What you have written is not true of us. It's true of you Chinese people and those people over there, but we're all right over here." And this happened especially with feminism, and you know I come out so strong for feminism, and everybody said—and the critics say, "Well, look at the way they treat women over there in China." No. I am talking about the way we're treating women right here.

We were talking about critics. And what's so unfortunate is that this is the way *critics* see it. It's the reviewers that look at your book and only notice what you have to say about race.

CJ: The dialogue was black and white for a couple of hundred years, and it cannot be that way any more. It has to be a dialogue that involves black people, 15 percent of whom are foreign-born, from all kinds of other cultures, like Africa, the Caribbean, and so forth. It has to involve Asian Americans. But even that term lumps many kinds of people together. The dialogue has to evolve beyond just black and white. It's got to be black and Asian. And it's got to be black and Hispanic. And it's got to be Asian and Hispanic.

But Maxine made another point, too, that I wanted to take up about being labeled Asian American. I had long talks with August Wilson, and some of them were very illuminating. August keeps *promising* that he's going to boycott certain book stores in which you go in to find his plays and they're over in the black literature section and you go over to look for Edward Albee, he's over in just "plays." Okay? Segregation, apartheid, you know, in book stores! It's really *divisive*.

He tells a very interesting story, too. And it's about being on a panel with other playwrights and one of the other playwrights is talking, and he says something about, "August writes about race." And he says, "Wait a minute. I write about race, but you don't?" Okay? It's because his characters are black and, therefore, it must be about race. But why isn't this white guy writing about race as well? He never thought about it that way, in those terms. August says, "What he's doing—he's not writing about race. He's writing about people. And they happen to be from Pittsburgh in a certain economic group that he understands."

The work of an Asian-American writer or black-American playwright is about humanity. It is not about race problems. It is not about reaction to what white folks did. This is about *human beings* and how they relate—what they discover through their interactions. Until at least we get to the point where we can do that and we find its universality—as we do with Updike—we haven't made any progress at all.

MHK: What little progress. At the 92nd Street Y with Sandra Cisernos, there was a little announcement in one of those newspapers that they give away out in the street, and it said Maxine Hong Kingston and Sandra Cisernos will be appearing together and talking about ethnicity. No!

CJ: I just looked at the catalog copy for my new collection. At the end of the first paragraph, it says "all these stories are about identity and race." No! No! They're not.

MHK: I *know*! What about love and kisses?

CJ: Yeah. It's about being human. That's what we lay on writers of color all the time. My question—it's a mantra with me—is, What does it actually mean to be a writer of color in a predominantly white and very Eurocentric society?

What role is set aside for us to play in that society? If you're James Baldwin, you've spent your entire life explaining to white people what they're doing wrong. And they're deeply appreciative:
"What are we doing wrong, Jimmy?"
"Okay. Well, I'll tell you what we're doing wrong."
"Well, come over here and tell us about that. Over here, Jimmy. We'll pay you lots of money."
I was not put here on this earth to spend my time educating white people. I was put here to create art. If it educates people, great. But that is not the role I can inhabit in this society. I can't, because it's a funny kind of service you're doing and it's still subservient in a particular way. I just can't do that.
That's why I said at the National Book Award: "No, I'm not a racial spokesman. You've got all these millions of black people out here. Go ask them what they think." This is post-civil rights era. During segregation when people were kept apart and white folks wanted to know what black people thought, they'd pick one guy, the minister in town, and say, "Well, you—what are these people thinking." "Well they're thinking this, boss." But after segregation, you could talk to anybody you want to and find out what the—go down the street. Don't ask me what I think about reparations. Talk to me about my last book. And don't ask me what I think about reparations. You know? Did I write about reparations? No. So why are you asking me a question about reparations? If I write about reparations, the question's fair. But then you don't need to ask me because I've already told you!

Will Nash (WN): I recognize the concern about being pigeonholed, but it seems to me, and maybe I'm naïve, that one of the gifts that you have in the ability to dream a world that is not exactly the world we walk around in is to also dream what it might be like if we could make this one work better.

CJ: In a recent interview I was told, "Well, you are an 'unelected legislator.' " But I'm not anybody's unelected legislator. I'm not a politician. We don't *begin* there. You can just have a character who is human.

Gary Storhoff (GS): You and Maxine both do so well at imparting and joy, but the one thing I still want to ask about the race of the protagonist in "Moving Pictures"—what is it?

CJ: Who knows?

GS: Who knows? When I teach *Middle Passage* or *Oxherding Tale*, or I teach *Woman Warrior*, my students respond to the depictions of race very emotionally.

Your books are richly comic and very, very funny, but there are some really grotesque scenes and horrible scenes. Especially the death of Minty in *Oxherding Tale*.

CJ: Sure.

GS: These moments really stick with the student. So to say these books are raceless would not be an accurate reflection of at least how my students respond to that. I don't see how my students can read such stories and not think about the race of the protagonist. Obviously, you don't pontificate in either book at all about race, but for these students, it's very difficult to read such a story or novel and say, "Well, slavery happened in the nineteenth century and now it's over with and there are no lasting effects." Or students reading the *Woman Warrior* may say, "My family is a lot like that," but they'll also need to recognize the special difficulties faced by an immigrant family.

CJ: The ideal thing is to leave an emotional impact on the reader—that's got to be the beginning. Otherwise, it's not going to succeed as a work of art. What do you do when you sit there and create a character? I'm thinking about the world that character's in, the time and place in which that character is living. If it's Rutherford Calhoun who is a free black person in the 1830s, then obviously whatever I know about what happened to black people right during that period is going to impinge on his movement through the world. It has to.
   Enough on race. Have you guys seen this new book, *Nixon Under the Bodhi Tree and Other Works of Buddhist Fiction*? It's the first contemporary anthology of Buddhist fiction. There's a story in there about the Buddha's mother before he's born. There's a story in there about a guy who's got a lawn-mowing service, and he has a Cambodian helper who is always slipping into meditation when he should be, you know, working. It's a great story! There are stories set two-thousand years back at the exact moment that Buddhists began to move from the oral tradition to writing down the sutras. In that story, a monk has memorized everything—he has a photographic memory. "Nixon Under the Bodhi Tree," the title story, is an O. Henry Prize fiction about a gay actor who plays Nixon on stage. In between two of his performances Nixon dies, and the actor's dying of AIDS. Very powerful story.
   I wrote the introduction, and one of the things I say in it that I think I got right is that Buddhism is first and foremost an experience, one each individual must confirm firsthand. Nevertheless, we are enriched by these wonderful stories, fingers pointing to the moon while recounting episodes of impermanence and interconnectedness.

JWB: So there is no tension between Buddhism and storytelling?

MHK: William Burroughs said there's no such thing as a great Buddhist novel. The book Chuck's talking about sounds like it's the answer to Burroughs.

JWB: William Burroughs made the statement in response to a Chögyam Trungpa intensive meditation retreat, and we have to remember that Trungpa did not allow anyone to write or read for distraction, but Burroughs negotiated and was able to have a notebook. Burroughs felt that all art needs conflict. This is central to modernist aesthetics, and Robert Penn Warren put the matter directly in one of his textbooks: "No conflict, no story."

I'd like to read a passage from *Dreamer*, my favorite, that is more-or-less about a conflict-free character, Mama Pearl:

> The staff fell in love with her that day, with her feathery wig that knocked 20 years off her total of 78, with the way she worked her toothless mouth like a fish, while listening to King explain his plans in Chicago, bobbing her head and asking, 'Is you really?' with her hands pushed forward, wig askew and feet planted apart in two shapeless black shoes. She was utterly unself-conscious. Egoless, and flitted around the room as though she had feet spun from the air, descending on the twin trees in her checkered dress with two vein-cabled legs, lumpy in places, bowed. But it was her voice that everyone remembered most. Thinking she might be thirsty, I offered her a soda, which she declined, shaking her head and explaining, "Thank you, darling. I'm tickled but I better not drink no pop. I might pee myself."

CJ: I have to tell you something about that passage. When I was a student at Stony Brook, my wife's grandmother stayed with us for a couple of weeks. We went fishing. She was so fascinating to me that I started taking down notes, and I kept them for decades, never using them until I wrote *Dreamer* twenty years later. I hoard all this sort of writing material. She gave me that line, "I can't drink no pop. I might pee myself." All Mama Pearl's lines are from my wife's grandmother, who was the model for that character. She struck me as totally unself-conscious as a human being.

JWB: She is what she is, with no evasion. As a character, beautiful, wonderful. As Maxine, borrowing from Lew Welch, puts it in *Trip Master Monkey*, you should sometimes just look at yourself in the mirror and say to yourself, "So it's come to *this*." [*laughter*]

CJ: That's a good line. Well, John, what we mean by enlightenment is supposed to be nonconceptual. You can't express this in the language. We try, fingers point to the moon. We use words like nondualistic, intuitional, and nondiscursive, right?

MHK: And it comes and goes. Wouldn't it be really great if one could get enlightened once and for all and say, "I've got it."

CJ: Get your degree!

MHK: But, you know, it's gone! In a second it's gone, and "So Thus Gone!" [*laughter*]

CJ: I think this is the important part to recognize. I have read that the longest time anyone has stayed in the awakened state without interruption is two weeks. You cannot maintain that state. We are incarnated *in bodies*. My favorite image for this state begins with an island, out in the middle of the ocean. The ocean represents enlightenment. We're standing on an island, which is *samsara*, delusion and ignorance. The ocean keeps wearing away at the island. It gets smaller and smaller and smaller until pretty soon there's only enough for someone to stand on the remains of the island with one foot. Think of that statue, the Dance of Shiva. Shiva is standing on one foot, actually standing on a demon representing *samsara*. Shiva's other foot is raised off the demon. What this famous, ancient image says is that as long as we are alive, embodied, we always have one foot in *samsara* or delusion and dualism. If that stepping-place were gone and if the island completely disappeared, we merge completely with *nirvana*, or emptiness; we would not exist as embodied humans. As long as we are incarnated in bodies, there is going to be some degree of *samsara*. One of Shiva's four hands says the universe starts with a bell. The other says it will end in fire. A third gestures, "Don't worry." And the fourth hand points to the one lifted foot, meaning, "There is liberation from illusion." But the other foot is still on the demon.

Until we depart this incarnation, there's always going to be a tincture of delusion and of ego, the illusion of self. And that's not a problem so long as you can recognize it at the time. You know what your mind is doing at that moment. You're not caught up in it. You say, "Well, I just had a terrible thought of envy and anger. But guess what? I'm not my thoughts. You let it go. Then we'll see what the next one looks like. Ah, there's a thought of benevolence. Let's hang onto that for a while. Let's water that seed for a little bit. The whole point is that you are free. You are free. That's why I wrote *Turning the Wheel,* because I think black people have always been driven, historically, by the question, *"How do I become free?"*

Does being free mean I act like characters in *The Cosby Show*? Is freedom owning a Lexus? No, freedom has to mean something else. Freedom means being totally in control of me so I direct *my* destiny. We're not the body. We're not our possessions. We know that. We're not our car. We're not our clothes. But we have a hard time accepting that we're not our thoughts. We're not the mind. But, as Buddhists, we are *aware* of this. We are consciousness. Thoughts simply arise and pass away, as do all things impermanent. What I'm describing here is *Vipassana* meditation. You recognize your thought for what it is. It's not controlling you, it's a product of you. That's the difference. You can be still on that little sliver of *samsara*, the island, before you merge with the One, but you're aware at every moment of what's happening with your own mind. That's the important thing.

I think that's why the Buddha has that little enigmatic, Mona Lisa-like smile in the statues after the experience of enlightenment. There's the awareness of suffering, within and without. He's looking at the world and he's in the world, not yet having passed over completely and finally to *nirvana*. And we know that at first he didn't want to teach—

JWB: He didn't want to grade papers.

CJ:—but some god said to him, "You've got to teach." Shakyamuni said, "I don't want to teach people about this. They're going to hate me. They're going to attack me." And the god said, "If one person understands, if only a few have a little dust in their eyes and understand, then it's all worth it." And so Shakyamuni spent the next forty-five years teaching. Forty-five more years in the realm of *samsara*. It has to be the case that he's looking at human beings and thinking, "How sad. How sad. But let me see what I can do to help." And so he uses skillful means. *Upaya kausalya*. Adjusting the teaching, the *dharma*, to kings and to people working in the fields, adjusting the wisdom to the level on which his listeners can receive it. Because they can all understand. That's the mark of a *truly* great philosophy. Like Marxism. You can reach the farmer in the field with Marxism, and you can also reach the theoreticians in the academy. The same is true of Buddhism—it speaks to genuinely universal concerns, since everyone suffers. I think that's why he's got this slightly sad, slightly pleased expression in some of those statues.

JWB: In John Stevens' book about Aikido, there's a description of Morihei Ueshiba's *dojo*. And over the door, there's a calligraphy that says "Art is the mother of religion." Some Buddhists have a humanistic-aesthetic approach, but some think about how many lifetimes it will take to wear away that island underfoot. What do we think about multiple lifetimes?

CJ: The notion of past and future lives is clearly one with great poetic value. But the idea of past and future lives? I can't take or accept this idea in a literal way. My friend, poet Al Young, once told me he did "Rebirth Therapy," whatever that is, and figured out what his past lives were.

JWB: Did he go in the hot tub and get reborn?

CJ: I don't really know what it is. I have no idea what past lives are, and I don't know what happens after death. That is, for my practice, absolutely meaningless. I think about my actions right now and my actions in the next moment when that arises. But brooding on past lives and bad *karma*—I just think that's dangerous. I've got Buddhist books written for children, which you can find in many Asian Buddhist temples, and these books can be very troubling. They say, "If you do *this*"—and an illustration shows a certain action, perhaps the action of laughing at cripple—then, "In your next life you will be a cripple," and there's a frightening illustration for that. A very crude understanding of causal connection is expressed by these illustrations of *karma*.

JWB: There's a logic to the stories that makes them memorable: If you're bloodthirsty, you'll come back as a mosquito.

CJ: There you go. I was at Arizona State recently for a week. One day I was walking from one classroom to another with the person who was hosting me, and I stopped to look at a statue I'd never seen before. A guy was selling it, you know, on campus, with lots of other spiritually related material. The statue showed a man with a sledge hammer and a bull cowering beneath him. The bull is looking up and it has the head of a man. In other words, in its previous life, the bull about to be slain had been a butcher. This is a very Hindu notion of *karma*, one right out of the *Bhagavad-Gita*. And that's similar to what one finds in those Buddhist books for children I just mentioned. It was so stark. You kill the bull; you come back as a bull. There's powerful imagery in that. I like Yukio Mishima's use of reincarnation, how he uses it to open up his characters. I'd love to be able to figure out how to do that with the reincarnation theme in my own fiction. But on the deepest levels of my existence, I just don't think about it. In fact, a Buddhist monk I interviewed in Thailand in 1997 said emphatically that we shouldn't think about reincarnation. If we take care of this moment, and the one after, we need not worry about an after-life or a next life. Ultimately, if we make progress on the path, we cease to create "good" and "bad" karma. That dualism disappears. Those who still have *kleshas*, emotional defilements, can achieve merit or "good karma" when they practice the *bodhisattva* ideal of transference of that merit to others.

When we use words like *kleshas* and *karma*, it seems like Buddhism has nothing to do with Western thought, but some people have called early Buddhism a kind of primitive phenomenology. There's a great deal of similarity. We're talking in both phenomenology and Buddhism about how ideas—concepts—are like a kind of paint that obscures the direct experience of phenomena. About how we project our ideas and interpretations onto objects and others, and so there is a need to clear all of that away if we want our perception liberated. Buddhism is about giving up a lot, just letting all that conditioning go. Phenomenology, in terms of the *epoché,* involves the clearing away of presuppositions and assumptions.

The Husserlian idea of the *lebensvelt*—life-world—was quite useful to Merleau-Ponty, who interested me greatly. I was also drawn to the method of "bracketing" our presuppositions when we encounter phenomenon. This process can be seen as a Western attempt to do something that has a 2,600-year-old history in the *buddhadharma.* One of Husserl's students, I can't remember his name, was Japanese and went back to Japan. He taught for a bit and then left teaching and went into the monastery. I see some interesting parallels between the two approaches because they're about the same quest for freedom, liberation. As one of my friends once said, where existentialism leaves off, Buddhism picks up. That's the way he put it. Existentialism doesn't go far enough.

JWB: There was a conversation between Robert Haas and Gary Snyder, if I have the story right. The comment was, "Deconstruction without compassion is self-aggrandized; deconstruction *with* compassion is Buddhism."

CJ: That's a good way to put it. I like that.

JWB: In the earlier years of American Buddhist practice and writing, the interest in Buddhism was often a reaction to the "religions of the Book," but this seems less true of your work, which is in many ways an invitation to Buddhist-Christian dialogue. Also, you're wife's a Christian and you're Buddhist . . . so you've got a mixed marriage, yes? Do you see yourself primarily as a Buddhist?

CJ: Yeah. But what does that really mean? Jan Willis is a Baptist/Buddhist, as she has written. It isn't a disjunctive, an either/or thing. I mean, I'm not *non*-Christian.

MARC CONNER: Could you just talk about your take on how Christianity and Buddhism overlap, wrestle with one another, in your work? The fusion of religions that emerges in *Dreamer* didn't arise in the earlier books.

CJ: I don't think there's any way to talk about Martin Luther King, Jr., whom I've written about in a novel, a short story, and several essays, without talking about Christianity. Before I published the book, I was somewhere giving a reading from it. And there was an audience, academic, you know, students, faculty and a philosophy guy down in the front row. And he raised his hand. And he said, "My question is this. Is there any way we can have King without the Christianity? Because it makes me really uncomfortable." And I said, "Well, you can take it out, but you don't have King if you do that." He supposedly was the department crank, or so I was told me later.

But, yes, I deliberately put Christianity front and center in *Dreamer*. Buddhism is always there with me, but I reference Christianity. My wife is a real Bible scholar. I just ask her a question, if I need a quote for something, and she'll give me three or four books on the subject, with her cross-referencing of Bible verses. That's her thing. She's a Christian. We raised our kids as Christians. My mom and dad were Christians. My grandparents were Christian. All my family in this country, you know, going back to the late eighteenth century, were Christians.

Thich Nhat Hanh says he has a picture of Jesus on his mediation shrine. He regards Jesus as a spiritual elder or ancestor. With Buddhism, this is not a problem. So I often reference Christianity. I studied all that. I mean I had to. In philosophy, we had to know the medieval philosophers, from Augustine to Aquinas, and all the minor philosophers as well. So Christianity is very present in my background. I don't deny it. But in the academic environment in which we work, religion is almost a taboo subject. I was at an oral two days ago with a student, and we were talking about viewpoints and why she doesn't like third person omniscient. She said, "Because I'm agnostic. And I just can't buy that." [*laughter*] She said, "I've got to know who's telling the story." So it's first-person for her, which is fine. I don't mind first-person. Many modern readers prefer it. It's more authentic to them because they *are* agnostic or atheist. And we have all been educated in modern universities, which tend to be very secular—but that's not the background I grew up in.

So I have an emotional commitment to the history and philosophy of Christianity, and I wanted to write a novel that allowed me to explore that. I ought to show you a paper I presented at Harvard; I presented it as the sixteenth Paul Tillich Lecture about a year ago. It was quite a challenge. The topic was suffering and meaning in Buddhism and Christianity. I spent six weeks on that address. In it, I had to do justice to Tillich's position, and then present Tillich's interest in the *buddhadharma*. There are three interviews he did with a Zen Buddhist, an art historian, who was a visiting professor at Harvard. Their dialogue is really wonderful. Because what stops Tillich *cold* is what stops most Westerners cold. That is, "*Anicca, dukkha, anatta.*" In other words, "All things are impermanent; suffering is universal; and there is no self." Tillich was baffled by the idea of there being no enduring self or soul. As for everything else—impermanence, suffering—okay, he says, we have those in Christianity. But no *self?* When I was on a book tour for *Turning the Wheel: Essays in Buddhism and Writing,* I spoke at a store in Seattle. In the audience there was a young man from England, and he specifically asked me about the issue of no self in Buddhism. I could see the naked fear in his face, you know, because he was thinking, "What does that mean? I don't have a self, an enduring soul?" This is more or less how Tillich responded to *anatta*.

JWB: But you're talking about the three seals, the three marks of existence. All genuine Buddhist discourses acknowledge the three seals, right? Two of the three we can share with postmodernism. Postmodern thinkers are perfectly happy with absolute contingency and with forms of "no self."

CJ: Yes.

JWB: According to Thich Nhat Hanh, any Buddhist teaching must also emphasize enlightenment, the fourth seal that is sometimes discussed. There has to be this affirmation of enlightenment. When it comes to representations of enlightenment, you have been bolder in some ways than other Buddhist writers, and I'm thinking of the chapter entitled "Moksha" in *Oxherding Tale*. "Dr. King's Refrigerator" comically presents a revelation, but it's still a revelation. Isn't there a taboo of sorts against presenting enlightenment?

CJ: Okay. If you've enlightenment, then you've got a sense of interdependence and no self.

There is a *via negativa*, and there are positive ways of talking about it. In the kitchen conversion scene in *Dreamer*, the story segues from what is in King's actual writing about how he directly experienced God into a very Buddhist moment, in which he asks himself, "Who suffers?"

And then the story offers that line, "Not I, but the Father within me is the doer." So in *Dreamer*, my fictional King suddenly experiences a displacement of selfhood. This kind of displacement can be found in the history of Christianity. If you go to Meister Eckhart and look at his Rhineland sermons, you'll see so much that resembles Zen—as if a Buddhist could have written some of his passages. This appears in many of the Christians mystics. Because when they begin to push at the question of the relationship of this divine Other and themselves, ultimately dualism collapses. You just can't maintain that dualism. So I just don't see that these religions are radically opposed, as they are presented very often in popular terms. I want to hear Maxine. I want to hear what she has to say about all this.

MHK: Well, I very apprehensively and humbly try to represent moments of enlightenment. And I do not write about it philosophically or didactically. I try to write it with images and what happens in the body when that moment comes. And probably the closest I came was in an image of a firefly. At that moment it glowed, did we see a firefly, or was that enlightenment? "It can't be enlightenment, so it must be a firefly." But in that moment there was a light in which everything was included. In such moments, you forgive yourself for all kinds of things because the self *is* everyone. Separate parts experience interconnection like the circuits in a huge electric grid. Representing it takes about three lines, one paragraph. All *I* can do is three lines.

CJ: Three lines.

MHK: And that's it.

Chapter 8

Poetry and Practice at Naropa University

John Whalen-Bridge

Poetry, fiction, and literary nonfiction have been essential vehicles in the transmission of Buddhism from Asia to the United States, rivaling even canonical
texts in influence. From the mid-1970s onward, the institutional center for
American literary Buddhism has been Naropa University's Jack Kerouac School
of Disembodied Poetics. Naropa grew out of teaching programs put together
in the early 1970s by the Tibetan teacher Chögyam Trungpa Rinpoche, who
named Naropa after the Indian mystic, yogi and philosopher Naropa (956–1041
CE), the founder of the Kagyu lineage of Tibetan Buddhism. Naropa was abbot
of Nalanda, home to the world's greatest library until it was burned to the
ground in 1197 CE.[1] In 1974, Trungpa asked Allen Ginsberg, Anne Waldman,
Diane di Prima, and musician John Cage to develop a writing program, which
was iconoclastically named "the Jack Kerouac School of Disembodied Poetics."
In part this title, Ginsberg once said to me in a diner, was a joke: "Kerouac
was DEAD—it was a JOKE!" In part the title is a recognition of the heroic
efforts to conjure a program out of nothing—no desks, no library, no budget,
no salaries—meaning, "disembodied" in the sense of being free of institutional
resources, not just institutional constraints. Formal accreditation came in 1988,
and the name was changed from "Naropa Institute" to Naropa University.[2]

Naropa's primary achievements include becoming the first Buddhist-inspired
university in North America to earn accreditation and giving the Dionysian
energies of Beat poetics and writing an institutional foothold. The phrase
"contemplative education" can be traced back to Chögyam Trungpa. Naropa
now defines itself as "Buddhist-inspired" and "ecumenical and nonsectarian."[3]
The phrase "contemplative education," which is inspiring programs throughout
the United States such as Brown University's "Contemplative Studies Initiative,"
appears to be a product of Naropa. Trungpa put it this way in a 1982 discussion with Naropa faculty members:

Education becomes a real contemplative discipline if things work out to be continuously genuine. "Contemplative" here doesn't mean that one tames thought or one dwells on some particular theme a lot. Instead it means being with discipline fully and thoroughly, as a hungry man eats food or a thirsty man drinks water.[4]

Despite considerable accomplishments, Naropa is more often remembered for several colorful episodes that highlight its bohemian origins. Many still associate Naropa with Tom Clark's *Great Naropa Poetry Wars* (1980), an account of events that occurred at a Halloween party in 1975. During one of Trungpa's three-month Buddhist seminars, poet W. S. Merwin and his girlfriend Dana Naone refused to attend this party and behaved in other ways that offended Trungpa, who ordered his "Vajra guards" to force them to participate. This involved stripping them naked against their will. Trungpa's defenders argued that in this sexual assault the guru was attempting, out of compassion and a radical teaching mode called "crazy wisdom," to peel away the delusions of ego. Kenneth Rexroth felt otherwise, comparing Trungpa to Buddhism's Judas-figure, Devadatta: "Many believe Chögyam Trungpa has unquestionably done more harm to Buddhism in the United States than any man living."[5]

Between June and October 2009, I was a visiting Lenz Fellow at Naropa University, and I interviewed Andrew Schelling, Keith Abbott, Reed Bye, and Elizabeth Robinson about the relationship between contemplative discipline and literary creation. I also interviewed Joanne Kyger, a frequent Naropa visitor since the early days, about the extended Naropa community.

Joanne Kyger: "I never say, 'I am a Buddhist' "

Joanne Kyger is the author of twenty books of poetry, including her collected poems *About Now* (2007). She has been a regular visiting faculty member in Naropa's "Summer Writing Program." I interviewed Joanne on September 24, 2009.

John Whalen-Bridge (JWB): How did you find out about Buddhism?

Joanne Kyger (JK): I found out about it through a book, since there were no practicing Buddhists around me in Santa Barbara when I was growing up. It was of course, D. T. Suzuki's writings that gave most people access to Zen Buddhism.

JWB: Do you go on meditation retreats?

JK: I taught at a retreat the Zen Mountain Monastery at Mt. Tremper in New York; and a few years ago I was invited to go teach and read at the Montreal

Zen Poetry Festival at their center, Empuku-ji. This celebration was in honor of the one-hundredth birthday of their teacher, Kyozen Joshu Sasaki, who lives and teaches at Mt. Baldy in Los Angeles. He is also Leonard Cohen's teacher, and still living. After I returned I had a dream in which Myokyu, the Abbess of the center, asked me to introduce myself and say why I was there. I said, "I'm here because I read too much."

JWB: Have you had a teacher?

JK: A formal teacher, no. When I lived in Japan I learned to sit in formal Japanese Rinzai style, at Daitoku-ji Temple, and did that for four years.

JWB: Did you do koan study in Japan?

JK: I never had the command of Japanese that one needs to have formal koan study, so I was never able to study with a teacher there.

JWB: Why do readers think you're a Buddhist writer?

JK: Probably because I mention Buddhism in my writing. And have met some prominent Buddhist teachers in Japan and the Dalai Lama in India. I sat with Shunryu Suzuki, the Soto Zen teacher, when he first came to San Francisco in 1959, and later met Chögyam Trungpa in an early visit to San Francisco at the San Francisco Zen Center. Everyone was very excited to meet him, but the students really had no way to engage him in a dialogue—asking him questions like "What is reality?" No one, at that point, had any vocabulary of the Dharma.

JWB: Can you tell me how you teach at Naropa? How did you get to Naropa, and when did you teach?

JK: I was invited to attend by Allen Ginsberg and Anne Waldman. I usually start with a writing exercise, go on to present the poet being discussed in the class that day—giving an autobiographical background and a cultural context, and then have students read out loud the work of the poet being presented, so they can feel what it is like to voice the words. And then at the end of the class have students read their first writing exercise out loud. These are usually very simple five-minute "takes" on a subject. By the end of the class, enough time has gone by that certain self-consciousness has passed. Everyone writing at the same time is very egalitarian; you're all in the same space together. There need be no particular form except the voice, and the fact that you have to be able to read your own handwriting. As Ginsberg once said, "When Mind is shapely, Art is shapely." That's why it's useful to take a moment to do some deep breathing and center oneself before writing down the first word.

JWB: I want to ask you about the first time you taught at Naropa. Did you give lectures, presentations, or benefit readings?

JK: The first summer I went to Naropa, in 1975, I did a reading, and the second year I started teaching classes, which I did for the next thirty years or so. Trungpa was still there when I first taught. There is a good description in Rick Fields' *How the Swans Came to the Lake* of people waiting outside for an evening lecture, and how in an open convertible Trungpa arrived with his retinue. Trungpa, with his flash and panache, was so different from the more modest and austere presentation of the Japanese Zen I was used to.

JWB: The summer writing program is demanding; I thought I was going to meet people casually, but it was like trying to talk to someone going by on a train.

JK: When Naropa housed the faculty in student apartments during the summer, there was a certain amount of shared domesticity between faulty members that was very memorable. However, the academic demands of the program have become more exacting, and there never seems to be much open space time during the summer. I never went to any other classes, so I never knew what was going on with the teaching style of other poets. And often when I came home I had instant, exhausted amnesia. But I kept notes when I was there and copies of all my class lectures.

JWB: What is your feeling about what the "Naropa poetry wars"? Did you read Ed Sanders' report on Naropa, *The Party*?

JK: Yes. I was there the summer before the "incident" in 1975 and soon heard about the Halloween Party, since it attracted lots of attention. In 1977, Sanders and his class did an incredible job of reporting on it for his class in "Investigative Poetry." It was the class that chose the subject. They made lists of questions, tape recorded interviews which they transcribed, and devised a flowchart. From this they made an oral history. Then followed a poem written in an hour's time in the last class, by each member, who was given a section of the chronology as their subject. These were gathered into one document, which was read the following night at a public presentation of the work. It was very theatrical, but grounded in different perspectives, voices, and styles. I heard many accounts of the party, mostly hearsay. My favorite line is supposedly when Dana is dragged naked in front of Trungpa and he says, "What are you going out with this white man for?" It was like a very bawdy party. I didn't especially disapprove of it.

JWB: The party? Or do you mean the stripping?

JK: All of it, the whole thing. It was like a Halloween free for all!

JWB: So you're not shocked by dragging someone out of their room and ripping their clothes off?

JK: It was almost a form of theater. I can remember being at parties in the 1970s out here in the country, that seemed to go on for days, entering into another reality with entirely different energies manifesting themselves.

JWB: I haven't seen the Sanders book, but Clark represents the behavior of Trungpa and his students as violent. When people start pulling out knives and breaking beer bottles, it doesn't seem very Buddhist.

JK: Buddhist or not Buddhist, that's what happened, and you could make arguments about whether this was appropriate. Whatever happened at the party seemed part of a sensational situation which took on a life of its own. What happened afterward bothered me: that it was going to be a huge scandal, and that Tom Clark and others were going to moralize about it. I remember immediately there were sides, and attitudes, especially because it involved a religious teacher. It's a story, as a friend of mine said, that is going to attract a lot of flies. I certainly am not going to set myself apart from other religious teachings by labeling myself as a Buddhist. Not very useful or religious to be hampered by a category.

Reed Bye: "Buddha and Bards"

Reed Bye is a poet and songwriter. He teaches poetry writing workshops, courses in classic and contemporary literary studies, and contemplative poetics. I interviewed Reed on August 23, 2009.

JWB: I'd like to talk about your career at Naropa as a meditator and as a poet. You've just come back from a two-week retreat. Can you say what that means?

Reed Bye (RB): This is part of my continuing journey as a Buddhist practitioner and involves a particular set of practices that are designed to be done in solitary retreat; you prepare your own food, and you practice in four sessions from roughly five in the morning until nine at night. This is a continuation of the Buddhist teachings and practices of Chögyam Trungpa. In his presentation, there is the study of Hinayana, Mahayana, and Vajrayana views combined with meditation practice. These teachings are presented intensively during a three-month seminary. Completing that, one could begin *ngöndro* practices, which are the preliminary practices before formal Vajrayana practice.[6]

JWB: So this is a Trungpa curriculum, basically introducing Buddhism through the three yanas from a Tibetan point of view. Is the seminary experience more discursive, more practice-based, or is it a kind of balance? For example, when you're doing the first third, are you doing *vipassana* meditation while talking about its philosophy?

RB: It's balanced. Trungpa Rinpoche's presentation emphasized meditation practice since this was what his students needed at that time. At the seminary, there were classes and readings, but the majority of time was spent in the meditation hall. The seminary emphasized sitting meditation as the ground for proper understanding. Maybe that will change culturally, but at that point, in 1970s, that's what Trungpa saw we needed: more grounding and less philosophy.

JWB: You probably get more sitting meditation following the breath in a Shambhala or Vajradhatu *dathun* context than you would in any more traditional Tibetan teaching arrangement.[7]

RB: Probably so.

JWB: Many of the younger teachers are perhaps now influenced by Trungpa. The emphasis is on a curriculum, and you don't just take empowerments. There is a strong emphasis on practice-based events.

RB: Trungpa designed many practice-based events that included study of both philosophical views and lineage history. Following the seminary, then, there are the preliminary or ngöndro practices, and then, if one completes those, there are the empowerments for particular Buddhist deity sadhana practices.[8] And he laid out a curriculum for that too, with some flexibility. I'm beginning to practice what is called the six dharmas of Naropa.[9]

JWB: If you were doing the *ngöndro* portion in a Tibetan monastery, this might be done with everyone at once. But are you on your own for this part? If you are going to do your prostrations, for example, do you get up in the morning and do them and tell someone when you are done?

RB: I think it depends where you live and what you have access to in terms of a sangha or community. Boulder has always been fortunate because it was a center early and the main center for quite a long time. So people can get together as groups and practice together at times, and there are community practice spaces here. But it's mainly individual. You record your daily practice and go deeper into it over time. Some people move quickly through, but some take many years to complete the parameters of a given practice.

JWB: I'm assuming you were a student of Trungpa while he was alive?

RB: Yes, not an early student, more of mid-term student, beginning about 1976.

JWB: So there were ground floor students who are 1970, 1971 and then there are people who came in the mid-1970s or so, and then I suppose in the later years, maybe they wouldn't have seen the teacher very much, since the group was very large.

RB: That was true in my case.

JWB: When you were doing *ngöndro*, who was your teacher?

RB: Trungpa Rinpoche was my teacher, but individual instruction was handled within the teaching structure of the sangha so that more experienced students, students who had done what you were learning, could be consulted with questions.

JWB: How did you begin?

RB: I came to Boulder in 1969, and I went to CU, but I dropped out of CU and I stayed in Boulder. I was working here as a tree trimmer and a roofer, and I became part of the small but active literary community that developed before Naropa began. When Naropa was founded, that community and the Naropa writers merged in interesting ways. Naropa introduced legendary literary figures to us local creative writers. William Burroughs, Allen Ginsberg, Gregory Corso, Diane di Prima, John Ashbury, Philip Whalen, Anne Waldman, Joanne Kyger, and many others came here from year to year beginning in 1974 and really put Naropa and Boulder on the map. That was my entrance point to the Naropa community. I was not too aware of what was going on with Trungpa Rinpoche and his sangha, though there was quite a lot of suspicion about him from some quarters, and from the writers especially, since Trungpa Rinpoche was a complex and controversial figure. Around that time there were many spiritual scandals going on in the country. I went to quite a number of talks and teachings at Naropa in those years, and I went to a number of Trungpa Rinpoche's talks as well. I didn't have a particularly suspicious attitude; I just wasn't drawn toward it as a practitioner until later.

There was a lot of social energy. There also were a number of fields of exploration opening up at Naropa: the psychology, science, and literary fields; music, theater and dance; and the dharma field. And all of them were intersecting. One might find oneself at a party with a lot of people who were here for different reasons, but often with an interestingly common inspiration, whether or not we knew it ourselves. Through talking to an old friend at one of these parties, I came to take the first level of Shambhala training. At a certain point in the 1970s, Trungpa Rinpoche began presenting the Shambhala teachings alongside his Buddhist teachings. He and his regent had designed a sequence of Shambhala practice weekends, 75 percent of the time spent on the cushion, but including talks in the evening and a progressive curriculum. So in 1976 I began taking weekends and it was primarily the sitting practice itself that began to open my eyes, heart, and mind.

JWB: Did Trungpa first come to Boulder because CU invited him to teach a course?

RB: Yes, to teach an Introduction to Buddhism class at CU. He was invited at the encouragement of some professors who knew he was teaching in Vermont.

JWB: Was it important to you to make a distinction between Shambhala's secular view and Buddhism's religious view?

RB: No, and the distinction didn't seem so important to Trungpa as far as I could tell. It doesn't quite work to define the difference between Shambhala and Buddhism on the basis of secular and spiritual orientations, even though that is the most obvious way of presenting the difference. Buddhists often don't really feel that Buddhism is a religion in the normative sense of that term, although it's simpler to acknowledge it as such. However, the difference between theistic and nontheistic religious outlooks is very significant, and Trungpa Rinpoche addressed that difference explicitly. As a nontheistic religion, speaking of Buddhism as a religion is problematic. In contrast, the secular orientation of Shambhala teachings and practices specifically addresses the experience of human beings in society rather than individual spiritual liberation.

JWB: Stephen Bachelor's book *Buddhism without Beliefs* points out the conflict. And it's coming up more often now when discussing the meaning of Buddhism in an American context. Bachelor's Buddhism pretty much disowns belief, and he says these beliefs are extraneous to Buddhism. Alan Wallace, Robert Thurman, and others debate him in *Tricycle* and elsewhere. So is it fair to say that for Shambhala, you could have Buddhism without beliefs?

RB: "Belief," I would say, is not the word that expresses my understanding of Buddhist principles. I would say "faith," "devotion," and "trust" are more operative terms. I don't know where the boundary is between belief and an open sort of faith.

JWB: I have lived in Asia for sixteen years, and it seems to me that many of the high-ranking Tibetan teachers address crowds in a secular way in North America, and this is an adaptation for Americans. And I am troubled, since within the Asian context I'm not really doing it right, or I don't really want to get in other people's way with my questions. Whereas here in Boulder it doesn't create trouble to say "nontheistic." People aren't really disagreeing that Buddhism is nontheistic.

RB: There seems to be an American cultural difference about doubt and evidence. I heard a young lama last year, in a talk, say that in Tibet, questions about faith, belief in the teacher, or teachings don't arise so much. In Tibet, people do become enlightened on the basis of what we Americans might think of as blind trust, blind faith, but Tibetans experience a totally heartfelt faith.

JWB: When you are moving into *sadhanas* that involve deity practice, how is it discussed?[10]

RB: There are apparently thousands of *sadhanas*, but different teachers come from different lineages and those lineages have particular relations to certain deity practices. In encountering the lineage of Trungpa Rinpoche, I encountered the deity practices particular to that lineage, including Vajrayogini and Chakrasamvara.[11]

JWB: Vajrayogini is very attractive in the images I've seen: red-skinned female figure drinking ecstatically from a skull cup. There are different versions.

RB: Yes, there are different versions, and I'm no expert. But the *thangkas* and the images represent different aspects of awareness, and the inner and outer and secret practices are represented differently.[12]

JWB: Is the imagery a personification of an archetype? I mention this in relation to what I was saying before—some people practice with the protector deities who are real, and they will be personally offended if you behave in certain ways. One could think that this is a way to practice, or one could think that this is really simply how people believe. If you believe if there is a multitude of gods who are as real as you and I, that's pantheism.

RB: These *sadhana* deities are distinctly not gods but are symbolic manifestations. In Buddhism, the god realm is one of the six realms of samsara, so these deities are not existent divine beings at all in that sense. They are symbolic: The best I could say is that they are mandala centers.[13] They represent enlightened energy in one aspect or another—sometimes benevolent, sometimes wrathful, and sometimes semi-wrathful. Sometimes what's needed in a situation is pacifying and clarifying, and sometimes what's needed is a cutting kind of penetration, for those of us who are thicker.

JWB: It seems to me that you make few references to iconic Buddhist imagery in your poetry. What's your poetics about the relationship between Buddhism and poetry? Is it a decision to exclude?

RB: No, but I think I tend not to write from a conceptual design. I don't take an idea for a poem and then work from that. It's not a conceptual plan to *not* be conceptual exactly, but I think my poems tend to be written more in between things that I am doing. It's not a central, primary activity in my life as it is for other people. Often, I find what I've written, but I don't know when I wrote it. And when I am writing something, my method is to try to stay on the thread of something, even if not knowing what it is. It's a matter of feel at that point. So my poetry is more happenstance; things enter in as items of thought or perception or feeling and then they develop.

JWB: There seems an overlap between what you are saying and the phrase Ginsberg made famous: "first thought, best thought." Is it standard procedure for you to have a lyric expression that isn't calculated?

RB: Yes.

JWB: Have you felt that your deepening interest in contemplation and your processes of composition have modified each other?

RB: Yes, although one's growth in this way is subtle. But certainly, I attribute being able to appreciate the space of mind in an immediate way, and through that to appreciate the world as coming through more clearly, more directly to the meditation practice I've done. That also goes along with words and thought coming through with more distinctiveness and clarity. So what gets in as I'm writing and what doesn't is a little less hit and miss now. There is less indulging in mental stuff while writing and just hoping for the best.

JWB: I'm not following one part. When you use the word "indulging," are you talking about a stream of consciousness as opposed to labeling it "thinking" in the way one would in a meditative context?

RB: "Indulging" in the emotionalized wish that I could write something when my mind isn't at all settled. You could call it stream of consciousness, but more it's just "stuff," not even in a stream necessarily. There is another aspect of the indulgence: the desire to be a writer, thinking of myself as a poet, so I have to write now. The emotionalized wish to write something and the self-image of being a writer are both kinds of indulgence. I would say that as a result of meditation practice, I am able more to get to the energy, the moving line of energy of the mind at any given moment. When I write I can stay on that line better now.

JWB: Were you around during the great Naropa poetry wars? Were you at the seminary?

RB: No, my seminary was in 1984. My development was gradual and I wasn't at the 1974 seminary. I was not yet a student of Trungpa Rinpoche. I had been to some of his talks but I think it was 1976 when I began sitting. But I knew Allen quite well at that point, and Anne and I trusted their hearts and the way they did things, not that they were infallible in any sense, but they were extraordinarily generous and articulate people. The way they dealt with people across the board was a huge teaching for me. Also, I knew Tom Clark and Ed Dorn quite well and liked them, and admired them as poets.[14]

In a way, this conflict was unsurprising. The cultural clash in this town was inevitable. There was the guru's world and the individualist U.S. poet's world—that was the basic division. You could say somebody like Ed Dorn was iconically individualistic. In my mind, Trungpa was touching that nerve of individualism. And then there are the questions: What is an individual? And who is the guru? And what are those fears and hostilities aroused when those two edges get as close as they did here, with poetry or the arts being the site of the debate: Ginsberg on the one hand and Ed Dorn on the other. They were friends, old friends. Robert Creeley, where did he fit in? Anselm Hollo? These are important figures for U.S. poetic history. And within that particular artistic community, you could not have raised a redder flag than the one of Vajrayana Buddhist guru devotion. When you get into the factual questions about what happened at a Buddhist event or a poetry reading, accounts vary widely. Of course, I am a devoted student of the guru at this point, so I'm biased. In order to establish Buddhism on this continent, it has to be clear that Buddhism is centrally concerned with the cultivation of wisdom and compassion. These qualities arise when one achieves insights into what is called "egolessness," which is a word that has a lot of parts to it. The approach to egolessness, Trungpa taught, may be terrifying, but Buddhism is about reality, not terrorism. It's about reality, seeing things as they are.

It's a big journey, one that is not achieved through the reading of books or theoretical speculation. Buddhist psychology and practice focuses on ego and its operational modes, which can take anything, any inspiration, and then convert it to self-interest. Without practice it's impossible to know when ego absorption is happening and when it's not, at least it seems so to me. You can be a very good person, you can be a very good scholar, but the appropriation by one's ego happens very quickly. I think the only way to really taste that is in these moments where you've given time over to watching who you are, watching your mind and its patterns, watching space emerge as a more real thing than it had been. So that there's a gentleness, but a very definite discipline that's involved in really getting to the heart of that issue, which is the heart of these teachings and without which they can be appropriated by the hungers of ego.

Keith Abbott: "Typewriter Yoga"

Keith Kumasen Abbott teaches writing and art at Naropa University. His latest poetry book is *Next Door to Samsara* (Fell Swoop, 2005). I interviewed Keith on August 12, 2009.

JWB: I want to start by asking you about Buddhism. What is your relationship to this particular practice? How did it come to you and how did your practice change?

Keith Abbott (KA): I started meditation practice very early because as a kid I loved to sit in the woods in the Northwest, and if you got very quiet you could steady your breath. Then I noticed that the animals would come as if you weren't there if you were appropriately downwind. I had my first brush with Buddhism as such, and was reading Kerouac and Snyder at the age of fourteen or so. I then continued at the University of Washington where I studied with Vincent K. Shih; he taught the history of Chinese philosophy, and I became very impressed with Taoism and Buddhism from his very rigorous course. When I went to California in 1966, the practice of Buddhism was current among various writers who were going to Suzuki's Zen Mission, but I did not go there. I did not sit until I moved to Berkeley.

JWB: When?

KA: That was in1972–1973. There were many things on the television on PBS about sitting practice. I started sitting meditation to calm myself and make myself clear before writing. I joked that this was "typewriter yoga." You sat there, you didn't have to write, you just had to pay attention to what was on your big screen. And eventually you would write. So it was utilitarian in some ways.

JWB: Who were the main people involved as the San Francisco Zen Center?

KA: Britton Pyland, who was rooming with Philip Whalen, and David Schneider, who is now writing Philip's biography. I did not go sit at the Zen Center for various reasons: I just didn't like the ambiance of the Zen Center. It felt competitive, with a shadowy class consciousness that also seemed oddly exploitative. But then I decided that I would be interested in sitting. There was a Buddhist priory on Marin Avenue, and I would stop by there and sit, but I never said anything about that.

JWB: You kept meditation and social relations, sangha relations, separate.

KA: That's correct.

JWB: Was this compartmentalization necessary because socialization and meditation might short-circuit one another?

KA: Yes. There was an air about Zen being special that was not to my liking. When I heard people talking, it seemed to me that people were coming there for therapy, like studying psychology because of some serious personal problems. I did not want to enter into that kind of social pretense. Also, some students discriminated against certain practices. People made distinctions even about sitting in silence, and that behavior bothered me.

JWB: Were you your own teacher?

KA: No, I had friends who taught me all kinds of things. I had a dear friend in my first year at college, Doug Benson, who was a Coyote figure—a very strange, bizarre, marvelous person who taught me a great deal. Doug carried boxes of clothes in his car so he could change into different outfits for any social occasion and he assumed roles to suit each costume/event. Life always was an illusion for him; he doubted everyone and everything.

JWB: In your memoir about Kobun Chino, you have a line saying that a field or meadow can be your teacher.

KA: "Don't misunderstand, this teacher is not always a person. It can embrace you like morning dew in a field and you get a strange feeling, Oh, this is it, my teacher is this field." —Kobun Chino Otogawa Roshi, my teacher.

JWB: The field as teacher! That solves some problems, no?

KA: I attended a lot of people's lectures, always with the hope that this man could be my teacher, yet I did not find anybody that I could relate to that way. I believed that, as a writer, I had to experience life before I could comfortably indulge in institutional silent meditation.

JWB: You came as an adjunct in 1989 and availed yourself of some of the benefits of the Naropa culture. Were you sitting with groups here or were you mainly sitting alone?

KA: I was sitting in the main meditation hall at Naropa and there were others there. Somebody usually presided over the sitting, and I would sit for awhile with people. But I did not join, since there was not at that time a strong Zen Buddhist community or practice. It wasn't until Kobun came and there were several places where that kind of meditation can be practiced that I attended Martin Mosko's Hakubai Temple in Boulder.

JWB: Was he associated with Baker Roshi?

KA: No, he was a senior student of Kobun.

JWB: Kobun Chino, who became your teacher. Was Kobun's role at Naropa to be an art teacher? Did he also teach meditation?

KA: He came very reluctantly and was World Wisdom Chair at Naropa. He lived at the Shambhala Mountain Center, coming down two days a week to teach meditation. Then Naropa needed another class, so they asked if I would take him as a co-teacher, which is ridiculous given that he was a brush master. People were collecting his work from when he was nine in Japan! I taught brush with him, and he came to brush class. He simply stepped into my curriculum; he didn't change anything. Because I was teaching the meditation form of Tai Chi, the standing meditation—where the students could relax their body, breath and especially their feet before they sat down on chairs to paint calligraphy—he started learning that. I thought that this was very funny, that I was teaching a master such as he. He had a big voice, and when I asked him again if he preferred sitting meditation, he used his sutra chanting voice to intone, "Nooo! I'm learning a lot!" [*laughs*] I thought this can't be. I can't be teaching him anything he doesn't already know. Some Zen monks go through a practice similar to Tai Chi relaxation before they do public displays of calligraphy.

JWB: You seem committed to the idea that he wasn't learning something from you, although it seems like he had a sincere commitment to lifelong learning.

KA: Yes, that was just one of many times that it was both humbling and eye-opening to teach with somebody as alive as Kobun. And every day was a blessing—so wonderful! He was a wonderful person to have in class, even if he didn't do any brush work or say anything, which was sometimes the case. He watched students brush and his scrutiny changed their posture, attitude, and attention.

JWB: He was your first formal teacher of Buddhism?

KA: Yes.

JWB: And your last?

KA: And my last, yes. I've studied with Joan Halifax, among others, but I consider Kobun my root teacher. I did pledge to be his student for life.

JWB: Would you have moved a long way to be closer to Kobun Chino?

KA: I would have, yes. I'd learned so much from him in such a short period of time that I felt very strongly that I must work on the things that he gave me. And I'm still working on them.

Andrew Schelling: "The Wordless Core"

Andrew Schelling is a poet, essay writer, and translator. At Naropa, Schelling teaches poetry, translation, courses in bioregional poetics, and Sanskrit. He oversees the Kavyayantra Press, the Kerouac School's letterpress print shop, and currently is editor of *Bombay Gin*, the school's literary journal.

JWB: Two decades ago you were editing a special issue of your journal, *Jimmy and Lucy's House of "K,"* which explored the interface of Buddhism and poetry. At that time, was Buddhism only an incidental part of your relation to the Bay Area scene? The line between poetry and Buddhism in your work seems provocatively unclear.

Andrew Schelling (AS): In that very low-budget but somehow influential journal, my co-editor Benjamin Friedlander and I had a great many themes, ideas, and poetic or political interests we were paying attention to. I wouldn't say Buddhism was simply incidental, nor were most of our concerns, which extended far beyond literary studies. From 1984 to 1990, when we produced

Jimmy and Lucy's, I was deepening my Buddhist practice and thinking carefully about what a sustained Buddhist influence on North American poetry might be. A couple of close friends—for instance, Pat Reed, who was a regular contributor to the journal—were sitting regularly. The essays and poetry had begun to reflect it. Across the Bay from Berkeley where I lived, at Green Gulch Farms Zen Center, Norman Fisher was a practice instructor. He was a friend who proved enormously supportive to poets who wanted a retreat situation. Norman was known as a uniquely innovative poet. He hadn't emerged as co-abbot of the San Francisco Zen centers yet, nor had he founded his own sangha or dharma group at that point, and there were many who thought of him as a poet, not a spiritual teacher. I think he had studied at Iowa, along with Barrett Watten, one of the notorious and controversial figures of language poetry. But Norman's connection with language poetry might be a little like Philip Whalen's connection to Beat poetry, more an account of friendships and where he found himself in time and place, than of some dogmatic approach to verse.

Philip Whalen was certainly more than incidentally interested in Buddhism. He had become what he once called "a professional meditator," and during the 1990s served briefly as abbot of the Hartford Street Zen Center. His rigor about zazen or sitting practice interested me of course, because he was to my mind one of the finest poets of our day.

When Ben and I were editing the *House of "K,"* we insisted on a more expanded notion of what could go into poetry than the people we knew in San Francisco. Over there, the poets we were in touch with—at least those who were more or less our own generation—largely clustered around the Poetics Program at New College, which had important figures on the faculty: Robert Duncan, Diane di Prima, Michael Palmer, Duncan McNaughton, and eventually David Meltzer. New College had a formal poetics curriculum. It was scholarly in a recognizably academic way, and seemed to me largely European-centered. Di Prima, of course, was interested in Buddhism, both Tibetan forms and Zen, but Duncan and Palmer's influences were European poetics, with some traces of anthropology and a lot of Continental philosophy. Their students were studying and translating French and German.

By contrast, in the East Bay I was studying Sanskrit and translating Sanskrit poetry, sitting at the Berkeley Zen Center, and often hung out with neo-primitives and eco-activists. The bumper sticker on my 1964 Volvo said, "Back to the Paleolithic!" Ben Friedlander looked on the surface like a punk-era skateboarder, and I think rock 'n roll and jazz, as well as baseball and politics, were all important to him for poetry. Pat Reed liked to surf with her girlfriends, she backpacked, and wrote what I still think of as the finest poems we were producing. All of us liked to go into the Sierras or Coast Range mountains camping. Sometimes we'd drive down to Tassajara Mountain Center for retreats or just to visit for a few days. In the mountains above Tassajara there was a rugged wilderness and several primitive campgrounds that we got to know quite well. Then, through my wife, Kristina Lofton, we brought animal rights into our journal. Kristina worked with an organization called Buddhists Concerned for Animals. The organization eventually renamed itself the Humane Farming Association, when it dawned on them that if they wanted to talk to ranchers or veterinarians in California's central valley, calling themselves Buddhist didn't help their cause. We drew interesting material for *Jimmy and Lucy's* from their newsletters, and published articles and rough-looking collages on factory farming and the abuse of animals, particularly in medical and military research. Along with this range of concerns, Friedlander was bringing in record reviews during the punk rock explosion of the 1980s. And we ran obituaries—sort of culture memorials, like signposts along the way—not just for poets but for Buddhist thinkers, astrologers, musicians, and philosophers—a kind of odd mix of people, to show what our era was formed by.

JWB: You were part of a countercultural project?

AS: Maybe it was a countercultural project. I think we were just trying to dig down into what were the obvious cultural influences. We published essays on the plight of Tibetans in exile, on the mujaheddin of Afghanistan, on the vinyl records we had in our apartments, or on Michel Foucault's lectures at Berkeley. Buddhism was a strong part of that mix, and indeed a growing influence in the whole Bay Area.

JWB: Were you a part of the Buddhist Peace Fellowship from the beginning?

AS: No. I knew some people involved. I would see them when I went to the Berkeley Zen Center.

JWB: In 1990 or thereabouts you put together the contemplative poetics issue of *House of "K,"* "the poetics of emptiness." Was that central to your identity at the time?

AS: As I said, it was a strong part of my work, my studies, and my aspirations. But Buddhism, a fundamental practice for me, was not my principle cultural (or countercultural) activity. Poetry was my sphere of public action. Buddhism is a significant spiritual and cultural practice for many people in North America, but not for everybody. Poetry was my outward face to the world. Buddhism was a personal choice. Ben Friedlander's father was an Auschwitz survivor, and Ben felt hat he had to affirm his cultural legacy as a Jew and acknowledge the Holocaust and its impact on his family and throughout the world. He pointed out that as a Jew he did not have a choice about his spiritual situation in the world. "You Buddhists, you've taken this on as a *choice*. We Jews don't have a choice." He respected my Buddhism, and I respected his Judaism. We were able to be close friends and energetic collaborators in poetry.

JWB: In your view, what is Buddhism?

AS: Other people—some who have made talking about Buddhism their careers—have developed definitions. I'm not sure I can add anything unique. [*Pressed to come up with an answer, AS later responded: "Buddhism is Poison."*]

JWB: If you contrast American Buddhism to Asian Buddhism, there's a predisposition to existential experience in the American expression. So is "American Buddhism" different from "Buddhism"?

AS: I see what you're getting at. At the core of Buddhism is the belief that there is an experience of clarity, awakening, enlightenment—call it what you like—and that all the external trappings have been developed through long experiment to point toward that irreducible experience. Practices draw on all sorts of experiments developed in Asia. Practices can be various: sitting meditation, a faith prayer, prostrations, a mantra. I remember Lama Govinda suggesting that yoga meditation had been developed by Paleolithic hunters in the Himalayan foothills. But for Buddhism the "hunt"—if you can call it that—is for an experience called enlightenment, *samyaksambodhi*—some kind of existential clarity.[15]

JWB: There are more and less elastic conceptions of this thing called enlightenment. For some people it's a psychological yoga. It's like doing Pilates: If you have a bad back you do Pilates; if you have a bad psyche, you do some letting go breath by breath.

AS: There's nothing wrong with that. How many people have been drawn to Buddhism because they've seen their lives derailed by a failed love affair or some other kind of personal crisis that has made them want to study life deeply? My practice has always been zazen, although I've done a bit of koan practice. In koan practice, the effort is to take an insoluble problem and put it at the center of your psychic and spiritual self, and then live inside that mind-cracking problem until you wear out your pointless inner explanations. I don't think you need a koan to do that, since life is already a pretty weird problem. In some sense that's my practice: to find the insoluble aspects of life and put them at the center of awareness. Sitting helps.

JWB: When you say sitting, do you mean a formal practice? Visualization? Chanting? Do you do counting breath, or is breath-counting training wheels that you left behind?

AS: No, counting the breath is good. Training wheels that I'd never leave behind. Maybe leave parked behind the garage when you have had a bit more experience, or if you do something like koan practice. In recent years I've worked with a Bhutanese lama, Dzongsar Khyentse Rinpoche, and have adopted a few specific *sadhanas* or practices that involve visualization, chanting of mantras, the use of *dharanis*.[16] I've used these to supplement my sitting practice. Typically, when I sit I do Zazen and follow it with Tibetan style or *Vajrayana* sadhana.

JWB: How did you start, what happened, and where are you now?

AS: Like many young people, I was a seeker. I tried a lot of different things. By the time I was about twenty years old, Zen seemed to me the closest to my particular temperament. I went to a number of Zen centers and became increasingly interested in the practice. When I moved to Santa Cruz in 1974 for college, I began sitting regularly at the Zen Center. Kobun Chino Roshi's example drew me into Zen.

JWB: What was your relationship with Kobun Chino Roshi before you came to Naropa?

AS: He had a small center in Los Altos, California, and would drive over one evening a week to Santa Cruz. A group of us would meet in the Zendo, a slightly ramshackle bungalow by the armory of the old Santa Cruz Mission. It did have tatami mats in an airy meditation room. The group of us would sit, and Kobun would say a few words after zazen. Then he might ask for questions, or we might just sit around until it was time to go home.

JWB: *Teisho* or just to chat?[17]

AS: We asked informal questions, and he made himself available. He was going through a difficult divorce, and I'm not sure he wanted to present himself as an authority in any way. But he knew it was important for him to show up if people were sitting. He presented himself as a practitioner rather than an authority. That's what appealed to me: his modesty, his humility, his sense of humor. And the fact that he was suffering a great deal. It was his ability to be kind and gentle yet somewhat humorous and even wounded. Somebody asked, "Kobun, would you say something about the relationship between men and women?" He didn't answer for a long time. Finally, he looked up and said, "No." When pressed—"Well why not?" Kobun said, "Because I would break a vow." What vow? "Not to get angry." I think it was this kind of thing that drew me in: tender honesty. I would not have been attracted by a tough guy, certainly not by any know-it-all bullshit. The meaning I took away was that sitting zazen is not going to clean up your relationship. If you're here because you are having a hard time, that is appropriate, but this isn't marriage counseling. This is a place where you come to ask fundamental questions, and that's what I always appreciated about Zen and the wordlessness of Zen. There's a wordlessness at Zen's core that has always attracted me.

JWB: Was Kobun Chino your teacher?

AS: Not in any formal way. I didn't develop a relationship with a teacher until I moved to Berkeley in the early 1980s. There I worked with Mel Weitsman at Berkeley Zen Center. When I left the Bay Area and came to Naropa, I studied with Bernard Glassman and did some koan practice under his supervision. Bernie was on the Naropa Board of Directors, so he would come three or four times a year to Boulder. I also attended the first of his street retreats—five days or a week living on the streets around New York City's Bowery district. That was a memorable practice session. It was cold and it rained. We slept in cardboard boxes, or in the Port Authority waiting room. We ate food at the Bowery Mission, or hiked uptown to the Catholic Worker's soup kitchen. Rick Fields, Anne Waldman, and Peter Matthiessen also attended that retreat.

JWB: Do you have a kind of apprentice relationship to the teacher?

AS: My own teachers never set themselves up as authority figures, but were simply some people who had been over the territory and could show me a bit of the way.

JWB: You're allergic to guru devotion?

AS: I'm allergic to guru devotion, yes.

JWB: When you came to Naropa, after Trungpa had died, was it before or after the situation with the Vajra Regent had resolved itself?[18]

AS: It was after that. I never visited Naropa while Trungpa was alive or during that very difficult time that developed around his Vajra Regent. I was in the Bay area and only obliquely aware of the traumatic situation happening to Vajradhatu people. By the time I arrived I felt quite comfortable coming into the college, which has a remarkable poetics program. Finding Bernie Glassman on the Board of Directors was a delight. I've often felt that Zen and the Tibetan groups, although there's a lot more cross-fertilization now, were for years like two distant families united by marriage. They sort of liked each other, they certainly knew they had to get along, but each felt slightly superior to the other.

JWB: That internal difference at Naropa would have played itself out in hiring, renewal, and promotions. Is this difference less pronounced now?

AS: Naropa has made a long, careful, and sometimes hotly contested effort to become an ecumenical or nondenominational school. Honoring its Buddhist roots. There still exists a number of old guard Vajradhatu Buddhists at Naropa, and certainly the school's not free of a certain kind of conspiratorial politics that look to me like they are inspired by medieval Tibet. But Naropa University these days is comfortable with its expanded identity. I should note that the agents of change have generally been the students.

JWB: You would not have come during the Trungpa years?

AS: I might have come as a guest, but I don't think it would have been comfortable to teach here. At root I am a part libertarian, part anarchist, part redneck, democratic bioregionalist American, raised with socialist grandparents on one side, military people on the other. Democratic debate and political openness are deeply embedded in my psyche. The inherent hierarchy, the hierarchical ways of thought, and the hierarchal power structures of Tibetan Buddhism keep me at a distance.

Elizabeth Robinson: "Ways of 'Not Knowing'"

Elizabeth Robinson is the author of eight books of poetry. In 2008, she was awarded a Foundation for Contemporary Arts Grants to Artists Award. I interviewed Elizabeth on September 19, 2009.

JWB: You are not a Buddhist, so how does your practice fit into Naropa's "contemplative" approach?

Elizabeth Robinson (ER): I grew up in a Christian household. My father did not participate in religious practice and my mother did sometimes out of obligation. But I had a very rich mystical life as a child. As I grew up, my whole family became disenchanted with modes of evangelicalism in the United States, but I still felt some pull toward the Christian tradition. I went to college and did not participate in any community, and then in graduate school I went through a personal crisis at the end of a relationship. It caused me to re-evaluate what humans are capable of. If you act in good will or with your best effort and it still doesn't work out, what does that mean? How do people work together, how do we make change, how do we love? During this period, I went to a Quaker meeting and also worked in a Methodist soup kitchen. The Quaker meeting was such a revelation; I saw powerful things happen there. You could sit in alert silence with other people and hear things you couldn't usually hear. The Quaker idea that all people are equally legitimate before the divine was very powerful for me. I moved into an intentional community, an African-American community in a really rough part of Los Angeles, where I shared household duties and everything else with the people there. We simply worked with kids in the neighborhood, but I also did some adult literacy work. This was really a version of Liberation Theology, although none of us would have called it that.

JWB: How did the intentional community come together?

ER: It was started by an African-American family from Mississippi. The father in the family had been active in the Civil Rights Movement and had been ambushed and terribly beaten by some white men. He wondered, "Can I forgive them?" He was going to retire in Los Angeles, but when he got there the neighborhood was beset with drug problems and racial tensions. Central American people were moving into this black neighborhood. He started working in the community and started bringing people in, and part of his idea was that you need to be vulnerable to your circumstances. You can't help people from the outside; instead, you have to be in the community. And his commitment was also to an interracial community because it was the practice, his spiritual practice, so we were living together, sharing space, dealing with all the difficulties of living together across class and race barriers.

JWB: Was there a lineage to this spiritual practice?

ER: He probably was an African Methodist Episcopal. They liked a robust African-American church with a lot of music, a lot of solace, and a strongly evangelical iteration of Christianity, but they welcomed me. At that point I don't know if I would've said I was Quaker, or just in a more open sense Christian, but they were most definitely Christians. To this group, Christianity meant acting socially and politically in the world, and I think they were more radical than they thought they were. But it began as a family, and then slowly other people started joining.

JWB: Did you feel like you had sure footing, spiritually?

ER: I still feel myself to be a Christian, although many Christians would probably feel uncomfortable with someone like me saying so because of the way I interpret the Christian tradition. I have since gone to seminary, so I've had opportunities to look at different modes of interpretation and how that material can be used and understood. So there's much in it that I still find powerful and compelling.

JWB: Do you think Quakerism is "other" than Christianity?

ER: Its tradition is Christian, but its contemporary practice can really go anywhere. I know people who call themselves Jewish Quakers, or Sufi Quakers, post-Christian Quakers, and Buddhist Quakers.

JWB: Have you considered Unitarianism?

ER: I don't feel the same comfort or warmth from Unitarianism. To me it feels very cerebral. I'm also uncomfortable with some of the rationalistic evangelical approaches—"we can prove that Jesus did this historically." A lot of the Unitarians I have encountered, especially in seminary, have felt uncomfortable with the way I believe that grace can come into the world, but I find that Quakers are very open to grace and to "not knowing."

JWB: The Zen teacher Bernie Glassman has "not knowing" as one of the three main tenets of his Zen Peacemaker order. But it's less common to hear about "not knowing" as a Christian approach to life. How has your practice changed since you've come to Naropa?

ER: Before coming here I taught at a college, went to seminary, got married and had a family, and intended to be a chaplain in the Bay Area, where I had many friends die of AIDS. They didn't have good community support, especially in relation to spiritual practice. But then once I had children I couldn't really afford to finish the chaplaincy training. I was writing all through all of this, and I started to publish. At that time I thought I wasn't going to teach, so I didn't pursue it as a career. But it was still flowing, and I was getting published without focusing on getting published. After my kids were born, I did a lot of community stuff, like setting up readings and publishing. I'm still involved with publishing projects, especially publishing other people. My spiritual practice involved being in community and working with other writers. This led to teaching as an adjunct instructor, which I loved. I loved teaching and I feel like that's basically what I'm still doing here. I do feel like I have a real gift for teaching, and it's definitely a spiritual practice.

JWB: How did you first connect with Naropa?

ER: I was offered a job at the University of Colorado, and I saw it as a troubled place from the outside, but on the strength of my relationships with people at Naropa, I wanted to come. Teaching at CU was really the most traumatic experience of my life. It started when I applied and they saw on my CV that I had a Master of Divinity, and a faculty member said, "We shouldn't hire you because you're a Christian." But I felt an economic imperative, and I thought, "Well, the Naropa people will be there," and I thought I could just work through it. I was wrong. It never got better. It got worse and worse, and so I quit a tenure track job. It was a bad experience.

JWB: It sounds as if you experienced raw prejudice!

ER: I think so, although I believe that discrimination would not have been as intense if I were Buddhist.

JWB: It's not acceptable to have racial prejudice, but we literary folk can tee off on certain religious beliefs.

ER: I've taken a lot of flak for it among poets too. At one conference I was put on a panel about spirit, and everybody was eager to say, "Well, I'm not a Christian!" I thought there's no denying it—I'm in seminary—so I said "I am!" And a woman approached me afterward and said, "I can't believe you said that. It's like saying you're a smoker."

JWB: How did people let you know you were a "bad person"?

ER: The chair of the department told me that she would make sure that I didn't get tenure and that I couldn't get a job elsewhere.

JWB: Because of your religion?

ER: Not because of my religious practice, but the couple who initially said they didn't want to hire me because I was Christian also didn't want to hire me because I had children. There were several really actionable aspects, and people continued to be difficult. Also, colleagues at CU felt my close association with Naropa was inappropriate. Yet I have never felt that my religious practice was inappropriate or problematic. The students and the faculty at Naropa are much more tolerant, even though they're pretty left. Also, the poets here have been publishing for a long time. They're doing it because it's their vocation, not to get tenure or a pay raise. They're doing it for its intrinsic meaning to them. They're respected in the community, in the larger writing community. There's a real commitment to students that I did not feel at CU.

JWB: What was the cultural atmosphere at Naropa?

ER: It was the Old Guard when I came, and, I have to admit, I really wasn't that interested in Beat writing. Robert Creeley was going to be here, and I wanted to work with him, but I knew Anne as a poet—and I was really intimidated. But she was very available and supportive. Creeley was fantastic, and I was always very interested in what Ginsberg had to say. Philip Whalen's class was amazing. The students were very welcoming too.

JWB: Did your views about Beat poetry change?

ER: Somewhat. I had read *On the Road* by the time I came here, but I was reading some of Kerouac's poetry and was really captivated by Whalen and how he could combine a level of erudition with what he decided to do as a poet. I came from a kind of more Black Mountain training as an undergraduate, but the New York School poetic techniques were very exciting. Really loved it.

JWB: How do you bring your own spiritual interests into the classroom?

ER: Next semester I'm going to do a class on modernism and mysticism. I did a class in a summer writing program called Mystic Speech, and it was really fun. Where else could you do that, but here? And I set up classes where I asked people to do spiritual autobiographies, and it was exciting. I tried to set up a process of speaking in tongues in relation to literary composition, and the students were game. That's the great thing about students here: they might come from a Beat kind of background, so they are ready to go in all sorts of directions.

JWB: You've experienced glossolalia, speaking in tongues.

ER: I have, as in a charismatic context. I mean, like Christian charismatic, and I was in a Candomblé ceremony and ritual in Brazil, once.[19] It's like a syncretistic kind of Brazilian, Afro-Brazilian, Christian.

JWB: Are you able to bring this experience into your classroom in a playful way?

ER: Yes, but without the expectation that people could speak in tongues. I was trying to set it up by having them take their own writing and then look at sonic patterns. What does the sound mean to you? What sound would you use to comfort yourself or incite yourself? They were a little nervous at first, so I had them work collaboratively to put their sounds together. And then it becomes really remarkable.

Notes

1. Former President Thomas Coburn describes the founding of the university in his preface to *The Legacy of Chögyam Trungpa*:

> By 1973, plans were developing for an institute where students, scholars, artists and practitioners of Buddhism and other spiritual traditions would engage in dialogue, and where mindfulness practice could be applied within their various disciplines. That fall, Trungpa Rinpoche gave the approval to his students to begin organizing The Naropa Institute. Inexperienced, but dedicated and full of energy, they set to work inviting teachers and students to come to Boulder for the opening session of summer 1974. The faculty that summer included Kobun Chino Roshi, Allen Ginsberg, Anne Waldman, Ram Dass, Herbert Guenther, Joan Halifax, John Cage, Gregory Bateson and other notable writers, performers and scholars. The first of the two 1974 sessions drew over 1,500 students. . . . (7)

2. Naropa's web page does not make it clear when the change from "Naropa Institute" to "Naropa University" took place. Goss discusses "Naropa Institute" and subsequent publications discuss Naropa University.

3. See "Naropa University: A Naropa University Self-Study Report."

4. From Simon Luna, "The Spark of Wisdom: 25 Years at the Naropa University" (unpublished manuscript), page 96, quoted in Coburn 12.

5. Rexroth's words appear on the back cover of Clark's book as an endorsement. Kashner also comments on the salacious details of Naropa in the 1970s.

6. *Ngöndro* is the term for a set of foundational practices, the specifics of which alternate from lineage to lineage, common to most forms of Tibetan Buddhism. In one lineage, a student might be expected to 111,111 ritual prostrations, 111,111 ritual offerings, and so on before one is allowed to proceed to higher-level practices.

7. At Naropa and at other Trungpa-associated centers, a *dathün* is a month-long meditation retreat involving sitting, teachings, and meetings with teachers. *Shambhala* is a mythological kingdom within Tibetan Buddhist cosmology, sometimes pronounced "Shangri-lah." Trungpa developed an alternative path of meditative training called "Shambhala Warriorship." See Trungpa.

8. Tibetan Buddhism involves practices called "deity yoga" in which one invokes specific deities, sometimes imagining that oneself is transformed into the figure.

9. Commonly discussed as "the six yogas of Naropa," these practices include generating body heat as a way to channel energy and lucid dreaming.

10. A *sadhana* or *puja* is a meditative practice in which one recites a text, also including ritual gestures and sometimes periods of silent meditation.

11. The various figures within deity yoga practice have distinct associations, and the practices are intended to achieve distinct transformations within the practitioner. Vajrayogini is usually imagined as a red-skinned, naked woman with a semi-wrathful appearance. The practice channels the energies of desire. According to H. H. Sakya Trinzin, head of the Sakya lineage of Tibetan Buddhism, practicing such deity yogas as Chakrasamvara helps the practitioner "to accomplish excellent siddhis which means

ultimate enlightenment" Benefits include purification, the removal of obstacles and life extension. See "Following the Path, Reading the Signs."

12. *Thangkas* are paintings that portray deities, mandalas, or other symbolic images important to the meditational practice. They are not mere works of ornamental art, but are ritually sanctified objects that are aids to specific meditational practices.

13. The six realms, in Buddhist cosmology, extend from the god realms (above the level of ordinary human enjoyment) to the animal and ghost realms (below). The god realms are not superior to the human realm from the Buddhist point of view; the human realm provides the best opportunities from which to study dharma and escape cyclical existence.

14. Dorn (1929–1999) is associated primarily with the Black Mountain School, and his most well-known book is *Gunslinger*. Clark is a poet, critic, and biographer who wrote a scathing account of the Trungpa/Merwin episode called *The Great Naropa Poetry Wars*.

15. *Samyaksambodhi* can be translated as "supreme," "unexcelled," "perfect enlightenment."

16. "In *Buddhist Goddesses of India* Miranda Shaw defines a *dharani* as a mantra for a female deity; I've also heard it used in reference to a magico-spiritual phrase that holds no recognizable lexical elements, but is comprised of sheer energy that manifests a deity or a state of consciousness." *[Andrew Schelling]*

17. A *teisho* is a period of verbal teaching within a Zen *sesshin* (period of intensive group practice), but the speech is considered a demonstration of insight rather than an explanation of it.

18. Trungpa appointed Thomas F. Rich, Ösel Tendzin, as his "Vajra Regent." After Trungpa died, Osel Tendzin was found to be sleeping with students and transmitting AIDS to them even though he knew he had the illness, leading to a crisis in the Vajradhatu and Shambhala communities. The Shambhala organization's web page describes the events as follows: "In 1988 the Vajra Regent himself became gravely ill with AIDS and there was dissension in the community around the leadership of the organizations." http://www.shambhala.org/teachers/vrot/ accessed 17 February 2010.

19. Candomblé is an animist religion of African origin that developed in Brazil after being transported across the Atlantic by the slave trade.

Works Cited

Clark, Tom. *The Great Naropa Poetry Wars*. Santa Barbara: Cadmus Editions, 1979.

Coburn, Thomas. *The Legacy of Chögyam Trungpa*. http://www.naropa.edu/naropalibrary/documents/CTR-BROCHURE-final.pdf. Accessed March 6, 2010.

Dorn, Ed. *Gunslinger*. Santa Barbara: Black Sparrow, 1968.

"Following the Path, Reading the Signs." http://www.purifymind.com/DharmaTeaching4.htm. Accessed February 17, 2010.

Goss, Robert E. "Buddhist Studies at Naropa: Sectarian or Academic?" *American Buddhism: Methods and Findings in Recent Scholarship*. Eds. Christopher Queen and Duncan Ryuken Williams. Surrey, UK: Curzon, 1999. 215–37.

Kashner, Sam. *When I Was Cool: My Life at the Jack Kerouac School of Disembodied Poetics*. New York: HarperCollins, 2004.

"Naropa University: A Naropa University Self-Study Report prepared for the Higher Learning Commission of the North Central Association of Colleges and Schools 2009–2010 Self Study." http://www.naropa.edu/about/documents/SelfStudyWebVersion.pdf. Accessed 16 February 2010.

Trungpa, Chögyam. *Shambhala: Sacred Path of the Warrior*. Ed. Carolyn Rose Gimian. Boston: Shambhala, 1988.

Contributors

Jane Falk is Lecturer in English Composition at The University of Akron, at Akron, Ohio. She has contributed an appreciation of Philip Whalen's *The Diamond Noodle* to *Continuous Flame*, a tribute volume, as well as biographies of Whalen to the *Encyclopedia of Beat Literature, The Greenwood Encyclopedia of American Poets and Poetry*, and *The Collected Poems of Philip Whalen*. Her essay on Zen influences on Whalen's poetry is included in *The Emergence of Buddhist American Literature*. An essay on Joanne Kyger's video, *Descartes*, is forthcoming. Current research interests include the work of Joanne Kyger, Lew Welch, and Philip Whalen.

Allan Johnston lives near Chicago, where he teaches literature and writing. He holds a PhD in English from the University of California, Davis. His scholarly writings have appeared in journals such as *Twentieth Century Literature, College Literature, ISLE, AUMLA*, and *Review of Contemporary Fiction*. Besides his academic writing, he is a poet with two published collections and poems in *Poetry, Poetry East, Rattle, Rhino*, and several other journals. He is currently president of the Society for the Philosophical Study of Education and editor of the *Journal for the Philosophical Study of Education*.

Julia Martin teaches English and creative writing at the University of the Western Cape in South Africa. She has a special interest in ecological literacy, narrative scholarship and has a long association with the work of Gary Snyder. Her publications include *Writing Home* (2002), a collection of narrative essays, and *A Millimetre of Dust* (2008), a travel memoir about visiting archaeological sites in the Northern Cape. She is also the editor of *Ecological Responsibility: A Dialogue with Buddhism* (1997), an international collection of essays and talks.

Linda F. Selzer is Associate Professor of English at the Pennsylvania State University-University Park. She is the author of *Charles Johnson in Context* (University of Massachusetts Press, 2009), and co-editor of *New Essays on the African American Novel* (Palgrave, 2008). Her work on African-American literature and culture has appeared in scholarly collections and in journals such as the *African American Review, Callaloo, Massachusetts Review, MELUS,* and *Rhetoric Review.* In 2003 she received the Darwin Turner Award for the year's best essay in *African American Review.*

Jonathan Stalling is an Assistant Professor of English at the University of Oklahoma and is the author of *Poetics of Emptiness (Fordham), Grotto Heaven (Chax), and the forthcoming book* 吟歌丽诗/*Yingēlìshī: Sinophonic English Poetry and Poetics (Counterpath), and a co-editor of The Chinese Written Character as a Medium for Poetry (Fordham). He is also the co-founder and an editor of Chinese Literature Today Journal and the editor of the CLT Book Series from Oklahoma University Press.*

Gary Storhoff is an Associate Professor of English at the University of Connecticut, Stamford Campus. He has widely published in American, African-American, and Ethnic American literature. He is the author of *Understanding Charles Johnson* (2004), co-editor of *The Emergence of Buddhist American Literature* (2009, 2010) and *American Buddhism as a Way of Life* (2010) with John Whalen-Bridge. He is currently working on a book provisionally titled *The Family Crucible: Family Processes in William Faulkner and Toni Morrison.*

Jan Willis is Professor of Religion at Wesleyan University in Middletown, Connecticut. She has studied with Tibetan Buddhists in India, Nepal, Switzerland and the United States for more than four decades, and has taught courses in Buddhism for thirty-seven years. She is the author of *The Diamond Light: An Introduction to Tibetan Buddhist Meditation* (1972), *On Knowing Reality: The Tattvartha Chapter of Asanga's Bodhisattvabhumi* (1979), *Enlightened Beings: Life Stories from the Ganden Oral Tradition* (1995); and the editor of *Feminine Ground: Essays on Women and Tibet* (1989). Additionally, Willis has published a number of articles and essays on various topics in Buddhism—Buddhist meditation, women and Buddhism, and Buddhism and race. In 2001, she authored the memoir, *Dreaming Me: An African American Woman's Spiritual Journey* (re-issued October 1, 2008 by Wisdom Publications as *Dreaming Me: Black, Baptist, and Buddhist—One Woman's Spiritual Journey*). In December 2000, *Time* magazine named Willis one of six "spiritual innovators for the new millennium." In 2003, she was a recipient of Wesleyan University's Binswanger Prize for Excellence in Teaching. In September 2005, *Newsweek* magazine's "Spirituality in America" issue included a profile of her and, in its May 2007 edition, *Ebony* magazine named Willis one of its "Power 150" most influential African Americans.

John Whalen-Bridge is Associate Professor of English at the National University of Singapore. He is the author of *Political Fiction and the American*

Self, co-editor with Gary Storhoff of *Emergence of Buddhist American Literature* (2009, 2010) and *American Buddhism as a Way of Life* (2010), and editor of *Norman Mailer's Later Fictions*. With Tan Sor-Hoon, he co-edited *Democracy as Culture: Deweyan Pragmatism in a Globalizing World*. He is completing a study of Engaged Buddhism and countercultural writing in postwar America, focusing on Gary Snyder, Charles Johnson, and Maxine Hong Kingston.

Notes on Interviewees

Keith Kumasen Abbott teaches writing and art at Naropa University. Publications include the novels *Gush, Rhino Ritz* and *Mordecai of Monterey*, as well as the short story collections, *Harum Scarum, The First Thing Coming*, and *The French Girl*. He wrote a memoir of Richard Brautigan, *Downstream from Trout Fishing in America* and contributed to *Richard Brautigan: Essays on the Writing and Life*. His art/calligraphy appear in *Shambhala Sun* and *Buddhadharma* magazines.

Reed Bye is a poet and songwriter. His most recent book is Join the Planets: New and Selected Poems. Other published works include Passing Freaks and Graces, Gaspar Still in His Cage, and Some Magic at the Dump. A CD of original songs, Long Way Around, was released in 2005 by Farfalla/McMillan & Parrish. His work has appeared in a number of anthologies including Nice to *See You: Homage to Ted Berrigan, The Angel Hair Anthology, Sleeping on the Wing*, and *Civil Disobediences: Poetics and Politics in Action*. He holds a PhD in English from the University of Colorado and teaches poetry writing workshops, courses in classic and contemporary literary studies, and contemplative poetics.

Charles Johnson, a 1998 MacArthur Fellow, was until his retirement the S. Wilson and Grace M. Pollock Endowed Professor of English at the University of Washington. His fiction includes *Faith and The Good Thing* (1974), *Oxherding Tale* (1982), *Dreamer* (1998), and *Middle Passage*—for which he won the National Book Award (1990)—and the short story collections *The Sorcerer's Apprentice* (1982), *Soulcatcher and Other Stories* (1998), and *Dr. King's Refrigerator and Other Bedtime Stories* (2005). His nonfiction books include *Turning the Wheel: Essays on Buddhism and Writing* (2003), *Being and Race: Black Writing Since 1970* (1988), and two collections of comic art. In 2002 he received the Academy Award in Literature from the American Academy of Arts and Letters.

Maxine Hong Kingston is Professor Emeritus at the University of California, Berkeley. She is the author of many award-winning books, including *The Woman Warrior: Memoirs of a Girlhood among Ghosts*, which won the National Book Award (1980); *Tripmaster Monkey: His Fake Book* (1989); *To Be a Poet* (2002);

The Fifth Book of Peace (2006); *Veterans of War, Veterans of Peace* (2006), which was awarded the Northern California Book Award in Publishing; and *I Love a Broad Margin to My Life*, to be published by Knopf in 2011. In 1997, she was awarded the National Humanities Medal by President Bill Clinton.

Joanne Kyger is the author of twenty books of poetry, including her collected poems *About Now* (2007). She has been a regular visiting faculty member in Naropa's "Summer Writing Program."

Elizabeth Robinson is the author of eight books of poetry, most recently *Inaudible Trumpeters, Under That Silky Roof,* and *Apostrophe.* Robinson has an essay in the new book on Lorine Niedecker, *Radical Vernacular,* and work forthcoming in a new Norton Anthology called *American Hybrid.* Another book is *The Orphan & Its Relations* (2010). Robinson has been a winner of the Fence Modern Poets Prize, the National Poetry Series, and three Gertrude Stein awards for innovative poetry. She has also been a MacDowell Colony Fellow and a recipient of a grant from the Fund for Poetry. In 2008, she was awarded a Foundation for Contemporary Arts Grants to Artists Award.

Andrew Schelling is a poet, essay writer, and translator. His work is known for its focus on ecology and natural history, as well as a studied engagement with the poetic traditions of Asia. He has written or edited sixteen books. Currently he is at work on an anthology of India's medieval *bhakti* (devotional) poetry for Oxford University Press, Delhi. At Naropa, Schelling teaches poetry, translation, courses in bioregional poetics, and Sanskrit. He oversees the Kavyayantra Press, the Kerouac School's letterpress print shop.

Gary Snyder is the author of over a dozen collections of poetry, starting with *Myths and Texts* (1960), through *Danger on Peaks* (2005). He has also published more than a half-dozen prose works, including *Earth House Hold* (1969), *The Practice of the Wild* (1990), and *Back on the Fire* (2007). He won the Pulitzer Prize for poetry in 1975, the Bollingen Prize for Poetry in 1997, and the Ruth Lilly Poetry Prize in 2008.

Index

Abbott, Keith, 13, 158, 168; *Next Door to Samsara*, 168
Action Dharma: New Studies in Engaged Buddhism, 43
Adiele, Faith, 43; *Meeting Faith*, 43
affirmative action, 61
African American literature, 6, 11, 38, 46, 48, 61
Ambedkar, B.R., 51–52
American Buddhism as a Way of Life, 2
American Buddhism, 1–3, 6, 38, 42–46, 64, 174; black dharma, 6, 11, 38, 43, 48, 61; Black Power, 58, 59, 60, 61; race, racism and, 6, 11, 24, 31, 37, 40, 42–43, 44, 45, 48–49, 63, 141–48, 178
Anagarika Dharmapala, 39, 41, 47, 62, 65
anatman, 7–9, 11
anatta, 154, 155
anicca, 154
Aquinas, Thomas, 154
Ashbury, John, 163
Augustine, 154
Baker Roshi, 170
Baldoquin, Hilda Gutierrez, 43; *Dharma, Color, and Culture*, 43
Baraka, Imamu Amiri, 41; *Yugen*, 41
Bateson, Gregory, 182
Baumann, Martin, "The Dharma Has Come West: A Survey of Recent Studies and Sources," 42

Beats, the, 2, 11, 144, *see also* Burroughs, Corso, di Prima, Ginsberg, Kerouac, Kyger, and Waldman

bell hooks, 6, 38, 41, 43–45, 47, 49, 57–58, 60, 61–62; *Rock My Soul*, 49; "Surrendered," 61; "The King We Left Behind," 57; "Waking Up," 45
Bhagavad-Gita, 152
Blake, William, 127
Bodhidharma, 19, 20, 21, 27
bodhisattva, xiii, 22, 25, 55, 64, 73, 81, 134, 152
Boyd, Merle Kodo, 44, 45, 50, 57, 58; "A Child of the South in Long Black Robes," 44
Buddha (Siddhartha Gautama, Sanskrit; Siddhatha Gotama, Pali), 3, 4, 48, 54, 57, 63, 64, 65, 72, 73, 148, 151
Buddhism, *see also* American Buddhism, Chan, Hua-yen, Kegon, Pure Land, Theravada, Vajrayana, and Zen
Burroughs, William, 103, 149, 163
Bye, Reed, 13, 158, 161

Cage, John, 12, 90, 96, 99, 103, 157, 182
Chan Buddhism (Chinese), 93–94, 106
Chappell, David, 42, 43, 61
China Men, 142 (*see* Kingston, Maxine Hong)
Chögyam Trungpa, 12, 149, 157–65, 167, 176–77, 182–83
Choyin Rangdrol, 43, 46, 48, 49, 50; "Black Buddha: Bringing the Tradition Home," 48
Christianity, 4–5, 6, 9, 11, 20–22, 25–26, 30, 40, 41, 46–47, 56, 63, 122, 153–55, 178–79